A Naturalist on a Tropical Farm

A Naturalist on a Tropical Farm

ALEXANDER F. SKUTCH

Illustrations by Dana Gardner

University of California Press / Berkeley / Los Angeles / London

To Annette Cretien
who has helped many people to know tropical America

University of California Press
Berkeley and Los Angeles, California

University of California Press, Ltd.
London, England

ISBN 0–520–03802–9
Library of Congress Catalog Card Number: 78–64474
Printed in the United States of America

1 2 3 4 5 6 7 8 9

Contents

Preface

BOTH the naturalist and the farmer deal with nature, but with interests, occupations, and aims that are very different, and often contrary. The naturalist wishes to observe and understand nature; the farmer, to make it yield crops that can be sold at a profit. The naturalist is concerned chiefly with the native flora and fauna; the farmer, with cultivated plants and domestic animals that are nearly always of foreign origin. To clear land for his crops and herds, the farmer destroys the wilderness that the naturalist is eager to preserve; to prevent the depredations of free creatures, the farmer combats animals that the naturalist protects. The naturalist often exerts himself as strenuously for the immaterial rewards of experience and knowledge as the farmer does for the material rewards of food and money.

In view of these oppositions, it is clear that the naturalist who undertakes to farm, or the farmer who becomes deeply interested in wild nature, will often be perplexed and face difficult decisions. This is especially true if he farms in the midst of, or beside, tropical rain forest, with its vast diversity of plants and animals, some of which may harm his crops. To compensate for his often distressing dilemmas, his farm most probably will include areas of both wilderness and cultivation and will support a greater variety of living things than either forest or plantation alone would shelter. If he lives perceptively, his experiences will deepen his understanding of the problems confronting conservationists in an overpopulated world, and perhaps also bring more acute awareness of both the glory and the tragedy of life on an exceptionally favored planet that stubbornly persists in producing more living creatures than it can support.

In an earlier book, *A Naturalist in Costa Rica*,[1] I told how I came to Los Cusingos, the tropical farm where I have dwelt for nearly forty years, and established a homestead there. For the benefit of readers who may be unfamiliar with that book, I begin this one by repeating, in the first chapter, some of the things that I wrote earlier, including a brief description of the farm and the home that, with the aid of carpenters, I built upon it. The rest of this book contains wholly new materials, or fuller treatments of matters that, for lack of space, received only passing mention in the earlier one. The second chapter follows, month by month, the changing seasons of a tropical year and their influence on the vegetable and animal life and on the activities of the farm itself. Then I recount certain memorable experiences that I have not told elsewhere—stories of the most engaging birds with which I have long been intimate, of certain quadrupeds that live close to me, of trees, flowers, and insects, of domestic animals, of fishes that swim in rocky pools on the farm. Other chapters deal with certain problems that life in the teeming tropics has presented, and how I tried to solve them.

In the next-to-last chapter, I take the reader off the farm to a part of Costa Rica that, although not far distant, has a very different climate, which supports a different flora and fauna, and I tell of the enormous changes I have witnessed there. Without going into wearisome detail, I have tried to present a cross-section of the wonderfully varied life that surrounds me. In the concluding chapter, I speak of the attitude toward life, in its widest aspect, that brought me here in the first place, and that, over the years, has been modified and refined by my thoughts and experiences.

1. Alexander F. Skutch, *A Naturalist in Costa Rica* (Gainesville: University of Florida Press, 1971).

Acknowledgments

THREE of the chapters in this book first appeared in *Animal Kingdom*, published by the New York Zoological Society: chapter six appeared in volume 60, pages 75–79, in 1957; chapter nine in volume 68, pages 168–72, in 1965; and chapter thirteen in volume 70, pages 106–111, in 1967. Chapter eight was published in the long-extinct *Nature Magazine*, volume 45, pages 523–25 and 550, in 1952. Chapter fourteen originally appeared in the *Aryan Path* (Bombay), volume 23, pages 382–86, in 1952. *Audubon Magazine* published chapter seventeen in volume 61, pages 20–21 and 76–77, in 1959. All these articles have been carefully revised, most of them have been extended with new information, and the titles of some have been changed. I am indebted to the editors or publishers of these four magazines for permission to use in this book material that first appeared in their pages. I am also grateful to Frank Almeda and William Burger for naming botanical specimens, and to William A. Bussing for identifying the fishes in chapter sixteen. The artist joins me in thanking the Western Foundation of Vertebrate Zoology, of Los Angeles, for providing working space and materials while he drew the illustrations.

A. F. S.

1. The Farm

I WISHED to study living things, especially birds, to reside among them, and to live in harmony with them. Although not absurd, this threefold aim is far from common. Professional biologists only exceptionally make their homes close to wild nature; they carry the organisms they study into well-equipped laboratories, where, too often, they subject them to painful experiments. Or they work in museums situated in great cities, describing and classifying specimens that were mostly collected by others. Their occasional excursions into the field are often collecting trips on which many living things die to become specimens.

In contrast to these people, who will sacrifice almost anything for knowledge, whose greatest triumph may be to express their findings in a mathematical formula or a succinct "law," are those who live close to nature for the peace, beauty, and refreshment it offers. Their contacts with the living things around them, highly gratifying to themselves, rarely contribute to the sum of scientific knowledge. Rarely do they make the sustained, painstaking observations and keep the detailed records that may increase our understanding.

I wished to live simply in an unspoiled natural setting, while studying nature like a scientist, all without harming the objects of my study, or the other living things around me. This rather unusual combination of objectives was not easy to realize. For a decade, I wandered about tropical America, living for months, or

sometimes for more than a year continuously, in rented or borrowed cabins, on hospitable farms, occasionally at a research station, while I intensively watched birds and collected botanical specimens to pay my way. As the years passed, and my growing mass of records became more cumbersome to transport, always with some risk of loss, I felt increasingly the need of a permanent home, where I could gather my books and notes around me, prepare my observations for publication, and continue to study nature on my own land.

When I reached this point, I thought of the Valley of El General, at the head of the Río Térraba on the Pacific slope of southern Costa Rica, where I had already spent two and a half richly rewarding years, studying birds and collecting plants in various localities. In those days, before the Inter-American Highway cut through the length of the valley, it was an isolated region, surrounded by vast, scarcely broken forests, and easily accessible only by air. Only a long, rough trail, threading the forest and passing over the high, bleak summits of the Cordillera de Talamanca, connected it with the center of the country. San Isidro de El General, now a cathedral town and bustling commercial center, was then only a small village, with a few stores that sold cheap clothing and household necessities to customers who mostly came with bare feet. From this center, unpaved roads led in all directions, between patches of the original forest and farms carved from it so recently that charred logs and stumps still cluttered the fields. No motorcar ever raised the dust on these rustic lanes. The airplane brought mail and merchandise, and a radio station provided more rapid communication with the capital, San José.

On my bay horse, Bayon, I spent days riding about the country, visiting farms that were offered to the foreigner who had come with a little capital to this valley where money was scarce and went far. Finally, in March of 1941, I found

◀ FIERY-BILLED ARAÇARI

the farm that promised to fulfill my dreams. At an altitude of about twenty-five hundred feet, it stretched along the western bank of the Río Peñas Blancas, a broad mountain torrent that rushed clamorously over a bed strewn with huge boulders, bringing crystal-clear, cool water from the high, forested slopes of the Cordillera de Talamanca in the north. A steep ridge, still mostly wooded, ran almost the whole length of the farm. Between the ridge and the river lay nearly level terraces, which fell away by high, steep bluffs to the exceedingly stony but fertile benches of black soil, where in past ages the river had flowed. Three permanent streams traversed the farm, two near its northern end, the third on its western side. In the rainy season, two other rivulets also flowed through the land.

This farm belonged to Francisco Mora, known as Don Chico, a restless pioneer who alternated between seeking treasure in old Indian burials and converting wilderness into farms, which he soon sold to move on to new land. It contained about a half acre of coffee in full production, a small patch of bananas, extensive pastures, a scattering of fruit trees, and about two acres of sugarcane, with an ox-driven mill, beneath a big thatched shed, for converting the cane sap into hard, round bricks of brown sugar.

What interested me more was the forest. I was sorry to see that several acres of it had been felled and burned, so recently that prostrate trunks still smoldered. The pasture on the steep slope behind the terrace where I would build my house was littered with huge, decaying trunks. Nevertheless, a large tract of unspoiled forest remained, with trees towering up to a hundred and fifty feet, multitudes of palms with slender, soaring trunks, orchids and many other epiphytes on the trees, and beneath them many low palms, flowering shrubs, and great-leaved herbs. In this forest lived tinamous, guans, quails, trogons, hummingbirds, toucans, woodpeckers, woodcreepers, antbirds, manakins, cotingas, flycatchers, honeycreepers, tanagers, and finches, along with White-faced Monkeys, Coatimundis, Agoutis, Forest Deer,[1] and other mammals. The woodland contained nearly everything that unexploited rain forest in this region should have, except such large animals as Jaguars, Pumas, Ocelots, Tapirs, and peccaries, which the tract was too small to support, and which I could do without. To discover the nests and follow the life histories of all the birds would keep me busy for years—after nearly forty, there are still several species for which I have failed to find a single nest.

No one who hoped to grow rich by farming would have bought such rocky, broken land, so remote, as it then was, from railroad, highway, or navigable water. But the very features that would at times have made it a farmer's despair made it attractive to a naturalist. Its diversity of habitats assured a diversity of organisms. The streams that caused transportation problems, and needed bridges, which rotted or were washed away, attracted kingfishers, winsome Torrent Flycatchers, Neotropic Cormorants, fantastic Gray Basilisk lizards, and other creatures that enhanced the whole. When I found that Don Chico would sell his land at a price within my slender means, I bought it, fondly taking all this vast diversity of natural wealth under my protection. Now, at last, I could dwell in an unspoiled natural setting, study nature on my own land, and try to live in harmony with the teeming life around me.

Don Chico lived with his common-law wife, their small, fair-headed son, and several huge hogs, in a low, floorless, thatched cabin set at the very edge of a high, wooded bluff above the creek, a site that permitted the convenient disposal of ref-

1. When the common name of a species of animal or plant is capitalized, its scientific name will be found in the Index.

use by throwing it out the back door. The contract of sale gave him the right to remain there, without the pigs, until he finished a new house on land he had acquired across the Río Peñas Blancas—a period that stretched on to a year.

I decided to build my home on a high terrace that faced the rising sun, the mountains, and the river, whose voice, softly murmurous in the dry season, thunderous in rainy October, revealed its varying phases. The river, or the creek that flowed into it almost in front of the house site, would supply water when I could not catch enough for household needs from the roof, which seldom happened except in the dry season. (Years passed before I had water piped in.) This site, near water yet far enough above the river to be in no danger from its highest floods, had evidently been favored by my predecessors long ago. Digging in the garden, I found shards of Indian pottery and a clay spindle whorl. Stones that they had probably used for crushing maize lay about. The summit of the steep ridge behind the house was their burial ground. And the huge rock with a gently sloping top that rose beside the creek nearby was incised with curious spirals, of puzzling significance, that the aborigines had carved. This enormous block of andesite was to prove most useful for drying newly harvested beans and rice in the sunshine.

The five-roomed house that I planned would be made almost wholly of locally available materials. Only the hardware and a single bag of cement came from outside the valley, necessarily by air. The stones so abundant on the lower ground and in stream beds served as bases to raise the construction above the damp ground, termites, and snakes. A man skilled in the use of the adze hewed the heavier timbers from durable hardwood trees in the forest. Lighter timbers and boards were brought by ox-cart from a small sawmill across the valley in San Isidro, eight or nine miles away by winding roads. Since the mill lacked a planing machine, many boards had to be smoothed with a hand plane. Unglazed tiles for the roof were supplied by a farmer in La Hermosa, four miles away. By no means an expert tile maker, he made inferior tiles, but the best I could find. Hundreds broke as the ox-cart that brought them bumped over roads rough with rocks and roots, but with occasional shifting and patching, the survivors of this journey have kept the house dry for nearly forty years.

I planned my house to be economical and durable rather than elegant. For the walls I chose *bahareque*, a type of construction formerly widespread in Costa Rica, as in other parts of Latin America, but now rarely used, as it is time-consuming, requires much expensive hand labor, and, to be secure, needs heavy timbers that have become very costly. On both sides of the sturdy uprights, wild canes, which grow tall along the rivers, were nailed horizontally at intervals of a few inches. The four-inch space between the two series of canes was filled with clay dug from the hillside behind the house. The clay had been kneaded with water in a shallow pit, by horses walking around and around, until it had become very tacky. As it dried in the walls, the clay shrank, leaving wide fissures, which had to be filled with more clay. When the space between the canes had been filled solidly, the canes themselves were covered with clay, which required several applications to fill all the cracks. Next, the walls were thinly covered with fresh cow dung, an excellent binder. This at first made a horrible stench, but it soon dried to a soft gray, odorless surface, which was admired by certain visitors ignorant of its origin. Finally, the inside walls were whitewashed, the outside walls coated with the sack of cement that had come in the airplane.

Work on the walls proceeded slowly, in the intervals when farm tasks abated somewhat. Not until two years after the foundation stones had been set was the house finished. Meanwhile, I made simple furniture, including tables, stools, cabinets, and open shelves for books. I also bought the larger farm, with much woodland and little cultivation, that adjoined mine to the south. After I sold part of this land, I had about two hundred and fifty acres, about half in old forest and much of the remainder in second-growth woods. I decided to preserve all the forest and plant only on land that had already been cleared.

After long cogitation, I called my farm "Los Cusingos," for the Fiery-billed Araçaris, which are found only on the Pacific side of southern Costa Rica and across the border in Panama. I was not wholly satisfied with this choice, but settled for it because certain other birds that I admired more lacked names that my neighbors knew and could pronounce. Now I am convinced it was a good choice; these agile, colorful toucans have persisted here, while other, less wary birds have disappeared.

Except for rare visitors, for nine years I lived alone. But how could I be lonely with so much varied, vibrant life around me? How could I be bored with so much to see and learn and do? When nests of the resident birds became rare, it was almost time to watch for returning migrants from the north. Most of the time I had, living nearby, a family that included a farm hand and an unmarried daughter, who came in the mornings to cook, wash, and sweep the house for me. I had cows for milk, chickens for eggs, horses for riding, and all these dependents needed much attention. I seemed never to have enough time for all the odd jobs that continually turned up: gathering fruits, mending fences and gates, repairing leaky roofs, curing sick animals, extracting fly larvae from the skins of cows. Far from finding the frequent long, rainy afternoons depressing, I welcomed them as a time for reading, writing, or carpentry.

After nine celibate years, I married Pamela, youngest daughter of Charles Herbert Lankester, a coffee planter and self-taught naturalist of wide interests. She willingly relinquished comforts to live simply on a farm still lacking many things that city people believe indispensable. Some years later, we adopted Edwin, a quiet, promising boy, already in his teens, who had grown up on the farm (his father had worked for me, intermittently, for many years) and had been left unprotected by the disruption of his family. Then, with a larger household and a growing library for which there never seemed to be enough shelves, we added a wing to the originally L-shaped house.

Nothing prevents our building castles in the air exactly to our specifications. Perhaps this is a reason for not putting foundations beneath them. However, unless we try to bring them down to earth, embodying them, as best we can, in the stubborn world of reality, they can never be truly productive. But if they are capable of yielding joys and precious experiences, they may also—too often, alas! —bring disappointments and sorrows.

So has it been with Los Cusingos. Animals that I loved fell sick and died. Nests that I found after much searching and desired greatly to study were prematurely destroyed by predators—a frequent occurrence everywhere, but especially in tropical forests. The river, which is mostly a friendly presence, has sometimes misbehaved, damaging the farm. Labor and disputes with neighbors have also been a source of trouble. A few years after I came here, a neighbor drew up a writ accusing me of having closed a public road traversing the farm from end to end and persuaded other neighbors to support his claim. With the help of older residents of greater probity, I proved that such a road, which would have ruined the farm, never existed. But finally, as more dwellings sprang up around us, I had to consent to cutting a road through a tract of forest at the back of the farm that I had wished to preserve intact. From this dirt road and adjoining farms, fires have bitten into the edges of the forest, fortunately not yet for a great distance, since even in the dry season, rain forest is not subject to crown fires and ground fires spread slowly.

Most distressing has been my inability to protect the forest from trespassers and their dogs. The thousands of Palmitos—tall, slender palms with graceful crowns of feathery fronds—that graced the woodland when I arrived have been stolen for the few pounds of soft, edible tissue at their growing points. As the progeny of these vanished palms grow up, they are slashed down while so young and thin that they yield hardly a mouthful, thereby destroying the possibility of reproduction. With the disappearance of the Palmitos, marauders have been attacking the taller and originally equally abundant Chontas, which, being slightly bitter, are less esteemed as food. To discover the perpetrators of these clandestine depredations is difficult; to try to obtain a legal judgment against them, when they can be identified, a waste of time.

Poachers have exterminated some of the larger or more spectacular birds and mammals. Years have passed since I last saw a Chestnut-mandibled Toucan, Crested Guan, Red-throated Caracara, Rufous-tailed Jacamar, Forest Deer, or Coatimundi, all of which were formerly present here, some of them abundantly. Other species have become rarer. When a sedentary woodland bird disappears from an isolated tract of forest, it may be permanently lost, because birds that avoid open country are unlikely to repopulate the tract from distant forests. A recent study of nature sanctuaries of small or moderate size suggested that one twice as large is likely to retain four times as many species.

Although much has been lost, much has also been saved in a valley where, over the last four decades, I have painfully watched the destruction of nearly all the splendid rain forest that once covered it, followed by the disappearance of most of

its animal life. Our modest tract of ancient woodland stands, fairly undisturbed,
lds, coffee plantations, and corn fields, a small sample of the
is well-watered valley, a refuge for forest dwellers that have
in the surrounding region. Four kinds of trogons still repeat
ps of our woodland. As twilight descends on the forest, the
reat Tinamou proclaim its continuing wildness. The Black-
ounds its triple whistle as, with dainty steps, it walks over
or. A troupe of shy White-faced Monkeys still climb and
. The farm still contains much to enjoy, to observe, and to
ce, this valley is permitted to regain the healthy balance
woodland that I found here, Los Cusingos might serve as a
orest trees and their associated life repopulate land that once

alize our dreams in all details is a wildly extravagant hope,
fulfill them is to relinquish precious opportunities for en-
e chapters that follow, I shall say little more of the tribula-
who tries to preserve nature amid neighbors intent upon
ll instead of some of the rewards that this effort has brought.

2. A Tropical Year

In tropical lands where frost is unknown, the activities of living things are regulated, above all, by the monthly fluctuations in rainfall, as at higher latitudes they are determined chiefly by the seasonal changes in temperature. All those recurrent events, such as the renewal of vegetation, the nesting of birds, the sowing of fields by man, which in the temperate zones await the return of milder weather in spring, are in the tropics dependent chiefly upon the start of the rainy season. In the few tropical regions where the rainfall is almost uniformly distributed throughout the year, we find a corresponding monotony in the course of vital activities; but in most parts of the tropics seasons of heavier rainfall alternate with drier intervals, and the march of events in the plant and animal kingdoms is regulated by these changes.

Although in regions nearer the Equator the year may contain two periods of abundant rainfall separated by two drier periods, Central America has only a single well-marked dry season and a single practically continuous wet season. The dry season is called *verano*, or "summer"; the wet season, *invierno*, or "winter." These designations would naturally be given by immigrants from parts of Spain where a Mediterranean climate of dry summers and rainy winters prevails. They would soon forget that the season they now call "summer" coincides with the coldest months of the northern winter, while the wet "winter" includes the warmest months of the summer in the Northern Hemisphere, within which lies the whole of Central America.

To a traveler newly arrived from a northern land, it seems absurd to designate as "winter" the season when, because of plentiful rain, the earth is brilliantly green, birds singing and nesting, crops growing in the fields. But to the native, the association of the names "winter" and "summer" with wetness and dryness is so firmly established that when a bright, rainless day occurs in the midst of the *invierno*, or wet season, he will remark, "What a beautiful summer we have today"; while if a rainy spell interrupts the *verano*, or dry season, he will comment on the unseasonable "winter."

Although the Pacific side of Central America is, in general, much drier than the windward Caribbean side, in the foothills of southern Costa Rica the rainfall is heavier, and spread over more months, than in other parts of the west coast. This is reflected in the magnificent rain forests of this region, which are hardly inferior in stature and richness of vegetation to the best that the Caribbean coast can show. The nearest point from which we have meteorological data is San Isidro, five miles from Los Cusingos in a straight line, where, during the decade from 1960 to 1969, the annual rainfall averaged 116 inches, with extremes of 83 and 133 inches. Records kept by my friend Isaias Retana during the seven years from 1937 to 1943 at neighboring Pedregoso show an average annual rainfall of 120 inches, with extremes of 92 and 167 inches. San Isidro, in the rain shadow of the Coastal Range, is drier than Los Cusingos, which lies at the shadow's upper edge. During our long and very rainy wet season—which extends from late March or April into or through December—most of the year's rain falls, chiefly in the form of heavy afternoon or evening showers, and often accompanied by lightning and

thunder. Now and then we have dark or drizzly forenoons, or sometimes a succession of them when rainstorms are countrywide; but, even at the height of the wet season, we enjoy mornings of brilliant sunshine; and the year brings few forenoons wet enough to deter farmers from outdoor work.

Even here in a fairly stable environment, no two years are quite alike. Many of the differences between years are related to variations in the dry season, which may begin earlier or later, be more or less severe or prolonged. Trees may bloom in different months in consecutive years, or, after fruiting heavily one year, they may open few or no flowers in the following year. Some birds sing and nest sooner when the rains come early than when they are delayed. Nevertheless, variations in the course of natural events in this tropical environment are minor, and their regularity is more impressive than their fluctuations. In the following pages I try to depict, in broad outline, the march of life at Los Cusingos through the twelve months of a "typical" year.

JANUARY

Although over much of the Pacific slope of Central America the dry season starts in late October or November, here, in the southern foothills of the Cordillera de Talamanca, it is, in most years, hardly well established until January. Nearly always, this month brings the year's most pleasant weather. By night, the stars twinkle brightly. Cool air, flowing down from high summits where frost whitens open spaces and icicles grow long on dripping cliffs and roadside cuttings, makes one pull a heavy blanket over his bed toward the night's end.

In a blaze of light, the sun floats up above the wooded ridge beyond the river. The landscape, still intensely green after long months of rain, is soon flooded with

◀ RED-HEADED BARBET, FEMALE

sunshine so intense that it appears to be some palpable substance. Especially
during my early years here, when fewer homes sent up smoke from kitchen fires
and not a single motorcar polluted the air with exhaust fumes and dust, the atmosphere on such mornings was perfectly clear and transparent to the most distant summits; the earth sparkled like a precious gem. Such visual clarity tinges
one's spirit with a sense of cleanliness and purity, making one feel that this old
planet is still pristine and undefiled. The flood of light often makes me strangely
restless. I yearn to wander beyond the distant horizon, which appears so near in
the pellucid air, yet I can give no good reason for wishing to be anywhere except
where I am, since I am as deeply immersed in all the glory of this light-flooded
hemisphere as one could hope to be anyplace else.

Although the sunshine is warm, in the shade gentle, shifting morning breezes
are cool and invigorating, reminding one with soft caresses that it is good to be
alive. Even at noon, on our best days, the air has not lost its freshness. After midday, clouds that have been slowly piling up against the high mountains to the north
may spread over the sky. Sometimes they release their moisture in light afternoon
showers. Often, after a dry beginning, the month ends with a few rainy days.

Costa Rican country people have a curious notion, not easily dispelled, that
the year's weather is forecast by the first twelve days of January, which they call
pintas, because they "paint" the character of the coming months. Thus, if January
2 is rainless, February should be dry; and if January 3 is rainy, March should be
wet. If this were true, the present year of 1977, which began with an exceptionally
dry January, should be one of unrelieved drought, although actually it has rained
much from April onward.

Shrubs and herbaceous plants that started to flower when rainfall diminished

SWALLOW-TAILED KITE ▶

and sunshine increased in December continue through brilliant January days to adorn roadsides, weedy ground, and low thickets on resting fields. None of our more spectacular forest trees flowers so early in the year. Along the river, gnarled old Riverwood trees may clothe their twigs with crowded clusters of pinkish stamens, which, especially on still afternoons, fill the air with a heavy, "polleny" odor that is almost fragrant. The tree that most adorns our landscape in January is the tall, swiftly growing *Heliocarpus*, the "sun-fruited tree," locally called Burío, whose wood is as soft as that of the more widely known Balsa. After a rather modest display of pale yellow flowers in December, it becomes more beautiful as its tiny flat achenes, each surrounded by a ring of soft bristles, which suggest solar rays, become tinged with pale red. Light passing through the plumy bristles forms a colored halo about each fruit, suffusing the whole dense mass of them with a soft, warm radiance that is lovely when viewed against a clear blue sky. Much of the forest's color at this season is provided by new foliage, especially the bright red young leaves of the epiphytic heath *Satyria elongata*, which grows profusely on old trees.

Birds are strangely silent in these delightful days, which would seem to invite ebullient song and nesting. Now and then a finch or thrush sings briefly; but the chief vocalists are male hummingbirds, who gather in loose assemblies in treetops, or beneath woodland shade, and tirelessly repeat simple refrains in weak voices that are seldom musical. Some continue all day long, vying with each other for females whose developing eggs need fertilization. Although hummingbirds' nests are not as numerous as in December, the females continue to lay, and to attend eggs and young with no help from males, as long as abundant flowers promise a liberal supply of easily gathered nectar. Another persistent but inferior songster is the

Bananaquit, a nectar drinker and insect gleaner like the hummingbirds, who raises its young at the same time as they do. But the majority of birds, as though aware that leaner days are coming, sing little and nest less in January. Nevertheless, diminutive male Orange-collared Manakins begin to clear their "courts," removing all loose litter to make a small patch of bare ground, above which they will soon display to attract the greenish females.

In this month a multitude of migrants from temperate North America are settled in their winter home, sharing a diminishing food supply with more numerous resident birds. Now they are joined by a few species that come to nest, after passing their nonbreeding season farther south. Swallow-tailed Kites arrive, to soar gracefully through clear skies, catching insects in their feet, and to build their nests of sticks in high treetops. Piratic Flycatchers proclaim their arrival with breezy whistles, which they repeat with seeming insolence while waiting for resident birds to finish covered nests that the "pirates" will capture for their own broods. In some years, late in the month, the Yellow-green Vireo's persistent song reveals that it has already arrived from Amazonia, although more often I first hear it in early February. Now the small, gray Lesser, or Bellicose, Elaenia makes its presence known by dry little notes, having come from I know not where. A less-traveled visitor is the brilliant, silent Red-headed Barbet, who flies down from higher in the mountains to eat bananas at our feeder and to hunt for the insects that hide in curled dead leaves high in forest trees.

A good shower after a short dry spell may bring coffee into flower so early in the year. Last year's crop has all been gathered; and this is the time for removing branches from the shade trees so that more sunshine can reach the coffee, for pruning old branches and exhausted twigs from the coffee shrubs, and for cleaning the

ground between them, where weeds have grown tall. Toward the month's end, beans sown broadcast in October are ready to be pulled up and dried in the sun, so that the seeds can be beaten from the pods.

As the dry season advances, fresh fruits and vegetables for our table become scarcer, unless brought from a distance. Our orange trees, however, usually yield abundantly through the dry months. The bean field gives us green pods in early January, and maize plants scattered thinly through it supply green corn until February. In this season we vary our diet by gathering Red Poró flowers from the ground, beneath trees that I planted as slender living poles, which rooted and sent out widely spreading boughs. (As the wet season approached its end in November, the thorny branches shed their trifoliolate leaves, and by December the naked twigs bore vivid clusters of long, slender, red flowers, each shaped like a machete or sword.) Before sunrise on January mornings, chattering flocks of Orange-chinned Parakeets settle in the poró trees, pluck the flowers one by one, and lift each to their mouths with a foot. A bite to create a narrow perforation in the thick base suffices to extract the nectar; then the flower is dropped. Wintering Baltimore Orioles have a different procedure. Plucking a flower, the brilliant male or duller female holds it against a branch beneath a foot, while its sharp bill splits the base of the flower to make the nectar available to its tongue. These two kinds of birds leave the ground thickly strewn with bright red flowers, which we must gather quickly, before the horse eats them, if we wish to boil them for lunch or supper. Throughout the day, long-billed hummingbirds visit poró flowers that parakeets and orioles have left for them. Later, as the long pods ripen, White-crowned Parrots will settle in the trees to eat the full-grown seeds, which are not yet hard and bright red.

◄ ORANGE-CHINNED PARAKEETS, RED PORÓ FLOWERS (LEFT) AND SEED PODS (RIGHT)

FEBRUARY

January's delightful weather often continues well into February, and in our best years, when a few afternoon showers relieve the prevailing drought, almost to the month's end. Usually, however, by the last week of February the atmosphere loses its fine clarity as smoke rises from fires set to clear land for planting and pastures begin to turn brown.

The floral display on fields and roadsides wanes as weedy plants set seed and wither. Nevertheless, this generally dry month has no lack of flowers. Now the Golden Shower Orchids are at their best, their thick, drought-resistant pseudobulbs sending out gracefully arching sprays, a yard or two long, covered with hundreds of small, bright yellow blossoms. On trees and shaded rocks, the clustered stems of the orchid *Sobralia pleiantha* still display large, cream-colored flowers, which begin to expand at dawn, diffuse their delicate fragrance through the bright morning hours, and close around noon, never to open again. On large, globular, earthy nests built by tiny dark ants high in trees, the stiffly erect, clustered stems of another orchid, *Epidendrum imatophyllum*, are crowned with clusters of small pink flowers, visible from afar. On similar ants' nests, the much rarer Bucket Orchid somehow finds enough moisture, in this dry weather, to fill its large, cupped lip with the water that plays an essential role in its strange transactions with pollinating insects. In tall second-growth woods, the Scarlet Passion-flower displays its large blossoms on nearly leafless shoots near the ground, to be pollinated by shade-loving Long-tailed Hermit Hummingbirds, while the leafy vines scramble up toward the sunshine.

A good afternoon shower in this generally dry month will bring the coffee plantation into fullest bloom nine or ten days later. For a single day, the glossy-

◀ ORCHID (*SOBRALIA* SP.)

leafed shrubs are thickly covered with pure white, fragrant blossoms, which attract multitudes of small bees and other insects. By the following day the flowers are becoming discolored. Like the coffee, several species of *Miconia*, tall shrubs or slender trees of the melastome family, may bloom simultaneously in February, each species at its own time. On a certain day, every tree of the same kind on the farm is covered with small white flowers murmurous with bees.

As the Red Poró trees growing around the house pass from bloom, the Orange-chinned Parakeets turn their attention to the much taller Orange Poró that I started from a seed at a corner of the garden. They can extract the nectar from the more open flowers of this South American tree without plucking them. They share the feast with Baltimore Orioles, several kinds of honeycreepers, and brilliant hummingbirds that appear colorless against the sky. Another planted tree, the Carao, is adorned with deep pinkish, clustered flowers in this month when our most colorful native trees are still mostly flowerless.

When the moon is full during the dry months, Pauraques repeat their clear, plaintive notes all through the night. Blue-throated Golden-tails, Rufous-tailed Hummingbirds, Blue-chested Hummingbirds, and others that join in courtship assemblies continue to sing into February; but if the drought becomes severe and flowers scarce toward the month's end, they fall silent until April's showers refresh the vegetation. Other birds become increasingly songful in anticipation of their nesting season. Now in February, flycatchers, from big Boat-bills to tiny Black-fronted Tody-Flycatchers, sing at dawn the stirring or whimsical songs that are rarely heard in full daylight. Thrushes, finches, and tanagers repeat their songs increasingly during this month, although hardly yet with full intensity.

In February the work of cleaning and pruning the coffee plantation continues. Now, on well-rested, fertile land too rocky to plow, we slash down brush and rapidly growing trees, which quickly dry in the hot sunshine. At the month's end, we set fire to clear the ground for planting maize. If we waited long into March, when the ground and standing vegetation usually become drier, the fire would burn more fiercely, with greater injury to the soil and increased risk of spreading uncontrollably through the farm.

The increased attendance at the birds' feeder reminds me that wild fruits become scarcer as the drought continues. Fortunately, with an occasional brief intermission, our banana plantation yields enough both for the birds and for our household throughout the year. Our orange trees, too, still bear enough to eat and to sell. Now the Itabo, a species of *Yucca* with thick, fleshy branches and long, narrow, sharply pointed leaves, spreads its generous panicles of large white flowers that never produce seeds. Prepared as a vegetable or salad, they add welcome variety to our diet. Root crops such as Cassava and Tiquisque (a large-leaved aroid) can be gathered at any season, and our granary still holds corn for making tortillas and feeding the chickens.

MARCH

When I first came to El General, February was usually our driest month, but it is now more often March, a change probably wrought by the vast destruction of forest in the last four decades. Although government, radio stations, and the press urge farmers not to burn for their soil's sake, the annual burning continues on a large scale. Much of the land in the valley and on the surrounding hills—including some of our own best fields—is so stony or steep that plowing is hardly possible and burning the only economically feasible method of preparing it for planting maize and other crops that require considerable area. In addition to this necessary burning, much more occurs when farmers carelessly permit their fires to escape

from bounds and run wildly over neighboring fields and into the woods. Other blazes are thoughtlessly or spitefully started. Last year, some malicious trespasser set fire to several acres of drying brush that we had cut down for a *milpa* where maize would be sown but had not yet surrounded by a bare lane to contain the flames. Happily, the adjoining thickets were still moist and the conflagration did not spread far.

As March advances, the burden of smoke in the air increases, until distant peaks disappear, the sun rises with an angry red glare, the sky is no longer blue by day, and no stars twinkle at night. The atmosphere that was so invigoratingly clear and pure in January now becomes murky and oppressive. By midday, the thermometer has often risen into the high eighties and sometimes passes ninety degrees Fahrenheit. In the afternoons, charred fragments of vegetation drift down, on the lawn, the porch, even on my writing paper. Added to the effects of the sultry, enervating heat is the fear that Los Cusingos is burning; for it is difficult to judge whether a column of smoke, rising high above the treetops, comes from one's own farm or another at a distance.

In the forest, where the persistent *chirrilin* of the big cicadas is the prevailing sound, drying leaves drift down until the ground is thickly covered. Although now thinner than in the rainy months, the high, leafy canopy still covers much of the sky; few trees lose all their foliage, and some even find enough moisture deep in the soil to renew it in the driest weather. The more shallowly rooted woodland shrubs fare worse than the trees that shade them; in drier years, their leaves and green shoots droop forlornly—a depressing sight. Fissures appear in the parched ground. In woods and fields flowers are not wholly lacking, but rare. Pastures turn brown and grazing animals must subsist upon dry grass, unless specially fed. Here

◀ VIOLET-HEADED HUMMINGBIRD

in the foothills, we receive more rain than does the valley floor, and our pastures may remain green while those below us are parched and brown.

As though to cheer spirits depressed by polluted air and the sight of wilting vegetation, some of our most splendid trees bloom at the height of the drought. Now the tall Large-leaved Jacaranda trees, still in full foliage, cover their rounded crowns with a glorious show of lavender flowers. Along the fences, Madera Negra trees, planted as living fence posts, dress their leafless boughs in clusters of pink blossoms, beloved of orioles and hummingbirds. At the woodland's edge, a scrambling vine of the milkwort family, *Securidaca sylvestris*, displays pealike flowers of delicate pink. Toward the month's end, the abundant Mayo trees may sprinkle their heads with gold.

Scarcity of nectar-bearing flowers silences the hummingbirds, who have fewer nests in this month than in any other. The only species that I have found nesting freely in March is the Violet-headed Hummingbird, which builds its downy cups above or beside streams in the humid depths of the forest. Now, when drying herbs shed many seeds, pigeons and doves that forage over the ground are at the height of their breeding season. Woodpeckers also nest early. Other birds sing increasingly in March and start to build their nests; many even lay their eggs in anticipation of more favorable weather.

Beginning in early March and continuing through much of April, great flocks of Swainson's Hawks, migrating from South America to the western United States, often stream across the sky from horizon to horizon. Where heated air rises above a sunny slope, they pause in their onward flight to spiral upward and regain altitude lost in forward gliding. They take little or no food on their journey and are reluctant to expend energy flapping their wings. With them are often a few

Broad-winged Hawks, which also migrate northward in much smaller flocks of their own.

Here, where the dry season is shorter than along much of the Pacific slope, March is the month for planting. After a shower or two presages the return of wetter days, we sow maize in the field cleared by fire. Among the corn we plant pumpkins and sometimes also a bean that climbs up the cornstalks. If the banana plantation needs to be extended, this is the best time for doing it. Root crops—Cassava, Taro, Tiquisque—are planted now, just before the rains begin. On neighboring farms, where large fields of sugarcane have replaced the small patches that were formerly planted for making brown sugar in ox-driven presses, the cutting of cane continues throughout the dry season. Tractors haul trains of heavily laden trailers to a distant mill, which turns out tons of refined sugar.

In March, the farm gives nothing new for our table. As long as the dry weather continues, the Itabos produce large panicles of edible flowers. Oranges and bananas are usually still plentiful, starchy root crops can be dug from the desiccated soil, and last year's corn remains in the granary.

APRIL

As a youth in Maryland, I did not welcome balmy spring days after a hard winter more joyously than I now greet the showers that end a severe dry season. Often they come in March, rarely later than early April. As the morning advances, clouds gather darkly against the high mountains in the northeast. Gradually they spread outward, by noon covering the sky overhead, while we eagerly await their pent-up water. Too often they dissolve as the afternoon advances, permitting sunshine, no longer welcome, to beat fiercely upon us. Perhaps a few drops fall before the clouds melt away, frustrating our longing for a refreshing shower. But up in the hills they may have released a deluge, swelling the river until it roars loudly as it races past our parched land, laden with silt, leaves, and branches that accumulated in its channel while the current was low.

After nine rainy months, the advent of the dry season is pleasant; but far more delightful and gratefully received are the showers that wash the air clean of smoke and dust, bring brilliant stars back into the nocturnal sky, refresh wilting foliage, stimulate the birds to sing more blithely, and end the danger of brush fires. After a few such showers, the earth is transformed, fresh and green again, as though the stressful final weeks of the dry season had never oppressed it. This, not the bright, flowery days of January, is our true *primavera*, the spring when seeds germinate, resting bulbs and tubers send up new shoots, birds sing and nest. Unlike spring at higher latitudes, the early wet season is, above all, a time of vegetative growth rather than of flowering, although flowers are not wholly lacking.

In the dusk, large *Pyrophorus* fireflies, agleam with two eyelike, greenish lights on top of the thorax and a wider red one beneath the abdomen, weave erratic courses between the trees and often fly through open windows. If one falls upon its back, it bounces into the air with a click, in the manner of elaterid beetles.

Jacaranda trees often continue to flower into April, and in some years are at their best in this month. Now the trees that most add a different color to this green valley, the two species of Mayos, delight the eye with domelike crowns almost solidly covered with bright yellow flowers, attractive to bees and Snowy-breasted Hummingbirds. Here these tall evergreen trees continue to flower profusely in May, and into June on higher slopes, where we view them from afar. On certain April days, gleaming patches of white call attention to an abundant tree or shrub

PYROPHORUS FIREFLY ▶

of the melastome family with precisely timed flowering. More sweetly scented than the tiny melastome flowers are the white blossoms of the orange trees, which for a week or more send fragrance through our garden and into open rooms.

In April, melastome trees that flowered in February ripen small berries, which nourish birds of many families. Other trees and vines open their pods to expose seeds surrounded by soft arils that are eagerly sought by birds, who spread the indigestible seeds far and wide. The abundant oil in these arils may help migrants to store up fuel for their long northward flights; for this is the month when most of those who wintered with us disappear, leaving only a few who will depart in May. Now species that have passed the months of the northern winter chiefly or wholly in South America pause on their long northward journey to reap the bounty of our trees. Red-eyed Vireos become abundant; male Scarlet Tanagers flash amid the verdure; innumerable Olive-backed, or Swainson's, Thrushes flit through the woodland with much singing, far from their summer homes. Occasionally a flock of Eastern Kingbirds suddenly appears, lingers a day or two, then continues on its way. Like swallows and hawks, kingbirds migrate by day, instead of by night, as most small passerine birds do. With a rich supply of small fruits and insects, the resident birds now come into fullest song and breed most freely. In April I have found more nests with eggs, of more species, than in any other month. Before April is past, many have fledged young.

If the planting of corn, rice, and other crops has not been finished, it is still not too late to continue. After the rains become frequent, the vegetable garden should be planted. While waiting for things to grow, pastures can be cleaned of weeds, fences mended, hedges trimmed, and odd jobs done.

MAY

May is a month of brilliant, sunny mornings, during which clouds mass against the high Cordillera, to release their burden of water in torrential afternoon downpours that make the river rise and roar. It was in early May that one of these freshets broke into a side channel that the Río Peñas Blancas had abandoned long before, sending half its water through our farm and giving us an island difficult to reach.

With bright sunshine and no lack of water, animal and vegetable life reach their flood tide. In no other month is the wealth and vitality of tropical nature so impressive. The rain-washed air itself seems to be charged with fertility. Vital processes are contagious; to see and feel the plants and animals around me living more intensely intensifies my own life. Hearing birds sing, watching them build their nests and feed their young, contemplating the sprouting corn, I am myself incited to activity. Although the air may now be less invigorating than that at the outset of the dry season in January, I find the beginning of the rainy season more stimulating intellectually and physically. In January, the bright, dry days inspire a restless wanderlust; in May I have not the least desire to wander. There is so much to see and learn and enjoy close around me that the very thought of leaving the farm is disturbing.

The Mayo trees still display golden flowers above their glossy foliage. Now tall, shapely shrubs of *Palicourea guianensis*, which have sprung up in our garden from seeds dropped by birds, hold generous panicles of bright yellow, orange-stalked flowers above handsome, prominently veined leaves. Sometimes a Rufous-tailed Hummingbird claims one of these shrubs and tries to exclude all competitors, not only other hummingbirds but even large bees and butterflies. On certain May nights, tall shrubs of *Cestrum*, another wildling that grows spontaneously in the garden, open multitudes of small, greenish-white flowers that fill the air with fragrance. Although less flowery than December and January, the landscape in May has its share of floral adornments.

The woody melastomes still yield many berries, while other trees and vines attract the birds with oil-rich arillate seeds. The abundance of wild fruits is attested by the fact that now, even though they are feeding young on all sides, birds consume far fewer bananas at our feeder. Somewhat fewer nests are started in May than in April, but more hold nestlings. Even hummingbirds, whose nests were rare in March and April, begin to breed more freely again. The four species of dull-colored hermit hummingbirds at Los Cusingos—the Long-tailed, Little, Bronzy, and Band-tailed Barbthroat—fasten their nests with cobweb beneath drooping tips of palm fronds, or strips of banana leaf, which form green roofs above them; but even species that lay their two eggs in open downy cups incubate their eggs and rear their young beneath May's downpours. By the middle of the month, all the migrants except a few belated stragglers have left us. I do not doubt that many could breed successfully here, where they pass the greater part of their lives. Why, then, do they go so far, at such great risk, to reproduce?

The birds nesting in our dooryard trees and shrubbery attract snakes, including yellow-and-black Micas up to seven feet long and slender, bright green tree snakes, all of which we seldom see when the nesting season is over. Fortunately, venomous kinds rarely invade our dooryard. Squirrels, too, take their toll of eggs and nestlings. Wherever they breed, birds lose a high proportion of their young to hungry predators.

This is the month we clean the *milpa* and other plantings of swiftly springing weeds. Nearly always the unwanted growths are chopped down with a long ma-

BRONZY HERMIT'S NEST BENEATH BANANA LEAF ▶

chete or scraped off with a broad one, without breaking the ground and exposing it to erosion under the downpours of May.

JUNE

June has less rain than May but more cloudy mornings. After May's exciting days, it is somewhat of an anticlimax, with fewer arresting floral displays to break the monotony of lush, rapidly increasing foliage. Although flowers still bloom, they must be more attentively sought amid the verdure. Now, in the coffee and banana plantations and rocky places in the riverside pasture, an elegant herb of the gesneria family, *Tussacia Friedrichsthaliana*, opens pretty yellow-and-red flowers, which emerge from green, cuplike calyces filled with water. They are borne on large-leaved, fleshy stems, a foot or two high, which in April sprout from thick tubers that have rested dormant in the rich soil during the dry months—a habit of growth common enough in northern lands but rare here in the humid tropics. A vigorous epiphytic shrub of the potato family, *Lycianthes synanthera*, displays clusters of small lavender flowers that attract many pollen-gathering bumblebees.

With the decrease in the number of berries that woody melastomes provide for birds, they sing and nest less; but many, especially those that lost early broods, continue to incubate eggs or feed young in June. The diminutive seedeaters, who wait until the grasses that sprang up anew when the rains returned are ripening the seeds on which they largely subsist, are now at the height of their breeding season, later than most of our birds. I have found more hummingbirds' nests in June than in any other month, although only one more than in December, when eight species were represented, instead of six as in June.

Now the maize spreads its dusty tassels at twice my height above the ground. In years when occasional showers following dry intervals have brought the coffee into flower repeatedly from January to March or April, the coffee bushes begin to ripen their berries in June, and picking begins. At a time when the small, swiftly maturing wild berries that attract birds are dwindling, the larger fruits that we eat start to ripen. Soon our table, which in April and May had little variety of home-grown foods, is richly laden with the produce of our land. Avocado trees, which flowered as the dry season began, now yield their fruits. One compensation for a severe dry season is a heavy crop of mangos. Mango flowers do not endure wetting. The tree beside my study, which in a succession of years with occasional showers during the first quarter does not form a single fruit after profusely flowering, will in a truly dry season bear more mangos than we, the horse, and the Agoutis can eat, or neighbors want.

Pejibaye palms now ripen their fruits on slender trunks that grow to be fifty feet high and bristle with needlelike, black spines. To bring the heavy clusters of one-seeded fruits down from the taller trees is strenuous work; we use a long bamboo pole with a hooked stick tied to its end. These palm fruits must be cooked, for the solid, nutritious, orange or yellow flesh stings the mouth when raw. Now the vegetable garden yields mustard, Chinese cabbage, radishes, cucumbers, and okra, while the *milpa* gives us tender young ears of corn and green pumpkins, which are cooked like squash. Golden oranges from last year's flowering still hang on the trees, and the banana plantation does not fail us. June and July bring us our greatest abundance.

JULY

Although the weather continues wet, July is often the month of least rainfall between May and November, suggesting the second dry season that, a few degrees nearer the Equator, comes each year. If three or four rainless days, rarely more, interrupt the rains in late June or July, the country people speak of *el veranillo de San Juan*—"St. John's little summer."

Vegetative growth still takes precedence over flowering and fruiting, although a considerable variety of flowers and fruits can be found by those who diligently seek them. Now a tall shrub or small tree of the verbena family, *Cornutia grandi-folia*, lifts generous panicles of small violet flowers above large, furry leaves. If this wildling is permitted to remain in dooryard or pasture where it has plenty of room, it makes an ornamental as handsome as any lilac in Maytime. In the forest, an arborescent member of the coffee family, *Cephaelis elata*, displays a tight cluster of small white flowers between two large red bracts that attract the Blue-crowned Woodnymph and other hummingbirds. Also in the woodland, a heliconia, or wild plantain, spreads long, red-margined, yellow bracts in a striking display that draws hummingbirds to the slender yellow flowers that these bracts embrace. In more open places, a taller heliconia catches the eye with large, plain orange bracts. The *Tussacia* continues to flower profusely in stony places, lightly shaded. The most brilliant color in our landscape is provided by an alien from Africa, the red-flowered Flame-of-the-Forest tree (or Tulip tree), which has spread itself by means of winged seeds and now stands out flamboyantly amid the prevailing green.

Days now dawn without the many-voiced chorus that greeted them from March to June. The chief choristers, Gray's Thrushes, have fallen silent; and most other birds sing at most sporadically through the morning. Although I have found about as many nests in July as in June, they belonged to fewer species. Late-breeding seedeaters now provide much of the song and many of the nests. Toward the month's end, wood-pewees arrive, the first migrants from the north to return to us. If they remain silent, I am usually uncertain whether these small, severely plain flycatchers belong to the eastern or the western species.

As the tall Sandpaper tree at the end of the garden ripens its small green fruits, White-faced Monkeys come to eat the thin, sweetish mucilage that surrounds the single, hard, flattish seed. While they eat, seeds and empty husks rain noisily down, calling attention to these shy primates, who, with throaty protests, flee back into the forest the moment they find themselves observed.

July is the time to clear the pastures of swiftly springing weeds, chopping them down with long machetes before they shade out the grass. Perhaps the policeman will bring an order to trim the farm's *ronda*, the strip of bushy or weedy ground that borders the public road. If it has not already started in June, coffee picking now begins. By the month's end, the harvest of mangos and avocados has passed, but the Pejibaye palms continue to yield their heavy clusters of fruit and the Breadfruit trees are maturing their big, green, milky, seedless globes.

AUGUST

August, the month of ripening grains, brings some fine sunny mornings that are often followed by afternoon downpours, reminding us that the rainy season is approaching its climax. A pleasant feature of this valley, particularly agreeable to bird watchers, is the complete absence of long-continued winds. We may pass years with hardly more than light, transient breezes. However, at long intervals, a tornadolike wind blows up after a sunny morning in the rainy season. It may continue for only a quarter of an hour, and although it never affects a large area, it may erupt with such violence that it flattens a field of ripening corn, breaks limbs from trees, or cuts a narrow swath through the forest. The most damaging of these storms in my memory came in early August, many years ago.

Despite heavy rains, the Candelillo trees scattered through the pastures cover themselves with bright yellow, delicately fragrant flowers. A related tall shrub,

WHITE-FACED MONKEY ▶

Cassia bacillaris, which also springs up spontaneously in the pastures, competes with them for the services of pollen-gathering bees to fertilize its own yellow blossoms. In the forest, no tree is now so colorful as the tall Cerillo, laden with globular red flowers that, held high overhead, might be mistaken for clusters of cherrylike fruits. As long as its flowers last, the Cerillo is constantly visited by two kinds of hummingbirds that we rarely see here at other times, the plainly attired Brown Violet-ear and the elegant White-necked Jacobin. Now, too, one of the finest of our native shrubs, a furry-leaved, brittle member of the acanthus family, *Poikilacanthus macranthus*, adorns itself with slender lavender flowers, three inches long, which attract Rufous-tailed and Little Hermit hummingbirds to the tall second-growth woods where it thrives on rich soil. From the tree on which it grows, the *Stanhopea* orchid diffuses a strong spicy odor, which attracts large bees. The two incurved, hornlike projections on the lip of this curiously shaped and spotted orchid earn it the name *torito*—"little bull."

On a fine morning, one may hear many birds sing, but rarely as much as they do in April and May. The chief songsters are now the Blue-black Grosbeak and the Thick-billed Seed-Finch, both of which eat maize or other grass seeds and nest late. Often at dawn, a White-winged Becard, unseen amid the dense foliage of a tree, tirelessly repeats his dulcet notes. From the upper levels of the forest come the sharp whistles, always in a rapid series of three or four, of the Green Shrike-Vireo; its call reminds me that neither I nor any other naturalist, as far as I know, has ever found the nest of this abundant, widespread bird that is so hard to detect amid the verdure with which it blends. In August I have found as many kinds of birds breeding as in July, but they have fewer nests. Ground-feeding doves of the thickets and plantations nest for the second time, after an interval, in May and June, during which they rested while most other small birds were breeding.

Now, after raising their young, the last of the Swallow-tailed Kites depart for their winter home in South America, leaving a vacancy in our sky. About the first of August, Spotted Sandpipers appear along the river. In the following weeks, a few other migrants arrive from the north, but the main influx into our mountain-rimmed valley will come later.

Sometimes in August multitudes of the day-flying moth *Urania fulgens* pass overhead on their way to Panama and South America, or pause to sip nectar from the white, powder-puff flowers of the Inga trees. These handsome black moths, adorned with bands and spots of golden green, are the size and shape of a large swallowtail butterfly, for which they are readily mistaken. After a northward migration earlier in the year, chiefly in April and May, they return southward in largest numbers from July to September. In recent years, I have failed to see such spectacular flights as were more common in past decades.

By mid-August the heavy ears of corn begin to droop on their drying stalks. Now is the time to harvest them, before the protecting husks decay. If gathered ears remain on the ground overnight, awaiting the ox-cart, they are carefully covered to shield them from a drenching by the afternoon rain, which would make them mildew in the granary. With the corn come big, hard-shelled pumpkins of many sizes and shapes, which, stored in a dry place, will remain sound and edible well into the following year.

SEPTEMBER

Although September is usually wetter than August, it is not without sunny days; sometimes a week or more of fairly dry weather interrupts the rains. The Candelillo, the Cerillo, the Flame-of-the-Forest tree, and the *Poikilacanthus* shrub in the woodland shade continue to flower. On rocks in the riverside pasture, a *Sobralia*

opens its fragrant white blossoms at intervals throughout the month. All the plants in the vicinity flower on the same day, then pass two or three flowerless weeks before they all bloom simultaneously again. For a single day in August or September, the shrubby or arborescent Wayside Miconia covers itself with a vast multitude of tiny white flowers, whose minute petals drift downward like falling snowflakes on the following day.

Many birds sing sporadically but few are in full song. Among the most vocal are the Bananaquit and the Scaly-breasted Hummingbird. These two nectar drinkers, along with ground-feeding doves, account for a substantial part of the very few nests of few species that I have found in this month.

September, when the sun crosses the Equator to enter the Southern Hemisphere, is above all the month of migrations. Now the last of the Yellow-green Vireos, and almost the last of the Piratic Flycatchers, follow the Swallow-tailed Kites southward. To compensate for the loss of these summer residents, a host of winter residents arrive, chiefly toward the end of the month. Among them are eleven species of wood warblers, the Red-eyed Vireo, Summer Tanager, Dickcissel, Baltimore Oriole, Barn Swallow, Yellow-bellied Flycatcher, and Broadwinged Hawk. I do not see them come; one day I find not a single individual of a certain migratory species; next day it is present, acting as though it is perfectly familiar with the vegetation and foods of this region so different from those where it fledged thousands of miles away—a marvel of adaptation. Of these arrivals, only the swallows migrate conspicuously by day. They continue toward South America, as do the Red-eyed Vireo and Canada Warbler. The others remain for the winter, some, including the Chestnut-sided Warbler and the Baltimore Oriole, in such numbers that they are among our most abundant birds.

◀ *URANIA FULGENS*

In some years the *Urania* moths continue to pass through September, swelling the southward migration of winged creatures. But the most conspicuous movement is local rather than long-distance, and now, unhappily, largely a thing of the past. Beginning sometimes as early as July but rising to a peak in September, great flocks of Red-lored Parrots and smaller but no less conspicuous parties of raucous Scarlet Macaws came up the valley from the forests where they nested. Both the parrots and the macaws flew in pairs within the flocks, which also contained a few single individuals and trios. After feasting on the ripening fruits of forest trees, including the winged seeds of the Mayos, they returned down the valley. Now, with the destruction of forests, only sadly diminished flocks of the Red-lored Parrots visit us; the macaws, never.

Now July's abundance of fruits for our table has passed. The Pejibaye palms yield the last of their bunches. The main crop of oranges is over, but usually we find a few that come from off-season flowers. Some farmers are still harvesting their corn, but the chief activity throughout the valley is gathering coffee.

OCTOBER

In October the wet season reaches its drenching climax, with more precipitation than many a region that is by no means a desert receives in a year. The rain still comes mostly in afternoon deluges, which may continue well into the night. The swollen river roars and rumbles as it shifts the great boulders in its bed and dashes floating logs against them. But even now many mornings are rainless and some sunny. Occasionally the month brings a *temporal*—which may continue for a day or two or, rarely, for a gloomy fortnight—when, from a high ceiling of clouds, rain falls not only in the afternoons and nights but also in the forenoons, although it is

◀ RED-LORED PARROTS

then rarely as hard as in the afternoon downpours. This is the month when bridges are washed away and mountain roads blocked or carried away by landslides.

Even this excess of falling water does not inhibit flowering. One October no fewer than seven native orchids of the large genus *Maxillaria* bloomed on the trees around our house. Now the curious epiphytic orchid *Elleanthus capitatus* pushes its small purple flowers out from the head of glistening, colorless jelly that envelops the unopened buds and developing fruits. They remind me of a circle of crowded nestling mouths displaying their deep pink lining as they gape for food. On some nights the small, clustered flowers of a shrubby *Cestrum* perfume the air. In the woods where the lavender *Poikilacanthus* flowers are disappearing, another handsome shrub of the acanthus family, *Razisea spicata*, lifts spikes of bright red flowers with long, slender tubes, inviting pollination by the long-billed Long-tailed Hermit. Forest pathways are strewn with the broad white corollas that drop from tall Campana trees.

Berries of the abundant shrubs and trees of the melastome family are not as plentiful now as they were early in the rainy season, but a species of *Miconia* with pretty lavender inflorescences offers shiny, juicy, black fruits a quarter of an inch in diameter. A mistletoe with conspicuous orange flowers, *Psittacanthus americanus*, burdens the crowns of Mayo Colorado trees, where lovely Turquoise Cotingas come to swallow the mistletoe's large black berries whole. High on large-leaved Jacaranda trees, flat, brown, woody pods are splitting into two broad valves to release winged seeds that drift down everywhere, sometimes floating through open windows.

Bird song and nesting are at their lowest ebb. Nevertheless, pairs of constantly mated Rufous-breasted Wrens proclaim their presence as the male and female,

foraging unseen in vine tangles, answer each other with musical verses. Orange-billed Nightingale-Thrushes continue even now to repeat their quaint songs amid the thickets. The hermits that fasten their nests beneath green leafy roofs no longer attend them; but, surprisingly, at least three hummingbirds, the Rufous-tailed, Snowy-breasted, and Scaly-breasted, lay eggs and rear their young in open downy cups exposed to October's downpours. In this inclement weather, their young may take several days longer to attain flight than they do in less rainy months. In some years, little Yellow-faced Grassquits sing and nest in October, but in substantial covered structures with a round doorway in the side.

Migrants from the north continue to filter belatedly into this valley, which, at least in autumn, is not on a main flyway. Now the Yellow-throated Vireo, Golden-winged Warbler, and Rose-breasted Grosbeak appear in our trees, and an occasional Olive-backed Thrush, probably on its way to Colombia, is glimpsed in the woodland shade. High in the treetops, the grosbeaks skillfully bite the embryos from winged Jacaranda seeds. Other migrants join the resident birds at the feeder, where much more fruit is consumed than in May, when so many birds were busy feeding young. During long-continued rainstorms, the feeder board is busy with a colorful, constantly shifting crowd of tanagers, honeycreepers, finches, thrushes, Baltimore Orioles, and Tennessee Warblers, who are often hungry for more bananas than we can supply.

Although the birds' eagerness for our bananas suggests that it is difficult for them to find enough fruits in woodland and thickets, at least one kind of fruit now ripens profusely. The coffee bushes are laden with bright red berries, which in this wet weather soon rot and fall if not picked. On neighboring farms, every able-bodied man, woman, and child arises before daybreak, eats a meager breakfast, and hastens to the coffee plantation with a basket and lunch, in an effort to save the crop. Scarcely any girl will work indoors when so much more can be earned by picking coffee, amid chattering, laughing, often mischievous companions who make the time pass quickly. Nevertheless, if both the crop and the rains are exceptionally heavy, much coffee may be lost for lack of hands to gather it. Picking amid dripping foliage and hauling the morning's harvest to the receiving station over muddy roads, beneath afternoon downpours, bring on many a grippe, which is seldom regarded as important as the money that coffee picking brings.

Toward the month's end, if picking leaves some free days, beans are sown broadcast amid standing, low, lush second growth, which is then slashed down and chopped up to form a mulch through which the seeds will sprout. If all goes well, this planting will yield a crop when sunny days return in the new year.

NOVEMBER

By early or mid-November, the peak of the rainy season has passed. Elsewhere on the Pacific side of Central America, the dry season has already begun; but here many a day will dawn dark and gloomy, and many an afternoon downpour will swell the river, before we have steady dry weather.

Despite the continued wetness, many plants appear to anticipate the advent of sunnier days. The Red Poró trees around the house, which bloom when leafless, begin to drop their foliage and may even display the first of their vivid flowers. In some years, the sturdy Riverwood trees that line the rocky stream banks cover their thinner twigs with massed pinkish stamen-clusters. As though impatient to bloom, many other plants that flower best beneath sunny skies open their earliest blossoms while rains are still frequent and heavy. The Arenilla, a large tree of the myrtle family abundant in the forest, ripens bright red fruits, with soft pulp as astringent as unripe persimmons. From half an inch to an inch and a half in diameter, these

fruits are too big for most birds to swallow. Tanagers peck into them, but Gray's Thrushes and White-throated Thrushes barely manage to swallow the smaller of them whole. If a thrush plucks one too big to force down, it drops the fruit and tries another.

By November, migratory movements have almost ceased. The only new species to appear in this month is the Indigo Bunting, the males in dull winter plumage. Although song is still at low ebb, it is increasing. By the month's end, male Violet-headed Hummingbirds and Blue-throated Golden-tails gather in their singing assemblies, to practice the songs that they will repeat tirelessly through the coming months to attract the females. Gray-breasted Martins sing and defend old woodpeckers' holes, high in dead trees, where they will eventually nest. Variable Seedeaters and Yellow-faced Grassquits, both of which breed again on a reduced scale as the wet season ends, also resume singing. Buff-rumped Warblers sing profusely in November; and in the deep shade of the forest floor, Scaly-throated Leaf-tossers repeat their beautiful, vibrant songs. Among the very few birds that I have found nesting in November are three kinds of hummingbirds, the Yellow-faced Grassquit, and the big, red-crested Pale-billed Woodpecker. Our other large, red-crested woodpecker, the Lineated, begins to carve its nest holes, but I have not found it incubating before December.

Butterflies increase as rainfall diminishes. It was in late November, many years ago, that I found the largest gathering of sleeping butterflies that I have ever seen. The species was *Actinote anteas*, a medium-sized butterfly with pale yellow forewings and dull orange hindwings, both margined with black. One hundred and fifteen of these high-flying butterflies settled in the evening on thin twigs and old, dry inflorescences at the very top of a tall Burío tree, fully exposed to the rain

◄ *ACTINOTE ANTEAS*

and flying creatures of the night. Evidently bats and nocturnal birds did not find them palatable.

On the farm, coffee picking continues, on a reduced scale. Now, as its big, heart-shaped leaves die, we dig up the tubers of a variety of Taro called *malanga* or *papa de maiz*. Well boiled, their soft white flesh is as good as potatoes.

DECEMBER

In December rainfall diminishes but by no means ceases. Most comes in light after-noon showers, but occasionally a day dawns dark and gloomy, with a cold rain that continues until nightfall. Unpaved roads may remain muddy until the month's end. Often, as an afternoon shower ends, a splendid rainbow, or even two concen-tric rainbows, arch across the valley in front of the house, so near that I am almost tempted to seek the pot of gold at its foot. The rainbows fade; the last rays of the setting sun tint the ten-thousand-foot domed summit in the northeast with a lovely roseate alpenglow that slowly dims.

Responding to sunnier skies, shrubs and herbs that have been growing vigor-ously through long rainy months now burst into fullest bloom. This is, above all, the time when composites flower, displaying a profusion of white, yellow, or red floral heads. Here this largest family of flowering plants contains not only weedy herbs but tall shrubs, lianas that climb high into trees, and even a large tree, *Oli-ganthes discolor*, which now spreads ample panicles of small white heads ninety feet above the ground. Tall, strongly scented, weedy mints add small purple or laven-der flowers to the colorful scene. Morning glories that have scrambled over thickets or climbed into treetops cover them with a wealth of blossoms—pink, purple, blue, or white. In riverside thickets, a scrambling hibiscus opens large pink flow-

COMMON POTOO IN CRYPTIC POSTURE ▶

ers, and a Calliandra displays clusters of long, red stamens. Along rocky stream banks, the glossy-leaved *Begonia cuspidata* holds spreading panicles of whitish flowers at the summits of canelike stems two or three yards high. Pealike flowers of the pulse family—yellow, purple, and blue—also bloom amid the floral profusion.

Too delicate to compete with vigorous tropical growths on rich soil, one of my favorite flowers, a low, slender melastome known as *Pterolepis trichotoma*, grows in sterile spots, where it opens half-inch-wide blossoms with four pink petals. Of all the plants in this land of exuberant growths, this little evanescent annual most reminds me of the delicate herbs of northern woods and meadows. On rock surfaces exposed as the river falls, river weeds of the podostemon family, which resemble green algae or mosses more than seed plants, promptly put forth their tiny greenish flowers, to be quickly followed by diminutive seed pods, which look like moss capsules.

Some of the late-flowering woody melastomes—those most generous providers for birds—ripen their small berries in December; but this is a month of flowering rather than fruiting. Consequently, the birds that sing and nest now are nectar drinkers rather than fruit or seed eaters—small birds with minor voices. While thrushes, finches, and other major songsters are mostly silent, hummingbirds and Bananaquits do their best to make their weak notes heard. In December I have discovered eight species of hummingbirds nesting at Los Cusingos—two more than in any other month. (Although I have found one more nest in June than in December, this was because the hermits' nests I then studied were exceptionally easy to detect.) Bananaquits continue their almost year-long breeding through this flowery month. Variable Seedeaters and Yellow-faced Grassquits sing and nest again, but much more sparingly than they do early in the rainy season. The big, red-crested woodpeckers and at least two species of small flycatchers attend their nests in this month, and the only egg of the Common Potoo that I have seen was laid at its very beginning. From this small start as the wet season passes into the dry, the volume of nesting will steadily increase until it climaxes after the rains return in April.

In some years, when showers scattered through the drier months make the coffee bloom repeatedly from January to April, the last red berries are gleaned in December. After the crop has all been gathered, it is not too early to prepare the coffee plantation for the next flowering, removing weeds, lopping off effete branches, and thinning the shade that has become too dense during the rainy months. December is likewise a good time for cleaning pastures, for the sun shines enough to dry the severed or uprooted weeds before they root from the stems and establish themselves more firmly.

Almost the only fruits for our table that ripen now are oranges, bananas, and pineapples. For cooking, Cassava, Tiquisque, and the last of the Taro can be dug from the ground. A vigorous Chayote vine continues to yield its big, green, one-seeded fruits, one of Costa Rica's standard vegetables. With drier months ahead, this is not the time to plant anything, except in ground that can be irrigated.

Now, with the earth splendidly arrayed in verdure and flowers, the tropical year draws to its end. It was a year when, despite all vicissitudes, never a week passed without some plants flowering, some trees putting forth fresh foliage, some fruits ripening, some birds singing and nesting, some butterflies or bees sipping nectar. To one accustomed to the four strongly contrasting seasons of middle latitudes, such a year may appear monotonous. One may miss the diversity provided by snowy winter's leafless trees and barren fields, springtime's marvelous renascence of dormant life, summer's full verdure, autumn's fruitfulness and colorful foliage. Our seasons are only two, the wet and the dry, and throughout the latter the high forest, which not long ago covered this valley, remains green. The year's most abrupt change comes with the return of the rains; and even this would bring less contrast if man had not replaced evergreen forests with pastures and thickets that turn brown, if he did not annually pollute the air with smoke, which the first showers wash away, bringing blue back into the sky. Nevertheless, it is only to the superficial view that the tropical year is monotonous. When a seeing eye gives attention to details, it notices endless change, with more exciting natural events in every week than one will find at a latitude where a large part of the living world lies dormant through long, cold months.

3. My First Harvest

THE year I bought Los Cusingos, I planted no crops, as Don Chico had already prepared his fields for sowing and reserved their produce for himself. With so many other matters to occupy me, I was glad to be relieved of this additional responsibility. By the following January, 1942, I had arranged most of the preliminaries and was ready to settle permanently on the land. Early in the month, I went to San José and bought two horses—a stallion and a mare. I took them back to the farm, riding them alternately over the long mountain trail on a journey of four days. Then, for the next four and a half years, I hardly interrupted my residence in my new home, except for short visits to the capital at yearly or longer intervals.

On my way back to the farm with the horses, I noticed that farmers who intended to plant on newly cleared lands had already started to attack the giant forest trees. The felling of heavy forest sometimes begins in December; during my early years in El General, when much woodland still remained, I came to associate the crash of falling trees with the brilliant days that start off the dry season. When I bought Los Cusingos, I resolved not to sacrifice any of my forest, but to farm only land that had already been cleared—about half of my acreage. The lighter second growth that springs up on resting farmlands dries, after it has been cut down, much more quickly than the primeval forest, so that it was not necessary to begin so early to prepare my *milpa*.

Since the house that Don Chico was building across the river was still un-finished, he continued to occupy his little thatched cabin at the edge of the bluff, fifty yards from my new house. Wishing to profit by his long experience in farming and knowledge of local conditions, I suggested that we make a *milpa* together. I would provide the land, he his experience; we would share equally all expenses for labor, and each would take half of the harvest. He did not hesitate to accept this advantageous arrangement. We chose for planting a plot of about a dozen acres, which had rested for several years and was covered with a scarcely penetrable growth of young trees, bushes, and vines, eight to ten yards high. Later, I realized that this was a greater area than I could plant with maize each year without over-working my land and causing its rapid deterioration. But, this first year, I was eager to make my farm show a profit, not so much because I had immediate need of the money, as that I wished to prove that I could support myself here.

We found several young men who undertook to slash down the bush that cov-ered the field, at the rate of about one dollar per acre. Early in February, they set to work with their long, straight machetes, which easily severed the slender young trunks and the vines. They rarely worked more than half a day, because a six-hour day had become customary in this region where, through most of the year, rain is likely to fall soon after midday. Three weeks sufficed to cut down the field's lush vegetation, which dried quickly in February's bright sunshine. Much of the time while this work was in progress, Don Chico was absent on an expedition to search for gold in old Indian graves—a favorite occupation from which, even in old age, he could not desist. Still unfamiliar with all the finer details of making a corn field, I could not adequately supervise our laborers. Eager to earn their money promptly, they failed to sever all the vines, which continued to grow and spread after the sup-porting trees had fallen, to give us trouble later.

The year turned out to be exceptionally wet, with light afternoon showers even in February. Nevertheless, toward the month's end, smoke began to rise on all sides, from fields that were to be planted. At midday on March 6, two neighbors set fire to large areas of newly felled forest. Dense smoke rose in great columns far into the air, and its fine particles apparently supplied centers of condensation for the abundant water vapor in the atmosphere. In any event, before sunset a drenching shower cooled the embers of these fires, at the same time soaking the field that we wished to dry.

We could not plant corn without removing by fire the recumbent brush that made the field almost impassable. I had been growing uneasy about the weather, and repeatedly asked my partner when we would burn. He continued to advise delay, promising that we would eventually have a *verano de los pendejos*—a "lazy man's dry spell"—for the benefit of laggards who had been slow to prepare their fields for burning. From the sixth through the eighteenth of March, heavy showers fell every afternoon. At last, on the nineteenth, we had a rainless day, and another on the twentieth. The following day, I proposed to Don Chico that we burn. Although he tried to put me off with more promises of "the lazy man's summer," this time I was insistent. The morning of March 21 was bright, and shortly before noon we set fire to our field.

No great conflagration rushed with leaping flames and loud crackling over the field, filling the air with blinding smoke, as I have often seen in drier years. The ground was wet; even the topmost layers of the cut vegetation were hardly dry. Nevertheless, with much patient coaxing, we started here and there a fire that would spread. The part of the field that had been cut last burned best. Where the bush had been felled more than a month earlier, the unsevered vines had continued to grow, and new, green vegetation had sprung up, retarding the drying of the

dead stuff during those three sunny mornings and impeding the advance of our fire.

Soon after two o'clock that afternoon, a drenching shower fell, extinguishing our struggling fires and with them our prospects of a good harvest. Well over half of our dozen acres remained untouched by fire and represented so much lost labor. Most of the rest had burned poorly, leaving charred trunks and branches littering the ground to make planting and cleaning difficult. We had seized our last chance to burn, for the afternoon showers continued to fall, and soon our lost acres were covered with waist-high vegetation, so lush and dense that I could hardly force my way through it. Many other farmers in the valley were in the same unhappy plight as we. Before El General was connected with the rest of Costa Rica by airplanes or highway, a rainy "dry season" that prevented the burning off of the fields for *milpas* caused people to go hungry for lack of maize for their tortillas.

Although in later years I hired labor for all the field work, that first year I wished to participate in all the operations of the farm, the better to learn how they should be done. If dry weather continues after the field for maize has been burned, it may safely lie unsown for a week or two—a desolate, charred waste—until a few good showers have given an earnest of the wet season's return. But this first year, when the ground had long been soaked, it was imperative to plant the corn promptly, so that its young sprouts would not be overwhelmed by growths that quickly sprang from stumps, rootstocks, and seeds that remained alive in the hardly scorched soil.

I took my *macana*, a stout wooden pole tipped with a long, narrow iron blade, and tied around my waist a gourd containing the seed-corn, which had been moistened with kerosene to discourage the ants and other animals that might eat it. Thus equipped, I joined the men and boys we had hired to help with the sowing. With a single stroke of the *macana*, I opened a shallow hole in the ground, dropped in six grains of maize, and covered them loosely with my foot. Then I took two steps forward and repeated the operation. Charred logs and branches retarded my progress over the field and blackened my clothes. Thus I planted maize much as the Indians must have done on this same land, before Columbus came; except that, having no iron, they had probably used a sharpened stick of hard wood, as my neighbors sometimes did. In sowing my land, I felt that I established a closer bond with it, and possessed it more intimately, than if I held title to it in name only.

We never hoed or cultivated our *milpa*. When the maize was a foot or two high, the field was cleaned by chopping down the weeds close to the ground with a machete. Then the maize required no further care until it was ready to be harvested. On new lands, still nearly free of the grasses and troublesome weeds that come in with repeated plantings, it is sometimes possible to produce a satisfactory crop of maize without giving it any care between sowing and reaping.

While the maize was sprouting, I turned my attention to rice. The big field where we planted maize had not burned clean enough to sow rice there, as we had planned. But fortunately, soon after buying the farm, I had lent a small plot to a little old man for planting tobacco. In return, he had promised that, after removing his crop, he would leave the field free of weeds and ready for sowing. After being reminded, the man fulfilled his promise, giving me the best-prepared ground on the farm, a half acre suitable for rice and a few vegetables. Although in the Orient, as in some parts of the Americas, rice is grown in wet or flooded fields, varieties used in Central America thrive on well-drained ground. Indeed, rice, a thrifty plant, yields fairly well on poor soil where maize, which must feed gluttonously in rich earth to form its heavy ears, is hardly worth planting.

To help me sow the rice, I engaged Raul, a lad of twelve, son of an unmarried woman who lived on a small lot adjoining Los Cusingos. With a pointed stick, I jabbed holes into the ground, an inch or two deep and about half a yard apart. Raul followed with the rice seed in a calabash, from which he took a pinch of the grains, about a dozen seeds, and dropped them into each hole, then loosely covered them by brushing in the surface soil. When I found that my rows tended to converge, I returned to the house for a cord, although I had never known anyone else to plant rice with a guide line. Now rotting stumps and logs, remnants of the vanished forest, interfered with the cord and prevented our drawing it straight. We interrupted the sowing while we pushed and kicked over all the stumps rotten enough to yield to this treatment and carried or rolled off the sloping field all the logs not too heavy to be moved. When we attacked them with poles as levers, most proved to be movable; although one huge, charred trunk, which lay across the middle of the plot, was clearly there to stay. Then we carried away all the dead tobacco stalks and weeds that the old man had merely pulled up and left to dry where they fell. At the conclusion of our labor, the land, although not wholly free from the stubborn remains of the forest, was much cleaner than most rice fields in this newly settled district. Our effort to plant in straight lines was rewarded also with freedom from trash and economy of space.

Six weeks after planting, the rice, already a foot high, delighted me with its straight rows of vivid green. Now Raul was assigned the task of weeding the field, which he did by scraping away the unwanted growths at the surface of the soil with a broad, curved machete, like a scimitar with an exceptionally wide blade. Rice, a lower and more delicate plant than the coarse, rapidly growing maize, needed to be cleaned more carefully.

After sowing the rice, I set about to enlarge my fields of sugarcane, of which the farm already had about two acres in production. Here cane flowers in the middle of the wet season, sending up, from the top of each mature stalk, a long, slender spear that expands into an ample panicle of tiny florets. A flowering cane field, with the delicate tassels rising high above crowded ranks of nodding green leaves, is a pleasant sight; but these flowers fail to produce viable seeds.

Lacking seeds, sugarcane is readily propagated without them. One can lay a whole mature cane in a shallow trench, cover it lightly with soil, and have a new shoot spring up from most of the nodes, each of which also produces a cluster of roots. Or the cane can be cut into short lengths, which, when dropped into holes suitably spaced, will give new cane plants. The leafy tops, which are lopped off and thrown aside when the cane is cut for milling, also serve for propagation. Or one can detach the stout young suckers that spring from the subterranean rootstocks, and set them, upright or slanting, in rows that will soon give cane for cutting. This is the method that Don Chico advised me to use.

To plant with suckers makes the greatest drain on the parent cane field. I have heard this procedure described as "pulling up one cane field to start another." Later, I tried some of the more economical methods of propagation used by big cane growers. But digging trenches for laying down whole canes proved too laborious in our rocky ground. When I planted short segments of canes, termites destroyed many of them. Again and again, when I tried to substitute scientifically approved procedures for seemingly wasteful and inefficient local practices, I ran into trouble and reverted to the local methods. Today, with all-weather motor roads, tractors, fertilizers, and other aids unavailable to the early settlers, agricultural practices in the valley are rapidly changing; but, at the period of which I write, the local farmers seemed to be doing about as well as they could with time-honored means.

In this planting, I was assisted by Abel Cordero. He had already done odd jobs for me, when in March he asked permission to build a thatched cabin on my land. He selected a site near the river, where water would not be far to carry, and close to the new cane field we were making. Then he requested a loan of fifty *colones* (then about eight dollars) to buy boards and nails. With posts and poles cut from the woods, a cartload of rough boards, and cane leaf for the roof, he finished his *rancho* in two or three weeks. Then he moved in with his wife, Selmira, and their four young daughters, Beatriz, Carmen, María Luisa, and Luz Clara. After they were settled in their new home, with its few crude wooden furnishings, its battered pots and pans, they looked so contented and happy that I asked myself why I had spent so much money and time building a bigger, more substantial house.

Abel was tall and thin, with black hair, penetrating blue eyes, and a smile that was pleasant in spite of bad teeth. He wore a battered straw hat and went without shoes. Those blue eyes distinguished him from his neighbors, most of whom had dark eyes, derived from Spanish and Indian ancestors, whose blood ran mixed in their veins. An illegitimate child, Abel attributed his blue eyes to an unnamed German father. Although he had never gone to school, he had taught himself to read but not to write.

Abel's versatility was most valuable to me. He could plant nearly all the local crops. He was a good ox-driver and, with little assistance, could cut a cartload of sugarcane, press out the sap in an ox-driven mill, and boil it until it would solidify into the hard brown cakes called *dulce* (then commonly used by the country people instead of refined sugar). An accomplished axeman, he could cut and square timbers. He did most of the work on the *bahareque* walls of my house, including the whitewashing. He was full of ideas for arranging things and making improve-

ments. Always courteous and willing, he was an excellent handyman, and for nearly three years served me well. I paid him at the current local rate of a *colon* and a
half (about twenty-five U.S. cents) for a six-hour day. (Since I came to Los Cusingos, wages for farm labor have increased about twentyfold, but the prices of
many essential commodities have risen in about the same ratio.) A few months
after Abel came to live on the farm, his daughter Beatriz, a girl of fifteen with a
harelip, became my cook, a position that she filled intermittently for a decade.
Long before she finally left us, to bear an illegitimate child, her father had departed
for what he hoped would be a better job.

In February, I had been occupied with explorations of the neighborhood and
making bookshelves. When these were finished, and the books, released from long
confinement in boxes, stood patiently in rows, like old companions awaiting a
friendly greeting, the new house began, at last, to acquire the atmosphere of a
home. In March and April, when the rains began, I was busy planting; in addition
to maize, rice, sugarcane, and garden vegetables, we set out plantains, Cassava,
and Tiquisques for food, and hundreds of stakes of Madera Negra trees as living
fence posts. By May, when rain fell heavily almost every afternoon, the season for
planting ended. Now I could give more time to the birds, which in April and May
sang profusely and were at the height of their nesting. I found and studied nests
that I had never seen before, including those of the Great Antshrike, Black-faced
Antthrush, Tawny-bellied Euphonia, and Baird's Trogon.

Early in the year, my diet consisted chiefly of grains, including beans, rice,
and maize in the form of tortillas. Plantains, bananas, and starchy root crops like
Cassava and Tiquisque helped to vary it. About two months after the rains returned, my vegetable garden began to yield. How I enjoyed those first green things
after months without fresh vegetables! First to be ready were the mustard and

tender bean pods, which were followed by cucumbers and okra. Soon I had suc-
culent ears of milky young corn from the main field, which, if gathered at the
proper stage, I have always found so delicious that I have never planted a special
variety for the table. As the maize grains became more solid, Beatriz and her mother prepared a surprising variety of dishes from them, making custards, cakes, and
tortillas of unripe corn, until finally the grains hardened and we were back to our
standard breadstuff, tortillas made of boiled dry corn. With oranges, avocados,
pineapples, and other fruits, my board at this season almost groaned beneath good
things to eat, and sometimes I wished for someone to share them.

Planted in March, the maize had tasseled in May, and by mid-August the
heavy ears were drooping on their drying stalks, telling us that they were ready to
be gathered. It was wet work harvesting the corn in the early mornings, in the
field where weeds and vines were already waist high. Breaking the ears from the
stalks but preserving the husks intact, we tossed them into heaps, which were
gathered up by Abel in the ox-cart I had bought, and hauled through the forest to
the big thatched shed that Don Chico had made for his cane press. Here I divided
the corn into equal parts. Don Chico's share was carted across the river to his new
house, while mine was stored on a platform made of split trunks of the Chonta
palm, laid across the rafters of the shed. Ears that came naked from the field, because the husks were loose, were shelled out and the grain was sold. I had no animals to consume it before it became infested by weevils.

While harvesting the maize, I found an ear that had sunk down, leaving a loose
husk as a broad hood above it. In the space between the hood and the ear were a
number of long, finely branched grass inflorescences, forming a snug little nest,
which I surmised had been made by one of the small, brown Plain Wrens that
lived in just such low, tangled vegetation as now covered the part of the field that

we had failed to burn and plant. If my conjecture was correct, this would be the wren's dormitory rather than a nest for eggs and young. For breeding, the wren builds a well-enclosed structure with a doorway in the side; for sleeping, it makes a more open and flimsier nest, or may occasionally take advantage of some convenient shelter, such as this corn husk. I left this maize plant standing intact in the midst of the harvested field.

Early next morning, I went out under brilliant stars and the bright last quarter of the moon. Peeping in beneath the hoodlike maize husk, I found the wren sleeping on the ear, surrounded by the wispy pieces of grass it had placed there, which outlined rather than enclosed its bedroom. It rested with its long tail outward, its breast against the base of the husk that arched over it. Its brown feathers were all fluffed out, revealing much of their gray bases; its head was buried somewhere in the loose, roundish mass of down; only its long, brown tail with dusky bars, and the brown ends of its wing plumes, stood out as distinct features from the downy ball. Thus slept the wren, well sheltered from dew and wind and rain by the dry maize husk.

Undisturbed by the beam of light that I directed upon it, the bird slept quietly while the stars faded, the moon paled, the east grew brighter, and the earliest birds broke into song. Soon the sharp, clear *chin-cheery-gwee, chin-cheery-gwee* of another of its kind, doubtless its mate, reached me across the dewy corn field. A few seconds later, my wren lifted its head from among the feathers of its left side, revealing its long, sharp bill and the light streak above its eye. It smoothed down its out-fluffed plumage and looked around. Dazzled by the flashlight beam, it lingered motionless for a few seconds, then darted out into the dim dawn to scold me sharply amid the weeds.

By the time the maize had been gathered in, the long tassels of the rice were nodding with the weight of yellow, ripening grains. The tiny, black-and-white Variable Seedeaters and other finches flocked to eat them; the longer we delayed to harvest them, the less we would have. With poles cut in the neighboring thicket, we made a low frame, across which we tied horizontal sticks, an inch apart, to form a grating. Against this grating we beat the heads of rice; beneath it, we spread sacks to catch the rice; and around three sides of the frame we stretched sacks and blankets, to stop flying grains. While two men cut the rice with their machetes and brought it in sheaves, a third beat the stalks in double handfuls against the sticks to knock off the grains. After thoroughly drying the rice in the morning sunshine, we stored it in wooden chests, each grain still tightly enclosed in its ribbed chaff, which, like the husks of the maize, guarded it from the attacks of weevils. As the rice was needed for cooking, the chaff was pounded off by a heavy wooden pestle in a big mortar, made by hollowing out a section of a thick tree trunk. Such was the laborious simplicity of farms at the edge of the wilderness, still untouched by mechanization and unafflicted by troublesome labor laws.

In mid-September, I paused to review what I had accomplished since buying the land. Two of the chief crops, maize and rice, had been harvested and stored. The sugarcane was producing more than when I acquired the farm. The pastures were in good condition. My modest dwelling was nearing completion, and I had, with my own hands, made simple furniture for it. Around the house were promising young fruit and ornamental trees and much colorful shrubbery that I had planted. While making these improvements, I had managed to preserve a substantial part of the small capital I had brought with me the preceding year. And with all this, I had still found some time for studying the birds and even for writing.

At such a time, one is apt to feel contented with his accomplishments—a contentment spiced, perhaps, with a pinch of pride. Doubtless, it is not wrong occasionally to indulge in such satisfaction with our practical achievements, provided that we never lose sight of their smallness, whether measured on a cosmic or a human scale, nor forget the insecure foundation upon which material prosperity rests. Under his own roof, with his own land and trees, his own animals and stored grains and growing crops around him, one feels somewhat sheltered from the chill vacuity of the interstellar spaces, and even from the violent social agitations that torture mankind today. He can go about his work with unhurried deliberation, a sense of ample time for its completion, for which the rootless wanderer, with neither a home nor sustaining reserves, yearns in vain.

Perhaps it is not wholly a misfortune that we, like other animals, must devote a substantial portion of our time and strength to the satisfaction of material needs. The scientist is sometimes overcome by paralyzing doubts about the value of the facts that he toils to discover; the artist knows intervals of surfeit or disgust with his art; the philosopher may become entangled in bewildering mazes of speculation. I had known something of this devastating state of mind. The advantage of working to satisfy our basic needs is that we know exactly what we are working for, and its value. If we begin to question whether these things are worth the effort, a day without a meal, a wet night without a roof, an hour in a biting wind without warm clothing will dispel all misgivings. The interest of the daily task and the weariness when it is done leave little room for the intrusion of debilitating doubts. The worker's most distressing uncertainty is whether the product of his toil will satisfy his vital needs. Remove this incertitude, and the simple, honest man is content. The danger is that we become so engrossed in the pursuit of material things that we live for them alone, losing sight of all beyond. From this debasing blindness, I trusted to the living world around me, the mountains that rose before me, the sky above, and the books upon my shelves to preserve me.

4. The Thatched Shed

WHEN I bought Los Cusingos from Don Chico, a large thatched shed stood beside the creek that flows into the Río Peñas Blancas in front of our house. Beneath it was a *trapiche*, or sugar mill, consisting of vertical steel rollers for squeezing the sap from the sugarcane, and a stone hearth with a huge copper caldron. The press was operated by a yoke of oxen who walked around and around, beneath a heavy, rotating, horizontal beam that turned the cylinders, while a man or boy stuck the canes between them, one or two at a time. In the caldron, the juice was boiled and thickened over a wood fire, until, when poured into tapered holes cut into a wooden block, it would harden into the flat cakes of brown sugar called *dulce*. Dissolved in hot water, this made *agua dulce*, a favorite drink of the country people.

I did not buy the somewhat worn *trapiche*, which would have substantially increased the price of the farm. A year or so after my arrival, it was removed by the neighbor who purchased it from Don Chico. The roof that had sheltered the cane press proved useful for storing corn, until the thatch of sugarcane leaves decayed and rain poured in. Rather than rethatch the wide expanse of this roof, I decided to build a smaller shed to shelter the horses and store maize.

The spot chosen for the new shed was a slight rise of ground at the edge of the pasture, beside the creek. In the forest we cut four stout posts with forks at the top, from Cacique trees with smooth gray bark and hard, close-grained wood resistant to decay. With difficulty we dug four holes in the very rocky ground, which, ages ago, had been the bed of the neighboring river, and in these we set the posts upright at the corners of the shed. Then we laid a stout horizontal beam between each pair of the forked posts, and on them we erected, with thinner poles, the framework of a high-peaked roof, which we thatched with leaves of the sugarcane. When all was done, we had an open shed where the three horses could keep dry during the hard downpours of the long rainy season.

As harvest time approached, we pulled broad strips from the hard outer shell of a tall trunk of a fallen Chonta palm, and laid them as a floor above the space where the horses stood. Setting boards around the edges of this second story, we made a bin that would hold several cartloads of corn, all within the high-peaked roof.

Year after year, we grew a variety of maize called *tusa morada* ("purple husk") for its deep purplish husks, which tightly enclose the ear and extend beyond it in a long beak. These tough husks keep out the weevils that, in a continuously moist, warm climate, destroy so much stored grain; with such husks, most ears remain sound from one harvest to the next. As the years went by, neighboring farmers began to plant new varieties of maize, with larger ears that tended to outgrow their clothes. Poorly protected from weevils, this corn did not keep well when stored in the husks. If not sold promptly, it had to be treated with pesticides. Some sprinkled such dangerous poisons as chlordane over unhusked ears; others shelled their corn and stored the loose grains in large metal drums, with a preservative. Preferring to avoid pesticides that might contaminate our tortillas or the food of the horses and chickens, I continued to plant the old "purple husk" variety, sacrificing quantity for purity.

THE THATCHED SHED ▶

The thick husks were no obstacle to the sharp teeth of Cinnamon-bellied Squirrels from neighboring woods, who before long discovered the open granary where our maize was stored. The corn that they exposed attracted birds. The Blue-black Grosbeaks that nested in orange trees scattered through the pasture came with sharp, excited notes and broke the grain in their powerful bills. They did not disdain grains infested with weevils or softened by partial decay, which our well-fed chickens would not eat. Two related species of doves, the White-fronted and the rufous-naped race of the Gray-chested, often flew into the granary but, ever shy, fled whenever they saw me approaching. Grains that fell through the slats of the floor attracted Gray-necked Wood-Rails, who came, singly or in pairs, to glean them from the dusty ground where the horses stood. Their keen red eyes would spy me while still a long way off; with long strides of bright red legs they would run rapidly into the bushes that bordered the stream a few yards away. I could watch these handsome rails eat my corn only through binoculars from a distance. I never found them in the elevated granary where doves and grosbeaks feasted more abundantly.

In March of the year after the shed was erected, a brown Gray's Thrush built her nest in a dark corner; and in April a pair of Blue Tanagers made a much smaller and softer cup on the round ridgepole, in the very center of the high-peaked roof, equally distant from both ends. The outer wall of the thrush's nest contained much green moss and brown maize silk. In it she laid three pale blue eggs speckled and mottled with rusty brown, which she hatched in twelve days. Then she and her mate fed the nestlings, two of whom survived to leave the nest early on the morning when they were sixteen days old. The female tanager laid and hatched two smaller eggs, blue-gray mottled with brown, but raised only one nestling; the other

◀ GRAY-CHESTED DOVE

died in the nest. In the two following years, the thrush again nested in the shed, each time building on the ridgepole. In the first of these years, she again laid three eggs and raised two young; in the second, she laid the unusually large set of four eggs but produced a single fledgling. The tanagers built one more nest upon the ridgepole, but if they laid in it the eggs vanished before I saw them.

As the years passed, more and more squirrels formed the habit of carrying off our corn, sometimes dropping half-eaten ears at a distance from the granary. Evidently they were not the only thieves, for one day I noticed a larger gap in the pile than they could have made. Moreover, rising wages made the replacement of the cane-leaf thatch every few years increasingly expensive. All over the valley, the old thatched cabins of the early settlers were being replaced by dwellings with corrugated iron roofs, less picturesque but less liable to develop leaks and cheaper to maintain. Accordingly, when after serving a dozen years, the horses' shed again needed thatching, I decided to build another granary.

The new granary, set on stone bases behind the house, was substantially built of heavy timbers and sawed boards, with a roof of corrugated aluminum that would last indefinitely and never need paint. In front was a stone-paved porch where the horses could take shelter. A stout padlock on the door would thwart thieves. At first, a squirrel or two, not to be deprived of their accustomed diet of maize, found their way in through the narrow space that had been left for ventilation between the walls and the roof, but they soon discontinued their visits.

Now bats, which had never been troublesome in the old open granary, started to hang up by day in the dimly lighted interior of the new one. I never learned whether their body temperature dropped to near that of the air while they slept, as that of certain bats has been found to do by day and that of hummingbirds does on cool nights—a physiological adaptation that saves much energy for tiny bodies with a high metabolism. However, the bats' prompt flight when I tried to chase them out suggested that, in this mild climate, their temperature remained high. They would circle around exasperatingly above my head, doubtless avoiding obstacles by the echolocation that more or less blind bats practice, until, one by one, they darted under the eaves into the bright daylight that they tried to avoid. Because they foul whatever is beneath them, and to husk ears of corn that they soiled was most unpleasant, I repeatedly drove them away. But bats are stubbornly persistent animals, and they returned again and again to hang up in the same spots. Finally, I outwitted them by closing the space between the walls and roof with fine-meshed wire net, which keeps out most pests except rats, mice, cockroaches, and weevils.

Years passed. Each August the granary received cartloads of corn, and by the following August it was empty again. As the valley's population rapidly increased and roads were slowly improved, bus lines stretched out from San Isidro in all directions, and horses almost disappeared from the roads. Finally, the buses reached our farm, at first once a week, then daily, twice daily, and at last three times a day. However, a bus of moderate size could not cross the narrow suspension bridge over the Río General; going to town, or returning, passengers had to walk across the bridge to take another bus on the other side.

On my way to San Isidro one morning, I was waiting with other passengers by the bridge when a tall, powerful man accosted me. I recognized him as Bacho, a former neighbor who had lived on a few acres that had been cut from my farm before I bought it. Our relations had been somewhat strained, because Don Chico, who had sold this plot of land, had promised to give a deed for it after his farm had been titled. However, the property was not surveyed and registered until I signed a contract for its purchase. The surveyor's plan that I received omitted the land at its northern end that Don Chico had already sold, because this would have made the farm larger than he had claimed. Nevertheless, a succession of owners had pressed me for a title to their plot and were unconvinced when I explained that it was not included in my plan and that I made no claim to it. The best I could offer to do was to help them obtain an independent title if they took the necessary steps through a lawyer. This left a certain coolness between my neighbors to the north and myself.

Now Bacho, whom I had not seen since he moved away years earlier, wished me to accompany him to the middle of the bridge. Perplexed, and slightly apprehensive, because he was occasionally violent, I followed him. As we stood high above the river rushing down its rocky channel, beyond hearing of the other passengers, he asked, "Don Alejandro, did you ever miss any corn from your granary?"

"Yes, I thought somebody stole corn, but I was not sure who did it."

"I took it. My children were hungry, and I had no money to buy corn for their tortillas."

"I see."

"I confessed to the padre, who said I must pay for what I stole."

Then, taking a note of twenty *colones* from his wallet, he offered it to me. At that time, before devaluation and inflation had reduced the *colon* to a small fraction of its former value, a laborer like Bacho would have to work the better part of a week to earn so much. I hesitated to receive this compensation for a small theft made so long before that I had almost forgotten it, but I thought it would be wrong to refuse the money that Bacho's confessor had directed him to pay me in order to make peace with his conscience. Finally, I said: "I do not know how much corn you stole, but I will take what you think you should give me. *Muchas gracias!*"

We shook hands and went our separate ways. I have never seen the man again.

Like many people, I had been doubtful about the value of the confessional. Since the early Christian centuries, it has been alleged by opponents of the Church, notably by the Emperor Julian, that to receive absolution and feel free of guilt made the penitent only too ready to repeat his sin, perhaps again and again. Now I had direct evidence that, at least occasionally, confession is followed by repentance and desire to make amends for past misdeeds. As the bus bumped along the stony road toward San Isidro, I reflected how much better it is for the wrongdoer, no less than for the person whom he has injured, when the former gives just compensation instead of languishing in prison, at great expense to the state. Unfortunately, people commit crimes, including murder and other acts of violence, for which restitution can never be made.

The rustic open granary of my pioneer days was picturesque and provided some interesting observations on birds. Only the corn that the squirrels stole was never paid for. Nevertheless, in these days when thieves are increasingly numerous and bold, it is comforting to know that our harvested grain is safely under lock and key.

5. Small Mammals

NOT long ago, Jaguars, Pumas, Tapirs, Forest Deer, Coatimundis, Collared Peccaries, Tayras, and White-faced Monkeys dwelt in the forest on this farm. Now all have vanished from the well over a hundred acres of old forest and tall second-growth woods available to them, except a single troupe of monkeys, who remain because they have become exceedingly wary. Gone, too, are some of the larger birds, partly because they need a greater extent of wild woodland, partly as a result of persecution by trespassing hunters and dogs. Very rarely now we glimpse a wandering Tayra, who is not welcome because it carries off chickens; or the footprints of a Forest Deer reveal that it has passed unseen.

Squirrels, brownish above and bright cinnamon on breast and belly, seem to have become more abundant than they were when I came here. Certainly they are more numerous in the garden, where they plunder too many birds' nests that I wish to study and eat the leaves and bark of our hibiscus shrubs. Other foods that I have seen them take include Guavas green and ripe, fruits of the Scarlet Passionflower and the Pejibaye palm, and, of course, corn. Not long ago, I watched a squirrel tear apart, with its teeth, a thick decaying vine in the undergrowth of the forest. It discarded the fibers and ate something that it found among them. Examining the vine, I found a number of white insect larvae, large and small, deeply embedded in it, which were evidently the rodent's food. Once I saw a squirrel break small flakes of lichen-encrusted bark from a recently dead avocado tree, and, with its lower incisors, scrape something, possibly cambium cells, from the inner side, after which it dropped the flakes.

One morning, while watching a birds' nest in a wooded ravine, I saw a squirrel pluck the large inflorescence of a shellflower, a species of *Calathea*, and carry it to a horizontal branch. Sitting there on its haunches, the rodent held the flat inflorescence in its forepaws and started to remove the dull orange-yellow bracts, beginning at the base of the inflorescence, which it held upside down. As it bit away the thick, stiff bracts and dropped them, the animal ate something white, which may have been the axis of the inflorescence. The squirrel continued busily until it reached the apex of the floral stem, then hopped away. Certainly, these squirrels are opportunists who consume almost anything that will yield a little nourishment.

Probably these Cinnamon-bellied Squirrels have multiplied because of the decrease of their natural enemies, the larger predatory mammals and birds, and probably also snakes. Once I watched a squirrel behave queerly in the presence of a Mica, a black-and-yellow arboreal snake that preys insatiably upon birds' nests and also eats mammals at least as large as rats. One morning an agitated crowd of birds and a scolding squirrel drew my attention to a seven-foot Mica resting in a tree in front of the house. As I approached, the birds dispersed but the rodent remained, chattering excitedly. It ran all around the serpent, viewing it now from this side, now from that, advancing closer and closer to it. As the squirrel advanced along the horizontal bough where the snake's forepart rested, the latter drew back its head. I watched, fascinated, while the quadruped cautiously advanced to within a foot of the reptile's retracted head. Would the little mammal attack the Mica? Would the snake capture and swallow the squirrel? Finally, when the rodent was

hardly its own length from the serpent's retracted black-and-yellow head, the latter struck out, more defensively than aggressively, it seemed. Thereupon, the squirrel retreated. But for some time it continued to hop around and scold the snake, preserving now a more prudent distance.

What motivated this squirrel's puzzling behavior? Was it "charmed" by the snake, as birds are said to be (although I know no reliable observation of this)? Was the furry animal simply curious? Did it have young hidden nearby, for whose safety it was fearful? Did it regard the snake as a competitor for the eggs and nestlings of the birds now, at the end of May, breeding in the surrounding trees and shrubbery? I have neither seen, nor read about, a similar episode, which might help to answer these questions.

Although I have never known a Mica to catch a squirrel, I have proof that it pursues rabbits. One afternoon, alerted by a great commotion among the birds, my son found a large Mica on the hillside behind the house. At his approach, the snake fled, leaving a half-grown rabbit with several inches of skin torn from its back, evidently by the Mica. Since our small native rabbits are wholly nocturnal, the snake must have either driven or carried it out from its form to the sunny hillside pasture. We hoped to keep the poor animal alive until the great raw place on its back healed, but it refused to eat, so we released it.

Here in the tropics, as in northern lands, squirrels cache excess food in trees (never, as far as I know, in the ground). One day, high in the mountains, I watched a Cinnamon-bellied Squirrel carrying a *coquito*, the fruit of the tree *Calatola costaricensis*, which resembles an English walnut and is said to be edible, although the one that I tried made me feel ill. Digging a hole in the moss that thickly covered an inclined trunk, the squirrel pushed in the *coquito* and covered it with moss. On another occasion, a squirrel carried a green *Clusia* fruit, as large as a hen's egg, to the top of a tall decaying trunk and buried it in the rotting wood. A little later the animal returned, uncovered a similar fruit, which had been stored slightly lower in the same trunk, carried it down to the base, and proceeded to eat it. This seemed to be a premature use of the rodent's stored provisions, for a shrub growing on a neighboring stump bore many of these fruits.

One morning in March, I watched a Cinnamon-bellied Squirrel carry materials into a tangle of vines high in a grove of slender Burío trees, where obviously it was building a well-hidden nest. It bit off thin twigs with leaves of moderate size that had been partly eaten by insects, doubled the twigs in its mouth so that they would not drag as it went, then raced away with them into the tangle of vines. The animal appeared to be in a great hurry to finish its dwelling, for it carried away mouthful after mouthful of leaves in rapid succession, hopping airily to and from the vine tangle.

When, as I judged, the outer walls of the invisible structure had been finished, the builder turned its attention to the lining. Clinging head downward to the trunk of a dead Burío tree, it gathered up a mouthful of the soft, fibrous inner bark. When it had a full load, it started up the trunk toward its nest, only to be pulled up short by some stout fibrous strands that it had failed to sever from the tree. Gathering its hank of fibers more compactly in its mouth, the squirrel braced itself with its forelegs against the trunk, then tugged and jerked until the connecting strands yielded, and it was free to bear its load to its nest. In a moment it was back for more. It carried up about half a dozen generous mouthfuls of the buff-colored, fibrous stuff, to make a snug bed in the midst of its green bower, before a man and boy, passing along the woodland trail, interrupted its labors and my observations.

An animal whose numbers have definitely increased in recent years is the Agouti, known in Costa Rica as the *Guatuso*. About the size of a large domestic rabbit, this brown, big-headed rodent is much higher behind than in front. The advantage of this configuration appears to be that it helps a terrestrial animal of this size to move through tangled undergrowth: the Agouti can insert its low foreparts beneath creepers and twigs and push them upward over its hindquarters with a wedgelike action. The much larger Forest Deer is similarly constructed, doubtless for the same reason. The Agouti has large, dark eyes, small, erect, pinkish ears, and a minute tail. It walks with alternately advancing feet when unhurried, runs with a galloping action, and can swim.

Before I bought Los Cusingos, I knew that it sheltered Agoutis. While Don Chico was showing me the boundaries, one of his lean hounds started to bark at a hollow log lying in the deep, forested valley along the western side. Cutting a switch, he picked up the dog by the scruff of its neck and beat it until it filled the woodland with dismal howls. The poor canine had committed the error of calling attention to a *Guatuso*, when a well-trained hunting dog should concentrate upon the more highly esteemed *Tepisquinte*, or Paca. The Paca is a rodent of about the same size as the Agouti, most readily distinguished by large white spots along its flanks; the Agouti lacks light spots. The nocturnal Paca spends its days in deep burrows that it digs in the floor of the forest, emerging in daylight so seldom that I have never seen one while wandering through the woodland. The diurnal and crepuscular Agouti disappears in the late twilight, apparently to sleep through the night amid dense vegetation or in hollow fallen logs. Even in bright moonlight, I have seldom seen it abroad. Tied to the surface of the land, it neither climbs nor burrows, as far as I have seen. Its habit of seeking refuge in hollow logs is sometimes its undoing; cruel hunters seal it up in these retreats and permit it to starve, apparently because it distracts their hounds, as it did Don Chico's, from more coveted prey.

As I wandered through the forest during my first years on the farm, I was sometimes apprised of an Agouti's presence by a startlingly loud outburst of sound, like an unmuffled human cough or sneeze, from an animal that bounded away before I saw much of it. After a while, Agoutis became so scarce that I seldom saw or heard one. Neighbors' dogs that for hours raced through the forest with horrid yelping were probably responsible for their rarity. The local policeman told me that to shoot the marauders was illegal, but added that dogs sometimes die obscurely from something they have eaten. I did not act upon this hint, for I dislike spreading poisoned bait, which often kills animals for which it was not intended. Sometimes an Agouti, hard-pressed by the hounds, took refuge beneath our house, while we drove the curs away. During this period, an Agouti might timidly venture forth from the forest in the evening, to eat fallen Guavas in the garden beside it, but we saw little of them.

Then, four or five years ago, Agoutis began to increase and walk more boldly over the lawns around the house, even in sunshine. The yelping dogs still made their annoying incursions, running in circles in and out of the forest and over the pastures, so swiftly that, even when they came nearest, it was seldom possible to reach them with a stick, and often continuing their mad careers for hours, with tongues hanging out. Nevertheless, as far as I know, they never caught an Agouti. These animals had learned to outwit their persecutors, which probably explains why they became so numerous, around the house and in the woods.

Apparently, at times an Agouti takes to the water to throw its pursuers off the trail. Once, while resting on a rock beside a forest stream, I saw one swimming downstream with its head held high above the water. It seemed about to land, but, noticing me, it continued to swim with the current and was carried, head foremost, through low rapids, without appearing to be hurt. Finally, it passed beyond view around a bend in the channel. Although, on this occasion, I neither saw nor heard anything that might have alarmed the animal, I surmised that it entered the river to escape an enemy, possibly one of the large snakes abundant in this region.

When suspicious, the Agouti often pauses in its walk, with one foot raised in an expectant attitude, while it surveys its surroundings. Once, while I sat in my blind of brown cloth in the midst of the forest watching an Orange-billed Sparrow's nest, an Agouti wandered by, constantly shaking its head and twitching its ears to keep off the swarming mosquitos that followed it. Noticing the blind, the rodent stood erect on its hind legs and looked intently at the strange object, wrinkling its pink nose as it sniffed the air. Satisfied that all was well, it continued its walk.

Agoutis are among the most innocuous of animals. Those that spend so much time in our dooryard have never made themselves unwelcome by injuries of any sort. They do not dig up the lawn or things we have planted. They live at peace with the chickens, not attacking even baby chicks. Indeed, they are more afraid of the hens than the hens of them. But they are far from being sociable animals. Although I have seen no indication that Agoutis defend definite territories, at least not outside the forest, they remain aloof from each other. An Agouti who comes too near another is chased. As they bound away, pursuer and pursued raise and fluff out the long, golden-brown hairs on their fat rumps, making themselves look bigger and more formidable than they are. Moreover, a pursuing predator that tried to seize an Agouti by the rump would have only a mouthful of fur, while the intended victim escaped. Whatever makes Agoutis flee, man, dog, or fellow Agouti, causes this elevation of the pelage on their hindquarters. Despite their frequent chases, I have never seen them fight.

Our Agoutis always look sleek and trim; they seem to have few external parasites, but mosquitos annoy them greatly.

To eat, Agoutis sit on their haunches, with backs arched into a graceful semicircle, and hold their food to their mouths with both little forefeet. As far as I have seen, they are almost wholly vegetarian. Fallen Guavas, oranges, mangos, Breadfruits, and such bananas as we can spare for them are the chief attractions in our dooryard. They often carry a half-rotten fallen orange, probably for its seeds, which they bite open to remove and eat the embryos, discarding the seedcoats. They share the corn that we scatter over the lawn for the chickens.

Some years ago, I planted two African Oil Palms, which have grown tall and produce large clusters of fruits that attract a variety of finches, tanagers, and woodpeckers, along with numerous Black Vultures, all of which eat only the oily orange flesh surrounding the single hard kernel. These kernels, which litter the ground in large numbers, nourish the Agoutis, who, with sharp, rasping sounds, audible at a distance, gnaw a hole in the thick, woody seedcoat. When they have made the opening large enough, they remove the white flesh with their lower jaws, which are much shorter and narrower than the forepart of their heads. Holding a seed in their hands, they continue to revolve it until they have scooped out everything edible. Once, after I pruned the hibiscus shrubs, an Agouti ate the fresh green leaves on the fallen twigs.

Farther afield, where Agoutis are shier and harder to watch than they have become in our dooryard, I have seen them eat the soft, whitish berries of the Coronillo tree, which are one inch to an inch and a half in diameter and by far the largest fruits of any member of the melastome family that I know. Picking up a hard, woody, fallen pod of an Inga tree, they deftly bite it open along a suture, methodically remove the seeds, one by one, until they have taken all, then drop the empty pod. They eat not only the sweet white pulp, beloved of children, that surrounds each seed but also the green embryos. The hard round seeds of lofty Milk trees, which at certain seasons fall in great numbers, likewise enrich their diet. When seeds drop from opening red pods of a *Protium* tree, the Agoutis eat the soft, thick, white aril, then gnaw open the hard, black seedcoat to remove the embryo. Like other rodents, they sometimes dig a shallow hole to bury food not presently desired. Sometimes they retrieve these caches, but many seeds remain to sprout. Thereby Agoutis help to propagate forest trees.

Not always fastidious, Agoutis sometimes eat decaying leaves, possibly for a fungus that grows on them, and spoiled grains of maize that our pampered chickens disdain. Once I watched an Agouti pick up and try to eat a dry chicken's dropping.

Although adult Agoutis are nearly always solitary, in early January two fully grown individuals came repeatedly to eat corn in front of the house. They appeared perfectly friendly, displaying no antagonism even when they rested only a yard apart. This unusual behavior led us to believe that they were a male and female temporarily mated, but they were so similar in all visible features that we could not learn their sexes. The pair bond seems not to last long, for mothers with young are seldom accompanied by another adult.

Females apparently give birth to their young amid dense, concealing vegetation, as is prudent in woodland with many predators. I have not seen the young until they follow their mother, when they are about the size of a Guinea pig and perfect miniatures of their parent in form, color, and mode of progression. I have found baby Agoutis of this size in early April, and others, not much larger, sucking their mother as late as the first of October. I have never seen a dam with more than two young, who usually trail behind their parent single file, occasionally running ahead.

To suckle her offspring, the mother lies on her side with a hind leg raised; and the two young, if she has a full family, drink simultaneously, for she has at least four nipples. Before sunrise one morning, I watched a pair of half-grown Agoutis take their breakfast drink after they had eaten Guavas. The one nearer its mother's tail moved from nipple to nipple, while the other, nearer the head, did not appear to be getting as much. Soon it started to groom or lick its mother's neck and head. After it had finished sucking, the one behind seemed to groom her a little, too; and I clearly saw it pull up the skin of the parent's abdomen, a short distance from a nipple. This pinch made the mother sit up and end the session. Later, I watched another pair of young nibble the fur of their dam's neck and head, between drinks of milk. When satisfied, they scampered over the grass, while the mother sat up and groomed her face with her forefeet, as Agoutis frequently do. Less often, I have seen a mother groom her young.

After watching these charming scenes, I reflected sadly upon one of life's many tragic paradoxes. The nurture of dependent young, which has done so much to make animals, including man, gentle, social, and altruistic, too often, by the excessive multiplication of individuals for which it is responsible, throws them into the fiercest, most brutal strife for food, living space, and mates. Although Agoutis, like many mammals and birds of humid tropical forests, have small families, they are large enough to make these rodents the most conspicuously abundant terrestrial mammals in some undisturbed Costa Rican forests at low altitudes.

One evening, while I gave the horse his supper, two half-grown Agoutis emerged from the dense growth of ferns that covers the neighboring roadside bank and began to frolic over the close-cropped pasture. They ran erratically back and forth, passing each other. They leapt upward for nearly a foot, as I have never seen an adult Agouti do, and one even jumped over its playmate. After these Agoutis disappeared, two smaller ones, about the size of a squirrel, came out of the fern to gallop hither and thither, playfully throwing up their hind legs. One advanced toward the horse eating his bananas but was evidently awed by the animal so much bigger than itself, for it turned back when a few yards away. One sat up in the roadway and seemed to wash its face, but the light was now too dim to see this clearly. With them were two grown Agoutis, who seemed so friendly that I suspected they were mated parents, although this would have been most unusual.

The following evening, only two young Agoutis gamboled beside the fern patch in the gloaming. They galloped around with occasional low leaps, reversed direction, ran past each other, and reared up against each other as though in mock combat, but only momentarily. Then they started to eat something that they found under the edge of the fern and in the short grass, but it was already too dark to see what it was. Eating was punctuated by bouts of renewed playfulness, which continued until, even through field glasses, I could hardly distinguish their dark bodies. Finally, a boy coming down the road made the youngsters retreat into the thicket of fern, where apparently they slept, beneath the Black-striped Sparrows and Scarlet-rumped Black Tanagers who roosted in this tangled, impenetrable thicket. Only in the evening twilight have I seen Agoutis, always immature individuals, frolic in this manner. They play silently.

When the young are about half their parent's size and have for some time been helping themselves to solid food along with their mother's milk, she repulses them. If they persist in following her, she turns to drive them away. For a while, the two siblings so abandoned may keep company, but soon they separate to begin their solitary adult lives.

On an afternoon in early June, some girls coming to visit found two baby Agoutis along the road behind the house, beside the dense stand of *Dicranopteris* fern where these animals often take refuge. One of the babies escaped into the fern, but our cook caught the other and insisted on taking it into the house, just as a hard shower began. The mother Agouti was not seen. Hardly as long as my hand, the little Agouti already had teeth. When hungry or lonely, it rapidly repeated a clear note that reminded me of the Bare-crowned Antbird's call. It also complained with low whimpers and moans. All its utterances were quite different from any that I have heard from adults. At first the baby ate a little banana, but in the following days it took less and less and would eat only a little cooked Breadfruit. It was given milk from a pipette and with a nipple, but neither way would it drink much. After three days, it died.

Many years ago, while I sat in my blind in the forest studying a nest of the Chestnut-backed Antbird, I saw much of Agoutis in their natural setting. The nest and blind were beneath a tall Milk tree, whose hard, round seeds, strewn over the ground, attracted these rodents. They sat on their haunches to eat them, incessantly twitching their ears to keep off hungry mosquitos. The cup-shaped nest, in a climbing fern beside a small, spiny palm, was only sixteen inches above the ground and held a single nestling. An Agouti passed almost beneath the nest, then ate seeds less than a yard away, while the male antbird brooded the nestling. For half an hour, the rodent ignored the nest; and the parent antbird, after churring once near the Agouti, paid little attention to it. After its meal, the Agouti came close to the nest and sniffed at it with uplifted head. Thereupon, the antbird jumped out and flew away low over the ground, while the Agouti bounded away in the same direction, probably startled by the bird's sudden movement rather than pursuing it. When beyond view in the undergrowth, the antbird scolded with a rattling *wittit wittit wittit*. Soon the Agouti returned to its former position near the nest but showed no further interest in it. After a few minutes, the animal wandered away.

When I again watched the nest, five days later, the antbird brooded quietly, while an Agouti moved around within a yard, ignoring it. After two more days, when the antbird nestling was in long pinfeathers, the male parent, who was its more assiduous attendant, became more concerned about the Agoutis' presence. When the Agouti, one of two in sight, came close to the nest, he dropped to the ground in front of the quadruped and fluttered away as though injured. As the Agouti approached, he flew up above its reach. The Agouti followed the antbird a short distance, then stopped to sniff the air near the nest, while the bird continued to scold. Again and again, he dropped to the ground and "feigned injury" in front of the Agouti, who each time stopped short after moving only a foot or so toward the bird.

These distraction displays, which might have led a dog or some predatory mammal of the forest racing after the bird until it had been lured well away from the nest, served only to stimulate the Agouti's interest in it. Although for at least a week Agoutis had eaten seeds all around the nest without paying much attention to it, now the one that the parent had tried to lead away sniffed and sniffed, wrinkling its broad nose, while moving all around the little clump of vegetation that supported the structure. Finally, the Agouti touched the nest with the tip of its snout—at which point I violently shook the cloth that concealed me, sending the animal galloping away with its usual sneezelike note of alarm.

The Agouti left the nest slightly tilted. Presently it returned, coming directly toward the nest, whereupon I burst out of my blind and chased it away. Soon the parent brought another insect to the nestling. At midday I propped up the nest and left. On the following dawn, I found the mother antbird calmly brooding. When I returned in the afternoon, the nest had been torn away from its supports and the nestling had vanished, along with the nest lining to which it had been clinging. Was an Agouti or one of the many habitual eaters of eggs and nestlings that lurk in the forest responsible for the destruction of my first Chestnut-backed Antbirds' nest? In any case, I am sure that if Agoutis made a practice of preying upon low birds' nests, this one would not have survived so long in their midst. I surmised that if the parent had not become so excited by their presence, thereby arousing their interest, they would have continued to ignore the nest, as they did at first.

Recently I watched an Agouti lick the glair that coated the inside of the shell of a hen's egg, which had been emptied in the kitchen, an observation that suggests that these rodents may take eggs from birds' nests low enough to be accessible to them. However, they certainly are not professional plunderers of nests; if they ever do indulge, this is probably only an occasional peccadillo. How pleasant, in a world where so many animals are fiercely predatory and others troublesome in various ways, to find one that is always welcome among the free birds and chickens in our dooryard, to which it brings interest and animation, without once, in many years, giving cause for complaint!

NINE-BANDED ARMADILLO ▶

Another animal, rare when I first came to Los Cusingos, that has increased in recent years is the Nine-banded Armadillo. Since armadillos are largely nocturnal, I do not often see one, but I frequently find the soft earth of the roadway that leads into the forest plowed up by them. In the rainless season, when the ground nearly everywhere becomes dry and hard, they dig for earthworms in a drain beside the house and are not easily discouraged from rooting in this productive ground. To repair their damages is often laborious. After returning rains soften the ground in the woodland, they cease to be troublesome.

One morning in July, as I passed through second-growth woods on my way to the *milpa*, I noticed a young armadillo, less than half grown, in the pathway ahead. It was rooting in the wet ground, sometimes pushing its whole head beneath fallen leaves and getting its long snout very muddy. It continued its eager search for food while I advanced and stood only a few yards away. Finally, noticing me, it ambled, still rooting at intervals, down the slope below the path and entered a newly dug burrow, with a pile of freshly moved earth in front. When I reached the spot, the mouth of the burrow was already blocked with a large mass of dead leaves, so that I could not look in.

Returning after I had gathered a knapsack full of green corn, I found the little animal standing on its hind legs in the burrow's mouth, holding its forefeet up while it sniffed the air and peered around with little beady eyes. When I approached, it slipped inside its burrow. I had never before seen an armadillo so active in midmorning. It must have been very hungry, so to expose itself in full daylight. I surmised that during the preceding night it had dug its burrow in the hillside, losing so much of its usual foraging time that it could not satisfy its appetite before daybreak.

An animal that I see even more rarely is the Tropical Porcupine. One cloudy morning, as I walked beside the thicket that borders the coffee plantation, deep scolding notes of a pair of Chisel-billed Caciques caused me to investigate. Two small animals rested beneath the thick canopy of vines that covered a low tree. They were difficult to see in the dim light, and at first I took them to be sloths. One was rolled up into a ball, just like a sleeping sloth, and the other, somewhat smaller, was stretched out beside the first, much as I have sometimes seen a sloth with her half-grown young. The blunt, bare snout of the smaller animal was sloth-like. As I cut my way deeper into the thicket with my machete, the large animal unrolled to climb higher into the vine tangle, and I saw that it had a prehensile tail, an appendage that sloths lack. Then I noticed that both animals had grayish marks amid the dark brown fur on their heads and necks. They were evidently spines, which if present on the rest of the body were so well hidden by thick fur that I could not distinguish them. These animals were doubtless a mother and her young.

In a later year, while pruning the shade trees of the coffee plantation, I noticed a porcupine coiled up at midday amid the clustered foliage of an Inga tree, well above the ground. This appears to be the porcupine's usual way of passing the daylight hours, to become active after nightfall, when it eats foliage, young shoots, and bark. I have heard of dogs, here in Costa Rica, so covered with porcupine spines that they died miserably. Country people believe that the porcupine can throw its spines to a distance, which is doubtless false. Unlike most mammals with prehensile tails, which they roll downward to grasp a branch by the ventral surface, tropical American porcupines of the genus *Coendou* have the upper surface of the tail bare and bend it upward to seize a support. In *"Mamíferos Neotropicales,"* José Ignacio Borrero reports that the related Colombian species is eaten by the Puma, in whose stomach were found porcupine quills that did not wound its internal organs.[1] Be this as it may, a naturalist whom I knew well, who roamed Costa Rican forests while they were vaster and wilder than they are today, once found a Jaguar whose mouth was horribly lacerated by porcupine quills. This experience of nature's harshness shook my friend's belief in God.

1. José Ignacio Borrero, "*Mamiferos Neotropicales*," mimeographed (Cali, Colombia: Universidad del Valle, 1967).

6. The Friendly Bicolored Antbird

ONE may wander far through tropical forest, meeting only here and there a solitary bird. Just as the wanderer begins to suspect that the accounts he has read of the variety and splendor of tropical bird life were greatly exaggerated, his attention may be drawn by a chorus of small voices somewhere in the distance. Following the sounds, he comes in view of winged figures flitting through the shrubs, low palms, and ferns of the dimly lighted undergrowth. It seems that a large part of the feathered inhabitants of the surrounding forest have congregated in this one spot. Most wear subdued colors— browns, olives, grays—which blend with the bark of trees and the dead leaves on the ground. Some perch on low twigs, others grasp slender upright stems, yet others cling woodpeckerlike to thick trunks. From time to time, they dart rapidly back and forth, or drop momentarily to the ground.

The excited feathered crowd sends forth a medley of churrs, cheeps, rattles, whistles, and trills. In intervals of relative silence, the keen ear may detect a low, rustling sound, made by countless tiny feet pattering upon fallen leaves. Looking down, one sees that the ground beneath the birds is covered with swarming ants— dull brown or blackish, sightless army ants. As the hunting ants push beneath fallen leaves and file up the trunks of trees, all the small creatures that hide in such places make a dash to save themselves. Crickets, roaches, moths, spiders, centipedes, as well as an occasional small frog, lizard, or snake, rush forth from concealment, and many that escape the ants are snatched up by the attendant birds. It is the ease of finding food above the foraging army that has brought together this motley crowd of feathered creatures.

Conspicuous among the followers of army ants is a sparrow-sized bird, with rich chestnut-brown upper plumage and a broad band of white along the central underparts from chin to abdomen. Each large, dark eye is set in an area of bright blue bare skin, below and behind which the cheeks and ear coverts are black. This is the Bicolored Antbird. It stays within a yard of the ground, clinging to slender, vertical stems in preference to horizontal twigs. By stretching the lower and flexing the upper of its bluish gray legs, it manages to hold its body almost upright, despite its peculiar manner of perching. Whenever its keen eyes spy some small invertebrate desperately trying to escape the ants, it drops down to seize the fugitive, returning in a trice to a low perch, with the victim in its blackish bill. It is a voluble bird, constantly repeating its half-whimsical, half-mocking call, which consists of a series of clear little notes rising in pitch toward the end: *we we we we we we we wheer*. Or sometimes two or three notes falling in pitch terminate the series—this call has many variations. Often three or four, and sometimes as many as six or seven, of these attractive birds gather about a swarm of ants, with many associates of other species.

As I walked through the forest one cloudy morning in February many years ago, I noticed a lone Bicolored Antbird in the undergrowth close beside the trail. It stayed so persistently in one spot that I was led to look for its nest. I searched the more eagerly because I had never seen a nest of this species, although I had hunted much for it in forests where the bird is fairly abundant. While I peered into the hollow center of a palm stump and scrutinized the crevices between its crowded

prop-roots, the antbird appeared to be examining me from the bushes only a few feet away. I found no nest. As I started to walk away, the antbird followed me. Moving slowly and watching it out of the corner of an eye, I saw that it was snatching up insects driven from fallen leaves by my passage. Taking care to stir the ground litter and to avoid abrupt movements, I led it through the undergrowth for nearly a hundred yards, a leisurely journey on which it was rewarded with many small edible creatures. Clearly, it was using me in lieu of army ants to stir up the insects so difficult to find while they hid motionless and camouflaged beneath fallen leaves.

This was the first of many similar excursions that this antbird and I took together. As we became intimate, I needed a name for my little woodland friend, and "Jimmy," short for *Gymnopithys bicolor*, seemed as good as another. As we walked together through the forest, I would repeat this name, in order to accustom him to my voice. But I was doubtful about the appropriateness of this masculine appellation. The sexes of the Bicolored Antbird look alike, and Jimmy may well have been a female.

Sometimes, as I walked through the forest near the house, I found Jimmy— but more often he found me. While I stood watching some other bird, he might apprise me of his presence by a low, questioning note. Looking down, I would see him clinging to an upright stem, a foot from the ground and hardly a yard away. Often he would wait patiently close beside me, perhaps preening his feathers, until I finished my observation of the other bird. Then, if I could spare the time, we would begin the leisurely journey that he liked. He would not try to keep up if I walked fast.

I frequently used a stick instead of my shoes to stir the ground litter. When-

JIMMY FOLLOWS THE AUTHOR DOWN A STEEP SLOPE ▶

ever a suitable item was exposed, Jimmy would dart up and seize it with a *clack* of his bill. He had definite preferences and paid no attention to certain insects that to me looked just as appetizing as those that he eagerly devoured. Among the creatures he disdained were certain moths, although he ate other kinds of moths. In the wet season, he varied his diet with small frogs, an inch or less long, which he beat against his perch before he swallowed them. If he saw an escaping insect dive beneath fallen leaves, he would alight on a low twig or the ground and flick them aside with rapid sideways movements of his bill, just as antthrushes, antpittas, and many other ground-feeding birds do. Sometimes, while seeking a fugitive, he would fall some yards behind me; but soon a rapid flight, low above the ground, would bring him to my side again. Or, if I delayed too long in one spot, he would remind me of his presence by repeating his low, throaty note, while clinging to a sapling close beside me.

In the breeding season, Jimmy sometimes followed me while I searched for birds' nests to study. These trips were more profitable to him than to me, for they provided many insects for him and rarely a nest for me. At times our travels together continued for an hour or more, and once we went an estimated half mile, which seems a long distance in the forest. This must have taken Jimmy far beyond his home range. Although he refused to follow when I returned along a little-used wood road, he apparently had no difficulty finding his way home. A few weeks later, I found him in the part of the forest where he lived.

Jimmy could not be enticed beyond the border of the heavy woodland into the brighter light of adjoining second-growth thickets or pastures, where I might have chased up fat grasshoppers for him. Although he picked up insects at my feet, he always flitted away when my advancing hand was a few inches from him, never permitting me to touch him. However, he did not object when I ruffled his feathers with the end of a short stick. After he had become thoroughly accustomed to me, I tested his reactions to noises and found him unmoved by my loudest clapping or shouting. Nor was he alarmed when I shook the sapling to which he clung. He was not estranged by a long separation, and, after an interval of several months in which we did not meet, he would come to me as though our last journey together had been yesterday. No other free bird has ever been so intimate with me. His trust in my innocence was heart-warming.

Since I had neither known nor heard of any other Bicolored Antbird, or bird of any kind, that followed humans through tropical forest, I concluded that Jimmy was an original genius, who had discovered that featherless bipeds may serve as purveyors of food; just as Cattle Egrets and anis use cows and other grazing animals to stir up insects, and, in the Orient, certain hornbills employ arboreal monkeys. My walks with Jimmy extended over an interval of sixteen months, after which, for nearly three years, I could induce no antbird to follow me. I missed his quiet companionship on my solitary woodland walks.

Then, one day, a Bicolored Antbird accompanied me much as Jimmy had done. In view of the long interval when no antbird had followed me, I concluded that this was a different individual, perhaps a descendant who had inherited Jimmy's peculiar trait. Accordingly, I called him "Jameson." In subsequent years, I have, from time to time, been followed through the forest at Los Cusingos by Bicolored Antbirds, sometimes by two together, apparently a mated pair. Probably because I did not try so hard to become intimate with them, none of these other birds would follow me as far as Jimmy did.

Sometimes young Bicolored Antbirds, easily recognized by their darker underplumage and the yellow corners of their mouths, have come almost within arm's length and even followed me for short distances; but they could never be induced to take a longer trip and catch the insects I stirred up, perhaps because they still received food from their parents, who were nearby. They were either curious or simply friendly.

At times, especially in June, the antbirds who followed me, instead of eating at once the larger insects that they caught, would carry them off through the underwood, suggesting that they were feeding young. To my great disappointment, I never succeeded in following them to a nest, if nest they had. But, as I passed along an indistinct forest trail in mid-August, a Bicolored Antbird clung to a stem close beside me, with a fat insect in its bill, repeating over and over a low, scolding *churr*. This prompted me to search through the undergrowth, and as I moved around, the bird darted so close that its wing brushed my leg. Then it dropped to the ground, groveling and beating its half-spread wings, in an excellent distraction display. It "feigned injury" repeatedly in several spots only a yard or two from my feet.

Finally, I discovered two nestlings lying close together on the ground, as though they had been tumbled there. They appeared to be about six days old, for they bore long, lead-colored pinfeathers and their eyes were already open. They had great, white flanges at the corners of their mouths. They were cold and sluggish in their movements, and one had fresh blood on its flank.

A little more searching disclosed whence they had come. Nearby was the stump of what had been a tall feather-palm. It was only about six inches high, and all the central part had decayed away, leaving a deep hollow surrounded by a papery shell. The frail stump had somehow collapsed, spilling nest and nestlings onto a palm frond that lay close beside it. The nest had consisted of large pieces of partly decayed palm leaf, forming a thin mat, above which was a lining of coarse fibrous roots and similar materials.

While I examined the remains of the ill-fated nest, the parent behaved in a most extraordinary fashion. With an effort, it gulped down the fat insect it had been holding and, with empty bill, incessantly repeated a somewhat churred *per-r-r-r*, at once plaintive and protesting. Several times more it groveled on the ground in front of me, beating its wings in an effort to lure me away from the nestlings. When I held them in front of the parent in the palm of my hand, it advanced and bit a finger three or four times, not hard enough to hurt. With the exception of a male Slaty Antshrike, who nipped the finger I placed on his nest while his mate "feigned injury" on the ground to lure me away, no other forest bird has ever dared to attack me. Spreading a handkerchief on the fallen leaves, I placed the torpid nestlings on it, while I arranged a new home for them. The parent lay or sat on the ground, facing the handkerchief with its young, and remained motionless, watching or guarding them, for the ten minutes or so that I left them there.

After I improvised a nest in the hollow sheath of a palm frond, I laid the nestlings in it, while the antbird intently watched me. Then I went away, confident that so devoted a parent would not neglect its little ones. But, when I returned next morning, both were dead, one in the palm sheath, the other lying on the ground close by it. Probably they had not been brooded in the makeshift nest.

After this, I looked into every hollow palm stump that I found, and also into the long, almost cylindrical, sheathing bases of great fallen palm fronds, for Josselyn Van Tyne had, a short while before, published an account of the discovery of a Bicolored Antbird's nest in such a situation in Panama.[1] The following May, not far from the spot where I had found the fallen nestlings, I peered into a low palm stump and found a Bicolored Antbird sitting in it, returning my gaze. It

1. Josselyn Van Tyne, "The nest of the antbird *Gymnopithys bicolor*," *Univ. Mich. Mus. Zool., Occas. Pap.* no. 491 (1944): 1–5.

stared up at me for nearly a minute, then jumped out and gave a distraction display on the ground close in front of me. Its departure revealed two creamy eggs, thickly marked with elongated blotches of rufous-chocolate, which lay on a nest composed of a double handful of leaf fragments, with a thin lining of rootlets and other fibrous materials.

The stump, about ten inches high, had been reduced by decay to a thin shell, so fragile that I did not dare to insert a hand into the deep, narrow cavity in order to pick up and measure the eggs. All the while that I examined the nest and made notes, the antbird circled close around me, voicing a churred *per-r-r-r*, punctuated by a higher, sharper note. Once it tried to lure me away by approaching within arm's length and then walking in front of me with little, mincing steps. When, finally, having completed my notes, I walked off, the parent followed me for a yard or two. Then, without delay, it went to look into the stump, to see whether its eggs were still there. After a second examination, it returned to incubate, while I stood watching a short distance away. Rarely have I seen a bird evince such obvious concern for the fate of its nest.

Setting up a blind, I spent two whole mornings and all of an afternoon studying the antbirds' mode of incubation. Their sessions on their eggs were amazingly long, even for antbirds, which, as a family, sit for longer intervals than songbirds. One morning, a parent incubated continuously from 6:25 to 12:04—nearly six hours. On another morning, I timed a session that lasted four hours and four minutes. These were long fasts for a small bird. Afternoon sessions were shorter, but one continued for about three hours. Nevertheless, I never saw one parent replace the other. Sometimes, after sitting for hours, the bird would go off, leaving the eggs unattended. At other times, the mate would come and call the sitting bird from the nest, then both would fly away together. In either case, the eggs might be neglected for periods ranging from five minutes to an hour and a half. Often the bird returning to the nest brought a rootlet or fiber to lay beneath the eggs.

Since I was unable to distinguish the members of the pair, I could not tell whether incubation was performed by the male, the female, or by both sitting alternately. Remembering that Jimmy would permit me to touch him with a stick, I wrapped a little cotton around the end of a long wand, dipped it in paint, and, touching the parents as they flitted close around me, protesting my intrusion, I placed white stains on one and vermilion spots on the other. Continued watching of the marked birds left no doubt that both male and female took turns warming the eggs, as seems to be the invariable custom in the antbird family. In species in which the sexes differ in coloration, it is not difficult to learn that the female regularly takes charge of the nest by night. The parent on whom I had placed the white marks sat through the night, whence I inferred that this was the female.

Fourteen days after I found the eggs, I visited this nest by moonlight. Looking into the stump in the beam of a flashlight, I saw a mass of feathers so loosely spread and disheveled that they appeared not to be attached to a living bird. Such complete relaxation of the body plumage is typical of antbirds sleeping on their nests. The parent marked with white continued to slumber while the light increased and woodland birds gradually became active. Even after waking, she would not leave, though I bent over her and gently tapped on the side of the stump. Soon weak peepings, filtering through the maternal coverlet, told me the cause of this increased attachment to the nest. When, finally, the antbird jumped out, it was to grovel at my feet in realistic "injury-feigning" acts repeated again and again, until I put an end to them by withdrawing a few paces. Thereupon, the parent promptly returned to her newly hatched nestlings. The empty shells had not yet been removed.

The newborn antbirds had dark flesh-colored skin, wholly devoid of down, and the interior of their mouths was orange-yellow. On the second day after they hatched, they were fed eleven times between daybreak and noon, seven times by their father and four by their mother. On each visit, the parent brought a single insect, which it held in its bill and delivered while it clung inside the stump in an inverted position, its tail in the air. Both parents took turns brooding the nestlings, each of them sometimes sitting for well over an hour at a stretch.

When the nestlings were five days old, they bristled with long pinfeathers and their eyes could be opened, although most of the time they drowsed. Their parents had by now simulated injury before me dozens of times—far more than any other bird I have studied. Yet, when a predator arrived, their wiles failed to save their nestlings, possibly because it came in the night. On the sixth day after the young hatched, I returned to find that their nest had been raided, as happens to the great majority of nests in the tropical forest. But, from the tremendous loss of eggs and nestlings, one may deduce the pleasant thought that the adults must be long-lived; otherwise, they could not rear enough progeny to replace themselves, and their kind would vanish from the earth.

On the same long, forested ridge where I met Jimmy and found my first two Bicolored Antbirds' nests, I discovered, in later years, four more, one of which was used in two consecutive years. All were in stumps that had been reduced by decay to frail, hollow shells, and all but one of the stumps were of palm trees. In height they ranged from twelve to thirty-four inches, and each held, on the usual mat of dead leaves lined with fibers, two beautiful eggs. One of these stumps had a hole in the side, through which the eggs were visible and part of the nest material projected. When a parent incubated, its light ventral plumage filled the gap.

Since all my nests were found after the set of eggs was complete, I could not determine the incubation period, which Edwin O. Willis, who for years studied Bicolored Antbirds in Panama, found to be fifteen days at one nest and sixteen days at another.[2] From the six nests that I found with eggs, twelve in all, only three young were fledged, at ages of fifteen and thirteen or fourteen days. One third of these nests, or 33 percent, produced one or two fledglings, which is slightly better success than Willis found in Panama, where only five of eighteen nests, or 28 percent, yielded fledglings. From my nest with the hole in the side, the eggs rolled out. In another, the eggs were abandoned. From one, eggs were taken by a predator, and from another the nestling was taken. Both of the successful nests were in the highest stump, in consecutive years.

As I recall my companionship with Jimmy, after the lapse of a third of a century, it remains one of the most memorable experiences of a lifetime devoted to the study of tropical birds. No other free bird that I have known has trusted me so greatly, has so unhesitatingly approached the human form, which most wild creatures dread. Nevertheless, our relationship lacked something to make it wholly satisfying. For this, it needed some exchange of thoughts, some mutual revelation of sentiments or feelings. Our intercourse was too objective, too superficial. But I ask too much. He gave me his confidence; he never questioned the honesty of my intentions. Simply to be trusted by a shy wild creature enhances one's self-respect.

2. Edwin O. Willis, *The behavior of Bicolored Antbirds*, Univ. Calif. Publ. Zool., 79 (1967), pp. 1–132. A more detailed account of Bicolored Antbirds is also given in the present author's "Life histories of Central American birds," vol. 3, *Pacific Coast Avifauna*, no. 35 (Berkeley, Calif.: Cooper Ornithological Society, 1969).

7. The Banana Plantation

AT the northern end of Los Cusingos, the alluvial deposit of light, rich, black loam, mixed with innumerable rocks of all sizes, spreads out broadly between the Río Peñas Blancas, which brought it there, and the tributary creek. Here, separated from the house by the creek, we for years grew food for home use, including bananas, plantains, and such underground crops as *Yuca* (Cassava), Tiquisque, and *Malanga* (Taro). The last two are members of the aroid family, distantly related to Jack-in-the-Pulpit and Skunk Cabbage. The banana plants, which despite their impressive size are giant herbs devoid of wood, bore generous bunches of fruit for only five or six years; and the plantains—large, solid bananas, which are cooked rather than eaten raw—yielded well for only two or three years. Accordingly, we at intervals planted more of each, on fresh ground, until we had covered several acres with bananas. Each time we set out more bananas, we interplanted with coffee, which continued to flourish after the banana plants grew feeble. Finally, we had a coffee plantation across much of the farm's northern boundary.

In spite of the difficulty of maintaining a bridge of logs, which rotted if the creek did not first rise and carry it away, this was the part of the farm most convenient for a provision plot. But it had one great disadvantage: beyond sight of the house, it was near a public road that made it easily accessible to thieves. Moreover,

BANANA PLANT WITH HERMIT HUMMINGBIRD'S NEST BENEATH A LEAF ▶

it was frequently invaded by neighbors' pigs, which rooted up the crops, despite pleas and threats to their owners, who should have kept them at home, and an occasional legal shooting of a trespassing pig. Tired of having our produce stolen, when it again became necessary to plant bananas, I decided to set them in a sequestered spot less accessible to marauders with either two or four feet.

The area that I chose for the new banana grove was near the river, in the midst of woods, where it was much less likely to be seen by trespassers than the old plantation was. The rich, stony land, an ancient river bed, had been cleared of forest and planted before I bought the farm; but after resting for more than thirty years, it was covered by second-growth woods where trees of the linden family (*Goethalsia meiantha*) grew straight and slender to well over a hundred feet. In August they bore a profusion of small, pale yellow flowers that were followed by winged fruits. In their shade flourished a great variety of ferns, aroids, small palms, and heliconias, with two lovely shrubs of the acanthus family, whose long, tubular flowers were visited by long-billed hummingbirds. The first of these to bloom was always *Poikilacanthus macranthus*, which in August and September displayed delicate lavender blossoms above small furry leaves, on brittle stems rarely ten feet high. These were followed by the bright red flowers of the more robust *Razisea spicata*, which continued to glow in the woodland shade from October until the dry weather began in the new year.

Among the ferns that flourished on trunks and on the deeply shaded ground was a most curious kind that grew on and between rocks, *Leptochilus cladorrhizans*. One of the "walking ferns," its larger fronds ended in ribbonlike projections, sometimes a yard long, which bore at intervals three buds. Where they touched the ground, these buds sprouted into new fern plants. Nearby was a species of *Dryopteris* with a bud near the tip of each larger frond.

Before this woods grew so tall and heavy, a singing assembly of male Blue-throated Golden-tail Hummingbirds was established among its treetops. For years I heard them, chiefly in the early months of the dry season, repeating their sharp little notes all day long, each male at his own station, within hearing of his neighbors, trying to allure females with eggs to be fertilized. Here, too, I found, in a decaying stub, the only nest of the elegant Rufous-winged Woodpecker that I have ever seen, and, nearer the ground, flimsy nests of the Ruddy Quail-Dove and Streak-chested Antpitta.

To have sacrificed all of this beautiful woods to the prosaic needs of the stomach would have been unbearable; but I chose for the banana grove about an acre toward its lower end, remote from the pasture that it bordered. The first step in the preparation of the land was to sow an "after crop" of maize. In rainy September, the corn was broadcast thinly through the woods, then the undergrowth was cleared with long machetes, and, finally, the tall trees were felled, making an almost impassable tangle of trunks, branches, and vines. The sturdy corn plants grew up through the clutter of dying vegetation, which meanwhile decayed, making it easier to clear the ground for banana plants.

The clearing where we sowed the maize adjoined the old forest, through which a band of White-faced Monkeys wandered, isolated from all others of their kind by surrounding farms, and, by their extreme wariness, escaping poachers year after year. In January, when the corn was reaching the milky stage, these monkeys found it and left little for us. Their depredations did not alarm me, for I knew that they would not steal the bananas, which would be cut green and ripened in the house. Unlike horses and cows, White-faced Monkeys do not relish green bananas.

In February, after the remnant of the corn crop had been harvested, we planted part of the clearing with banana suckers, regularly spaced in quincunxes, taken from an older grove. We left the remainder to grow up into a dense thicket of bushes, young trees, and creepers, until we needed it for later extensions, when the first planting lost its vigor. The following year, after the banana plants had grown tall and bore fruit, the small plantation began to yield a double harvest, one expected, the other an unanticipated bonus.

Over the years, at Los Cusingos and elsewhere, I had found a number of birds nesting on banana plants. Big birds, such as Brown Jays, sometimes build their bulky, open nests of coarse sticks in the center of the rosette of huge leaves. Here the nest lies upon the elbow of the stout stem that bends over to support the hanging bunch of fruit, after the stem emerges from the overlapping leaf bases that form most of the plant's apparent trunk. Smaller birds, such as Gray's Thrushes, often build on top of the bunch, where the upturned "fingers" of the uppermost "hand" of bananas make a hollow, like that of a cupped human hand; in this spot the nest will not slip off the smooth-skinned fruits. I have also found Ruddy Ground-Doves nesting in this site. Small tanagers not infrequently hide their nests in the center of a bunch, between two hands of fruit. A pair of Blue Tanagers, feeding nestlings in such a situation, had increasing difficulty slipping in and out as the thickening fruits narrowed the gap between two bananas through which they passed. Their nestlings would probably have become inaccessible and starved if I had not noticed the parents' predicament and widened their doorway.

As long as the fruit remains too small to cut, the birds nesting upon banana plants are probably as safe from the many tropical animals that eat eggs and nestlings as they would be anywhere else—possibly a little safer because of the concealment that the bunches offer. But if the nesting continues too long, the eggs and young are in great peril, for in a well-attended plantation the fruits are always harvested while still green, and plantation laborers are not likely to spare the bunch because it shelters a birds' nest. Indeed, despite benevolent intentions, we have sometimes cut a bunch of fruit and afterward found a nest, occasionally still occupied, so well hidden in its midst that it was invisible. If the bunch is left to ripen on the plant, the birds are in no better plight, for the many kinds of animals that are attracted to the aromatic fruit might find eggs or tender nestlings a welcome addition to their fare.

Even the Black-cowled Oriole, who hangs her woven pouch beneath a banana leaf by means of fibers that she sews through perforations in the broad blade, must finish her nesting before the fruit is full, for to harvest it the whole "tree" is cut down—it would never bear a second bunch, but suckers that grow up around its base will continue to yield. Hummingbirds that attach their nests to banana leaves —in another manner, as we shall presently see—must likewise rear their young before the fruit is ready to be cut.

Although I had found many other birds using banana plants to support their nests, I had never known a hummingbird to do so; moreover, I had never seen a nest of either of the two species that I discovered nesting in or beside the plantation on the memorable August 2, 1967, the year after the bananas were planted. In all my years in Central America, I had never met a single individual of the Bronzy Hermit, whose nest I noticed first. While watching this newly found nest, I became aware that a Band-tailed Barbthroat was building nearby. Although, for many years, I had listened, enchanted, to the long-continued, plaintive songs of male barbthroats perching low in the dim undergrowth of the neighboring old forest, I had failed to find the female's nest. To find in one day two nests of kinds that I had never seen before, one of a bird quite new to me, on a farm where I had studied birds for a quarter of a century, was as exciting as it was unexpected.

In the elation of discovery, I might have thanked the thieves who made me hide the new plantation in this secluded spot.

The Band-tailed Barbthroat is one of the dull-colored hummingbirds with long, curved bills that inhabit the dim undergrowth of humid tropical American forests and are collectively known as "hermits." As in other hermits, the sexes differ little. The upper parts, including the middle pair of feathers of the rounded tail, are metallic bronze-green. When spread, the tail reveals three broad, contrasting bands, the inner one white, the middle one dull black, and the outer one white or pale buff. A dusky patch with buffy margins covers the cheeks and ear coverts. The chin and throat are dusky, the chest cinnamon-rufous, and the abdomen buffy gray. Sometimes, while I made my way laboriously through tangled undergrowth, a barbthroat has flown up to hover all around me at scarcely more than arm's length, obviously inspecting the strange biped that has invaded its domain. Nevertheless, while building and attending their nests, barbthroats are suspicious and must be watched from a distance, or from concealment.

Banana leaves tear readily from their thin margins to their massive midribs, which in windy places become long rods fringed with narrow, waving, green ribbons. In our plantation sheltered by tall trees, splits are fewer but by no means absent. The Band-tailed Barbthroat's nest that I found under construction on August 2 hung twelve feet above the ground, fastened beneath a strip of banana leaf, about an inch and a half wide, which formed a green roof above it, shading it from the bright morning sunshine and shielding it from the afternoon downpours frequent at this season. When finished, the nest was an inverted cone. From the hollow in the top, where the eggs were laid, it tapered downward to a slender "tail" that hung below the end of the supporting leaf strip. (See illustration, p. 35.)

The dark brown body of the nest was a rough, stiff, springy fabric, composed largely of thin, wiry, richly branched stems of mosses and liverworts, on which the few minute leaves that remained were dry and shriveled. Attached to the outside were small pieces of pale gray foliaceous lichens and fragments of green moss. The sparse lining consisted chiefly of a few filaments of black "vegetable horsehair"— fungal strands that creep over stems and branches in wet tropical woods. Although the walls were rather thick, they were so loosely constructed that much light passed through them. The builder sacrificed insulation for rapid drying after rain. The loosely hanging tail, composed of liverwort stems and small, shriveled leaves of seed plants, occupied over half the length of the nine-inch nest. The cup in the top, where the eggs rested, was only an inch deep by an inch and a quarter wide at the rim.

How does a bird attach a nest beneath a slippery, ribbonlike leaf strip, without any projection to hold the materials nor any place to perch while she works? Probably only a hummingbird, whose ability to hover motionless in the air and to maneuver in a narrow space exceeds that of all other feathered creatures, could build in such a situation. Although my first barbthroat's nest was nearly finished when found, I have watched the early stages of construction of similar nests. At first, the bird works wholly on the wing. She wraps strands of cobweb around the strip, or the tapering tip of a palm frond, while she hovers on rapidly beating wings and circles slowly around it, once or several times, keeping her bill pointing toward the leaf. She brings fragments of vegetable material and attaches them to the cobweb, then more cobweb to bind them firmly together. When she has accumulated enough material to form a little shelf on the underside of the leaf, she rests upon it, always facing inward toward the supporting strip, and often continuing to beat her wings into a haze, while she builds up the cup around herself. She uses her bill to tuck pieces in place and her feet to arrange those inside the cup. Sometimes a thin, wiry strand persists in sticking up above the rim, and, with her long bill, she tries again and again to make it stay down. Like every other hummingbird that I have watched, barbthroats build their nests with no help from a mate.

About a week after they were laid, the eggs vanished from my first barb-throat's nest; but, during the following ten years, I found eighteen more nests in the banana grove. One year two barbthroats nested in the grove, and in another year a third individual built a nest and laid an egg that was promptly lost. Once a second nest was built after the first brood was successfully fledged; and some-times a barbthroat renested after her first nest failed; but in no instance did the same female rear two broods in a year. The earliest eggs were laid at the beginning of June, after the rainy season was well established; the latest, at the beginning of September.

All these nests were attached to narrow strips of banana leaves, at heights of eight to sixteen feet above the ground. With two exceptions, each nest held two tiny white eggs, the second of which was laid two days after the first, around seven o'clock in the morning, an hour after sunrise. The nest with a single egg would probably have received another if it had not been so promptly emptied. A most ex-ceptional nest held three eggs, with a fourth on the ground below. Watching this nest, I repeatedly saw one barbthroat hover beside it, sometimes with material for it in her bill, while another incubated. Once, while the presumed builder and owner of the nest was absent, the intruding bird sat on it briefly, only to flee as the other returned. When, after at least twenty days of incubation, this nest with two claimants was abandoned, with three unhatched eggs, I opened them and found no trace of an embryo in two, a very small embryo in the third.

I love to stand in the banana grove early in the morning, while the sun rises above the hills and the river into a blue sky adorned with white clouds. Wherever the bright rays fall directly upon a broad banana leaf, wet with dew or rain that has fallen in the night, its pale, translucent green contrasts sharply with the deeper green of its shaded parts, and its fine, close-set, parallel veins stand out clearly. In the fresh morning air, the moisture evaporating from the leaves in the sunshine condenses in fine droplets that swirl upward in protean clouds. Around me flit colorful butterflies; and little, black, stingless bees visit the clustered white banana flowers, newly exposed beneath the latest upturned red bract of the massive bud that hangs on a knobby stem, beneath a bunch of developing fruit. Tiny, yellow-breasted Bananaquits cling to the flowers, head downward, to extract abundant nectar with sharp, curved bills.

These flowers of Old World origin seem to have evolved for pollination by hummingbirds confined to the New World, although, apparently, banana flowers and hummingbirds never came into contact until after Europeans introduced the plants into their American colonies. Hovering beneath the flowers, their bodies nearly vertical, the hummers push their slender bills almost straight upward into the long, narrow flower tubes, while they suck the sweet liquid through thin, tubular tongues. After visiting a number of flowers, the hummingbirds dart away with foreheads powdered with white pollen—pollen that will never fertilize, since the widely cultivated varieties of bananas are seedless. In this small plantation, I have seen thirteen species of hummingbirds, either passing through it or visiting the banana flowers. Four kinds have nested there.

Larger birds fly across the grove between the tall trees around it. From high, exposed perches, flycatchers dart into the air to seize flying insects. Colorful tanagers gather fruits and insects from leafy boughs. Occasionally, a flock of White-crowned Parrots fly overhead with raucous cries, or a family of Fiery-billed Araçaris straggle by in looser formation, voicing notes that seem too sharp and thin for these great-billed toucans. On certain bright mornings, this opening in the woods is a wonderful place to watch birds.

It was on such a morning in early August that I found my first nests of the Bronzy Hermit and the Band-tailed Barbthroat. I have told about the latter first, because it behaved as I expected a nesting hummingbird to act, attending its nest alone. The Bronzy Hermit was more puzzling, required closer study, but yielded the more surprising discoveries. Unlike most of the others, my first Bronzy Hermit's nest was attached, not to a banana leaf, but to a narrow strip of a rather similar leaf of a heliconia, or wild plantain, at the edge of the plantation. In construction, it was hardly to be distinguished from nests of the Band-tailed Barbthroat, and it hung, twenty feet in the air, in an exposed situation. Raising a mirror attached to a long, thin stick, I could barely detect the reflected images of two dark-skinned, recently hatched nestlings. With this same mirror, pivoted to the end of a short wooden handle that could be tied to a stick, I inspected all these nests attached to leaves, thereby avoiding the labor and disturbance caused by a tall, heavy stepladder. Sometimes, while I held the mirror above a nest, the parent hovered close around it, as though examining this strange, shining, intruding object, in which, perhaps, she noticed her own reflected image and mistook it for a trespassing hummingbird.

I sat on a log among the banana plants to watch this newly found Bronzy Hermit's nest. Presently a hummingbird arrived to feed the nestlings. Her upper plumage was metallic bronze, her ventral surface almost uniformly rusty cinnamon, and her tail, when spread, showed that all except the bronzy central pair of feathers were rufous-chestnut, with white tips and black subterminal bars. Clinging to the nest's rim with flesh-colored feet, her wings raised high and rapidly beating, her tail swinging up and down, she pushed her long, strongly curved bill down into the nest to regurgitate nectar and minute insects and spiders to nestlings that I could not see. Then she settled down to brood, with her breast toward the supporting leaf strip, her tail projecting over the outer edge of the cup. In this position, her head was necessarily thrown so far back that her bill pointed almost straight upward and the back of her head nearly touched her rump. Almost bent double, her posture, typical of incubating and brooding hermit hummingbirds, seemed unendurable; yet she could sit this way for hours.

All this was no different from what I had seen at nests of other kinds of hermit hummingbirds. But I had not watched long before I noticed that a second Bronzy Hermit was interested in this nest, and the relations of the two were far from friendly. Although in this species the sexes are hard to distinguish, the female's breast being only slightly more uniformly cinnamon than the male's, I concluded that the intruder was another female. During the first session of brooding by the mother that I watched, the other came twelve times to molest her, menacing her with the tip of her long bill, sometimes appearing to thrust its point at her. Often the intruder clung to the side of the nest, while the other sat warming the nestlings. To defend herself, the brooding bird turned her bill toward the assailant, sometimes bending her head back until it was almost upside down. Occasionally, the two hummingbirds briefly seized each other's bills, but they seemed never to injure each other. Much fine twittering accompanied these encounters, but I could not tell whether it came from one or both of the hummingbirds. Usually the disturber left while the parent continued to brood, but at times both flew off together, one apparently chasing the other until they were beyond view in the thicket. During nearly every session of brooding, the parent was repeatedly harassed by the intruder.

Two days later, I saw the parent alight on the nest's rim as though to feed the nestlings. Before she could begin, the other attacked her from the rear, poking at her back and apparently pulling at her feathers, making her crouch down instead of delivering food. The assailant returned again and again, often clinging to the nest's side. They struck their long bills together, and the one in the nest lunged violently at the persecutor clinging beside her. The nest with the young swayed widely on its narrow ribbon of leaf while the two adults fought. The assailant withdrew, soon to return and renew her attacks.

Throughout the twenty-four days that the young remained in the nest after I found them, the second bird continued to persecute the attendant parent. The intruder often looked into the nest while the parent was absent. Although I could not distinguish the two by their appearance, their behavior was quite different; I found no convincing evidence that more than one of them fed or brooded the nestlings. (When two birds attend a nest, continued watching will nearly always reveal them replacing one another, or feeding the young in quick succession.) The intruder spent much time perching on a slender, head-high twig just within the edge of the neighboring thicket, wagging her tail up and down in the manner of hermits. From time to time, she sallied forth to look at the nest, nearly always leaving promptly if the parent was absent, but molesting the parent if she found her there. Sometimes the parent entered the thicket to look for her persecutor. When the latter was present, one chased the other swiftly through the thicket and the adjoining plantation, to the accompaniment of high-pitched twitters.

This behavior was hard to interpret. Although hummingbirds contend with each other for the control of nectar-yielding flowers, this dispute obviously was not over a feeding territory. If the second female was motivated by parental impulses, why did she not take an unmistakable part in feeding and brooding the young? Or could I have mistaken the sex of a young male, still not in fully adult plumage, who misplayed the role of a male Bronzy Hermit? Be this as it may, long watching in the banana plantation showed me that the conspicuously hanging nests of the four species of hermits that bred there often attracted the attention of hummingbirds other than their owners, sometimes of individuals of different species. We have already noticed that two Band-tailed Barbthroats may lay in the same nest, an occurrence also recorded of the Rufous-breasted Hermit in South America. The less conspicuously situated nests of other kinds of hummingbirds that I have watched were only in exceptional circumstances molested by intruding individuals.

Despite the turmoil at and around their nest, the two young Bronzy Hermits throve. The whole time they were in the nest, they sat with their heads toward the supporting strip of leaf, and, after they were bigger, resting against it with bills turned nearly straight upward, just as their mother incubated and as all hermit nestlings lie, as far as I have seen. In this orientation, they could shoot their excrement over the nest's outer edge and keep it clean—while they were tiny, the parent sometimes carried it away in her bill. To feed them, she reached over their backs to thrust her bill into their upturned, open mouths, while, with rapidly beating wings, she clung to the nest's rim. After they had grown until their tails projected beyond the rim, she hovered in the air, as though she were visiting a flower. Sometimes, while delivering a meal, she clung to a nestling's rump, always with wings rapidly beating. Usually she fed both nestlings at each visit.

In the following year, the Bronzy Hermit attached her nest to a strip of another heliconia leaf, about fifty yards from the site of her first nest. At the beginning of July, two fledglings flew from this nest; and a fortnight later, the parent started to build a new one higher on the same strip that still held the first. In the upper bowl of this two-story or "double-decker" nest she laid two eggs, in early August. After incubating at least seventeen days, she hatched one of them, but the nestling soon vanished. During the next five years, this Bronzy Hermit or her successors built eight more nests, all beneath banana leaves within the plantation, in sites nowise different from those chosen by the Band-tailed Barbthroat. The ribbon of leaf that supported one of these nests was only five-eighths of an inch wide. One of these Bronzy Hermits' nests was built only nine feet from a nest where a Band-tailed Barbthroat was feeding a nestling. In another year, the two species had eggs and nestlings simultaneously in nests only twenty-five feet apart. When two barbthroats nested at the same time, they were much more widely separated.

After the first nesting, when the parent Bronzy Hermit was so persecuted by another of her kind, she was nearly always guarded by a male, recognizable by his paler abdomen. Only in one year, when I did not find the nest until the nestlings were well grown and watched very little, did I fail to find him in attendance. Throughout each of the other nestings, he was to be found, day after day, resting low at the edge of the thicket nearest the nest, or, in two seasons, in a coffee bush almost beneath it, from time to time singing or twittering in a high-pitched voice. After each excursion to forage or drive away an intruder, he returned to the same perch. At intervals, he flew up to hover beside the nest, examining it, or poking his bill into it. While a nest was under construction, he sometimes sat in it and briefly made the motions of building, although I never saw him bring a contribution to it. As the female flew to and from her nest, he often flew with her; but whether he was escorting or pursuing, or whether she was chasing him, I could not decide because they went so fast and so promptly vanished among the banana plants.

The male Bronzy Hermit never incubated or fed a nestling, activities in which male hummingbirds have very rarely been reported to engage, and which appear to be abnormal even in species in which they sometimes occur. His business was to protect the nest, chiefly from the intrusions of other hummingbirds—above all, other Bronzy Hermits—to which he gave chase the moment they appeared. Although occasionally the male seemed to be somewhat rough with the female, perhaps only importunate, in all the later nestings she was never so persecuted as during the first, thanks to his vigilance.

In 1974, for the first time in eight years, no Bronzy Hermit nested in the banana grove; but in early July, when breeding should have begun, I found a male resting in a tree fern that had been the guardian male's station, while the female was nesting on a banana leaf above him, in the preceding year. It was hard to doubt that he was the same individual, waiting for his mate, who failed to appear. This was the last time that I saw a Bronzy Hermit anywhere on the farm. Hummingbirds may live ten years or more, and, in view of the rarity of the species in this locality and the proximity of all the nest sites, it is not improbable that the same male and female were mated in six successive years. Whether the pair bond was maintained between breeding seasons is more doubtful. Only for the closely related Rufous-breasted, or Hairy, Hermit of South America has somewhat similar behavior been reported of any hummingbird. In Trinidad, Barbara Snow found polygamous males guarding the nests of several females,[1] who built above woodland streams. Breeding female hummingbirds are typically as solitary as the Band-tailed Barbthroats in the banana grove.

The third hummingbird that nested in the plantation was the Long-tailed Hermit. Although frequent visitors to the banana flowers, these big, brownish hermits with slender, white-tipped tails usually attach their nests beneath the tapering tips of fronds of low, spiny palms in the forest's deep shade; in only two

1. Barbara K. Snow, "Social organization of the Hairy Hermit *Glaucis hirsuta*," *Ardea*, 61 (1973): 94–105.

years have I found their nests on banana leaves. Instead of choosing a narrow strip such as the other two hermits preferred, the Long-tailed Hermit selected a large sheet of leaf, to which she attached her structure at a corner, almost a right angle, where the margin met a tear that extended to the midrib. Her nest was made of softer materials than the other species used, including fine fibers from decaying leaf sheaths of the banana plant, rootlets, and vegetable horsehair, all bound together and fastened to the leaf with cobweb liberally applied. Below it hung the usual loose "tail" of hermits' nests. Unlike the nests of the other two species, no light passed through the much thicker, softer nest of the Long-tail. If wetted, it would take longer to dry; but the broad sheet of leaf blade that folded around it gave much better protection from wind-blown rain than the narrow strip of the other hermits' nests would afford.

The single Long-tailed Hermit that I found in the grove raised two nestlings, who left the nest in mid-September of 1971. Five days after the second of these fledglings flew, she laid the first egg of another brood in a nest, twenty-five feet from the first, that she started while still feeding her first brood in the nest—a not unusual habit of hummingbirds. The single fledgling in this second brood did not take wing until November 2, the latest date that I have found any hummingbird nesting in the banana grove. Toward the end of the following May, this Long-tailed Hermit laid another two eggs in a nest near the sites of the first two. These nests, fastened to banana leaves at heights of thirteen to fifteen feet, were by far the highest Long-tailed Hermits' nests that I have seen.

The fourth and last hummingbird that nested in the plantation was the Little Hermit. As this bird is almost a miniature of the Long-tailed Hermit (with a relatively shorter tail), so her nest was a miniature of that of her larger relative, a thick-walled, softly padded structure attached at the corner of a large sheet of banana leaf. Twelve feet above the ground, this nest was unusually high for the Little Hermit, which usually binds its nest with cobweb beneath the tapering tip of a spiny palm leaf, only two to six feet up in the woodland shade.

The tiny, narrowly ellipsoidal eggs of hummingbirds take much longer to hatch than the very much bigger eggs of many songbirds, such as thrushes and finches. Moreover, the incubation period of hermits is somewhat longer than that of some other hummingbirds, which may be only fifteen or sixteen days. In the banana grove, the Bronzy Hermits' eggs hatched in about seventeen and a half days, counting from the laying of the second egg to the hatching of the second nestling. The incubation period of the Long-tailed Hermit was about eighteen days, and that of the Band-tailed Barbthroat eighteen and a half to nineteen days. The nestlings likewise remained in the nest a long while, those of the Long-tailed Hermit twenty-three to twenty-four days, those of the Bronzy Hermit and Band-tailed Barbthroat usually twenty-four or twenty-five days; although one young barbthroat, who seemed normal, delayed its flight until it was a full month old. The periods of the Little Hermit were shorter, only sixteen days for incubation, and twenty or twenty-one days for raising the young until they flew.

In the early morning, when they are wet with dew or rain, the blades of the banana leaves spread out broad and flat. As they dry under a bright morning sun, the two sides bend downward beneath the midrib, until at noon they have folded together, giving the plantation a very different aspect. It now looks much less lush than at sunrise; but in their nearly vertical position, with their lower surfaces almost in contact, the two sides of the leaf blade absorb much less radiant heat and conserve much water. It often becomes difficult to watch a hermit's nest when the supporting leaf has folded together. Probably, at this time, older nestlings cannot take their usual exercises, when they whir their wings rapidly, without releasing their hold on the nest.

To have these exercises permanently impeded can have disastrous consequences. One year, when the Bronzy Hermit built her nest near the tip of an old leaf that started to dry and fold around it like a tent, one nestling vanished when only about twenty days old, possibly having flown prematurely to escape the confined space. The other nestling could not take its exercises without striking its right wing against the drying leaf. During its final days in the nest, I noticed that when it whirred its wings it did not spread them equally, but kept the right one partly closed and held somewhat back and up. Nevertheless, continued impact against the leaf rubbed the feathers from the underside of this wing, until it became raw.

After this young hummingbird had delayed in the nest five or six days past the usual time for flying, it occurred to me that I might help it by pushing out the part of the leaf that interfered with its exercises. Since the nest hung high above my head, I could do this only with the aid of a long stick. As my stick approached the nest, the young hummer jumped out and fluttered to the ground. When I picked it up, my hand was stained with blood. Although its flight feathers were hardly damaged, the abrasion beneath the wing was so great that it could not fly; it could hardly perch. I set it on a slender twig of a coffee bush, with its breast resting against another twig, where it managed to stay. Next morning, its mother came to look for it there, and in the nest, but she could not find it; nor could I. Evidently, the wing exercises are so important to a nestling hummingbird that it practices them even at the price of injuring a wing. To avoid damage, the female must build her nest in a site that affords enough room.

Although the hermits' nests hang where such flightless nest pillagers as small mammals and snakes could hardly reach them, only a minority escaped disaster. In eleven years, Band-tailed Barbthroats laid thirty-nine eggs in nineteen nests. They hatched twenty-one of these eggs but raised only twelve young in seven nests. In seven years, the Bronzy Hermit(s) laid nineteen eggs in ten nests (omitting one nest of which I did not learn the outcome), hatched thirteen eggs, and raised eight young in four nests. In two years, the Long-tailed Hermit laid six eggs in three nests, hatched five of them, and raised all five nestlings. In the single Little Hermit's nest, both young lived to fly.

Although no animal was seen raiding a nest, the simultaneous disappearance of the entire contents of nine nests of Bronzy Hermits and barbthroats was probably caused by predators. Suspicion falls upon bats operating in the night, certain species of which are known to prey upon small birds. Five barbthroats' nests were abandoned while containing unhatched eggs, two sets of which I opened and found no trace of an embryo. One barbthroat's nest became detached from the leaf strip; and the old leaf supporting another nest sank down, apparently spilling out the nestling. Two nestlings of each species, including the Bronzy Hermit with the injured wing, probably died. Taking the four species of hermits together, 45 percent of their thirty-three nests yielded at least one fledgling, and 41 percent of their sixty-six eggs produced flying young. This exceptionally high rate of success for nests at the edge of lowland tropical forest is doubtless to be attributed to the difficulty, for all but winged predators, of reaching structures hanging free beneath slippery banana leaves.

After leaving their nests, the fledgling hermits of all four species vanished into the surrounding woods, and I lost track of all but one of them. This was a young Band-tailed Barbthroat that I found in a thicket through which I passed to reach the plantation. Considering the rarity of barbthroats, I had little doubt that this youngster was one of two that, three weeks earlier, had left a nest fifty yards away. Resting on slender horizontal twigs at no great height, it was so fearless that I could almost touch it. The young barbthroat was full-grown, with a tail much like that of adults, but it lacked cinnamon on its pale gray chest. While I stood watching, its mother came, alighted close beside it, thrust her bill into its open mouth, and regurgitated to it. After a while, the young barbthroat received another meal in the same fashion.

Morning after morning, for the next ten days, I watched the parent feed the juvenile in the same place. Sometimes, when the adult started to fly away after delivering a meal, the juvenile followed, causing her to alight on another perch a few yards away and feed it again. Occasionally, the pursuit was repeated, winning for the persistent youngster a third meal on a more distant perch. Between meals, the young barbthroat tried to feed itself, at first without much success. It evidently mistook some pale red young leaves of a vine for nectar-yielding flowers; and it tried to stick its bill into the expanded, slightly hollow base of the petiole of a large dead leaf caught up in the thicket, as though it were probing a corolla. From time to time, the young bird flew beyond view, but soon it returned to the same small area, the only place I saw it being fed. Since young hummingbirds do not follow their foraging parents, as many other birds do, it is important for them to have a definite rendezvous, where the adult can find and feed her dependent offspring.

As days passed, the juvenile spent more time hovering beneath green leaves, seeming to glean from them minute insects and spiders, invisible to me, in the usual manner of hermits. I last saw it receive food on November 3, when it was fifty-six days old and had been out of the nest for thirty-two days. This appears to be about the normal interval of dependence in tropical hummingbirds. A Rufous-tailed Hummingbird was fed until fifty-nine days old; a Long-billed Starthroat until at least forty-eight days of age; and a Scaly-breasted Hummingbird was still being fed at the age of fifty-two days. The most prolonged parental care that I have discovered in the hummingbird family was achieved by another Scaly-breast, unmistakable because of a wart on her bill, who was last seen feeding her progeny when it was sixty-five days old and had been flying for forty-one days.

Although our small banana plantation gave us many heavy bunches of fruit, it would have yielded more with less shade. Loss of productivity was amply compensated by greatly reduced theft and all the discoveries I made with the hummingbirds who nested there. Commercial growers plant bananas in full sunshine; naturalists eager to increase their knowledge should set them in a small clearing in tropical forest.

8. *Scarlet Passion-flowers & Hermit Hummingbirds*

BEHIND the house rises a steep hillside, where in past years horses cropped the short grass and picked up aromatic fruits that fell from scattered, brown-barked Guava trees. On its farther side, the narrow ridge falls as steeply into a deep vale, where, years ago, a cluster of tall tree ferns had been left standing, to adorn the pasture with their spreading crowns of intricately divided fronds. Beyond this moist hollow, a tall second-growth woods rose like a wall beside the open pasture. Along the edge of this woodland, in the bright days of January and February, brilliant spots of scarlet were visible from afar. These were Scarlet Passion-flowers, which open only in the dry early months of the year.

To push into these woods, through the barrier of bushes and interlacing thorny vines along its exposed edge, was not easy. But, at intervals, the cattle had forced passageways. Entering through one of these narrow gaps one bright January morning, I found myself in dim, subdued light, which contrasted violently with the brilliant sunshine in the neighboring pasture. Here and there, the fiery color of a passion-flower caught my eye amid the tangled undergrowth.

Bright blossoms seek bright sunshine; yet the most brilliant wildflower of the valley was displayed here in the dim light near the ground. I looked around for the foliage of the woody vine that bore these splendid blossoms. A few three-lobed leaves, like those of the grape, grew on the slender branches with the flowers.

But most of these leaves were small; there seemed to be too little foliage to support such long racemes of big blossoms. Following the ropelike ascending vines with my eyes, I caught glimpses of more of the three-lobed leaves far up among the branches of the trees. When I returned to the pasture and scrutinized the roof of the woods from outside, it became clear that the main mass of the vine's foliage was spread over the upper boughs of the trees, in the sunshine. But here I detected no scarlet flowers.

Why this separation of the foliage and flowers of the same plant? The situation is not unique in the vegetation of the tropics, where a number of trees and vines bear flowers and fruits low on the main trunk (a condition that botanists call "cauliflory") or on special, often leafless, basal branches; yet it is sufficiently rare to call for explanation.

While I stood pondering this puzzle, a big, brownish hummingbird darted through the undergrowth and poised beside one of the red blossoms, into which it pushed its long, strongly curved bill. As it hovered on wings vibrating too rapidly to be seen, it wagged its long, slender, white-tipped tail slowly up and down. It was a Long-tailed Hermit, a large hummingbird that lives in primary forest and heavier secondary woods, where it usually stays near the ground.

Over the years, I have found a number of its nests. With the exception of a few attached to banana leaves (as described in chapter seven), they are fastened beneath the tip of a frond of a small, usually spiny palm in the deep shade of heavy forest. From the cupped top, a soft pocket of vegetable down and fibers, the nest tapers downward to a point that matches the shape of the leaf-tip, to which it is attached by much cobweb. In this swinging cradle, sheltered from rain and prying eyes by the broad surface of the palm frond, two tiny, white eggs are hatched by a solitary female, and the young hummingbirds rest until, at the age of three weeks

or a little more, they are able to fly well. Throughout the breeding season, the male hermits, who take no interest in eggs or young, perch on twigs near the ground, in dimly lighted undergrowth, tirelessly repeating squeaky notes to attract the females, while they wag their tails rhythmically up and down.

As I continued, day after day, to watch the passion-flowers, I became convinced that, in this locality, Long-tailed Hermits are their principal visitors. Evidently the flowers are displayed near the ground to secure the services of this and related hummingbirds as pollinators. The Scarlet Passion-flower ranges, from Nicaragua to Peru, wholly within the range of the Long-tailed Hermit and other hummingbirds of the genus *Phaethornis*, which prefer the undergrowth of the woodland to its upper levels. Occasionally, at Los Cusingos, Scarlet Passion-flowers are visited by a Green Hermit, in size and form much like the Long-tailed, but bronzy green instead of brownish. However, the Green Hermit is at home higher in the mountains, and rare here at twenty-five hundred feet, except when driven downward by long-continued, cold rainstorms.

Once a Violet Saberwing, a hummingbird as big as the Long-tailed Hermit, with a bill nearly as long but more strongly curved, claimed a group of passion-flowers for a week or more. During this interval, the Long-tailed Hermit who had been a regular attendant could make only furtive visits; if discovered, it was chased away by the heavier saberwing, a species that only occasionally visits Los Cusingos.

Of the seventeen kinds of hummingbirds resident or frequent on the farm, I saw only one other make repeated visits to the passion-flowers. This was the Little Hermit, a smaller replica of the Long-tailed Hermit that is abundant in second-growth woods. With its shorter bill, less than an inch long, this small hummingbird cannot reach the nectar in the heart of the passion-flower. It confines its visits

◀ LONG-TAILED HERMIT HUMMINGBIRD

to the nectaries on the floral bracts, where it either sips the sugary secretions, or picks up small insects that are attracted to them, or, more probably, takes advantage of both sources of nourishment. Its mode of visiting the flowers made me certain that it does not transfer pollen from blossom to blossom. Of the four hummingbirds that I saw here, only the three with bills over an inch and a quarter long seemed able to reach the nectar in the flower itself and to serve as pollinators.

Although not absent from old forest, the passion-flower is here most abundant in tall, rich, second-growth woods. Rarely one of the vivid blossoms is displayed as high as forty or fifty feet, but the great majority are much lower. Perhaps most are not above a man's reach, and some even lie on the ground. They are borne, not on the main stems of the vine, but upon slender, whiplike lateral shoots, an eighth of an inch or less in diameter and up to ten feet long. These floral branches sprawl over the ground, rocks, or surrounding low vegetation, or, if arising higher on the main stem, they may hang limply in the air. Those that find some low support become longest. They appear never to branch unless their growing point has been injured. If in a spot where they receive a fair amount of light, they bear well-developed leaves of the usual trilobate form; but in the deepest shade the leaves are greatly reduced in size, at times to tiny rudiments that soon die.

Each leaf of a floral branch, if not too rudimentary, bears at the base of its furry petiole two, three, or four small, reddish nectary glands, cup-shaped and opening downward. In the axil of each leaf is a flower bud and a long, unbranched tendril, which is often rudimentary. Above these is an accessory bud that usually fails to develop but may grow into a branch if the tip of the floral shoot is destroyed. The flower bud is surrounded by an involucre of three pale, broadly lanceolate bracts, with a number of nectaries along their margins. Thus, in addition to the floral nectaries, the flowering shoot is equipped with numerous extra-floral nectaries, whose secretions attract ants, other insects, and Little Hermits.

The flowers start to open late at night. I have found the sepals and petals beginning to separate at three o'clock in the morning. When, soon after five o'clock, the first glimmer of dawn brightens the eastern sky, the big blossoms are half or more open, and the anthers have already split to release their pollen. An hour or less later, they are fully expanded. Often the sepals and petals continue to turn back until they are strongly reflexed and surround the pedicel. The five sepals and five petals are all much alike in size, shape, and intense red color; but the sepals are somewhat longer, fleshier, and broader. They are strengthened on the outer side by a keel, which the petals lack. When fully expanded, the great blossom measures five and a half to six inches in diameter. A single plant rarely has more than two or three open flowers, and usually only one on even the longest floral shoot, where they open in succession from the base toward the apex.

The flowers stay open and are visited by hummingbirds throughout the day. A few have perceptibly begun to close before sunset; others are wide open at night-fall. They close gradually during the night and are well folded up by dawn. After closing, the perianth gradually withers but persists around the stalk of the developing fruit. Even if pollination is prevented so that seeds are not set, the blossom folds up at the end of its single day of glory and fails to open again. Nevertheless, a constant succession of flowers adorns the plant, until the increasing dryness of March stops the blooming of the passion-flowers. The season's last flowers may be pale pink and only half the normal size.

Of the complex structure of the passion-flower, I need mention only a few salient features related to its pollination. The ovary is not, as in most flowers, situated between or even beneath the bases of the petals, but is borne at the summit of a long, slender stalk that emerges from the center of the blossom. From the summit of this exposed ovary diverge three styles, each of which ends in an expanded stigma with its surface receptive of pollen turned downward. The five stamens stand in a ring around the base of the ovary, with the five big anthers, each swinging by its middle, hanging between the stigmas and facing downward into the flower.

In the center of each flower, surrounding the long stalk that holds the ovary aloft, is the corona, a triple crown of long, slender fringes or filaments. Each filament is red, red and white, or sometimes almost wholly white. This "crown of thorns," and other less obvious resemblances of the floral parts to the instruments of Christ's Passion, or suffering and crucifixion, led early botanists to give the name "passion-flower" to plants of this genus. Below this crown, the central stalk that supports the ovary is closely surrounded by a collar or sleeve of thick tissue, fringed at its upper edge, and at its lower edge turned upward like a cuff. This complex structure investing the central stalk guards the nectar richly secreted by glands at the very bottom of the tubular base of the perianth.

The functions of this collar appear to be, first, to exclude insects and short-billed hummingbirds that might take the nectar without transferring the pollen; and, second, to control the posture of the preferred visitors, such as the larger hermit hummingbirds. To reach the nectar, they are compelled by the stout collar to hold their bills nearly parallel to the central stalk. Thus, whether the flower faces upward or downward, while sipping nectar the hummingbird must hold its head where its crown will brush against some of the five anthers and three stigmas that

SCARLET PASSION-FLOWER: a, anther; b, bract; c, corona; n, nectar well; o, ovary; p, perianth; s, stigma; ▶
st, stamen; sta, stalk bearing ovary and stamens (the foliage belongs to a different plant).

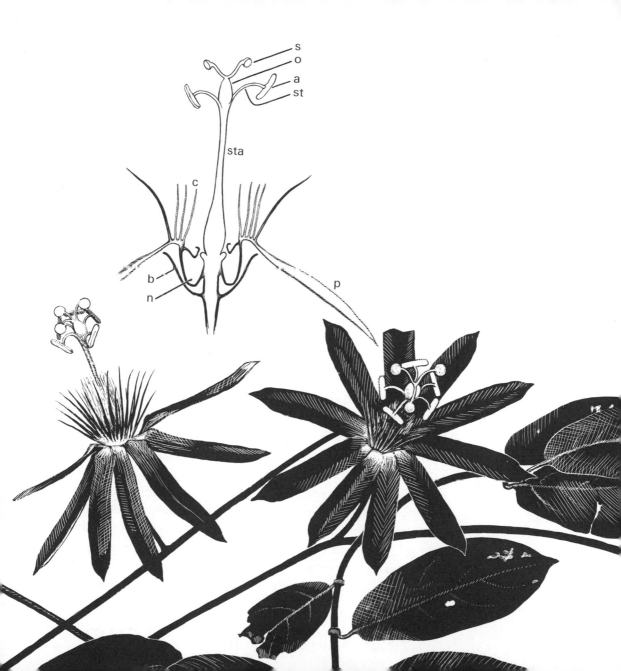

stand in a ring above it. The long-billed hummingbirds that I saw visiting the flowers had the tops of their dark heads heavily dusted with pale pollen. They were working for the bountiful plant, even if they did not know it.

The edible fruits of passion-flowers are called *granadillas* in tropical America, "maypops" in southern United States. In most, the digestible part is the soft, gelatinous aril that surrounds each of the many small, dark seeds that fill the cavity of the usually dry, tough fruit. The fruits of the several species vary greatly in size and edibility: some are hardly bigger than grapes, others almost a foot long; some are sweet and aromatic, others have an unpleasant odor. The Scarlet Passion-flower's ripe fruit, about the size and shape of a large hen's egg, is prettily mottled with green and white.

Once, in late April, in the tall second-growth woods where, earlier in the year, the scarlet blossoms had been conspicuous, I watched a squirrel eating one of these fruits. The furry little animal sat on a thick bush-rope that lay along the ground at the base of a tree trunk. It held its thick, auburn tail above its brown back, and the fruit rested on the ground before it. The rodent had opened one side, to expose the gelatinous mass that filled the cavity. Taking a double handful of the seeds between its forepaws, it ate eagerly, repeating this over and over. From time to time, it bit away and discarded more of the mottled rind to expose the interior mass. It swallowed the seeds along with the mucilaginous aril in which each was separately imbedded, just the way many people eat cultivated *granadillas*. Probably the seeds themselves would pass undigested through the squirrel's alimentary tract, thereby disseminating the vine.

With sticky pulp dripping from forepaws and chin, the furry rodent reminded me of a small boy blissfully immersed in a juicy mango, forgetful of cleanliness and clothes. The squirrel continued to eat for many minutes, until he had quite consumed the contents of the fruit—a big meal, I thought, for a small stomach. His feast over, he carefully wiped his dripping chin against the rough bark of the great vine on which he had been sitting, then scrambled up the long, slender trunk and hopped away through the treetops.

The rather disagreeable odor of the rind had, in the past, deterred me from eating the fruit of the Scarlet Passion-flower. But the squirrel had so obviously enjoyed it that I decided to sample it for myself. I found it pleasantly acid-sweet, but not quite as good as the common cultivated *granadilla*.

9. *Speckled Tanagers*

Of the two hundred and twenty-three species of tanagers in the Western Hemisphere, where alone they occur, forty-six are known in Costa Rica. Sixteen species have been found at Los Cusingos, of which thirteen are breeding residents. The Summer Tanager is here through half the year as a winter resident. The Scarlet Tanager pauses here in spring, on its long journey from its winter home in South America to its summer home in the north. Occasionally, Blue-hooded Euphonias come down from the Costa Rican highlands, where they nest, to eat mistletoe berries, but they do not stay long.

What a colorful assemblage our tanagers are! The most abundant species in the clearings is the Scarlet-rumped Black Tanager, of which the velvety male is well described by the name. The duller female has bright orange on her breast and rump. The subdued red Red-crowned Ant-Tanager, the black White-shouldered Tanager, and the three resident species of purplish black-and-yellow euphonias all have more plainly attired females. In all our other permanently resident tanagers, the sexes are too similar to be readily distinguished. These include the Blue, or Blue-gray, Tanager, with bright blue wings; the bright yellow Silver-throated Tanager with a silvery gray throat; the blue, black, white, and yellow Golden-masked Tanager; and the lovely Bay-headed Tanager, whose body is bright green and light blue. Generous as our representation of tanagers is, it hardly suggests the immense variety of color patterns in the family, especially among its South American species. Tanagers contribute more than any other family to the beauty of tropical American bird life.

The largest and loveliest genus in the tanager family is *Tangara*, with about forty-five species. These small, gemlike tanagers are most abundant in heavily forested foothills from southern Mexico to Bolivia, but they are by no means lacking in hot lowlands, and a few live permanently on cool, stormy mountain heights. Their food consists largely of small berries and the soft arils, rich in oil, that surround the seeds of many tropical trees and vines. They vary their diet with insects and spiders, for which they search by hopping along horizontal branches and bending over, now on this side, now on that, to see what may be hiding in the bark or moss beneath the boughs. They also glean insects from foliage.

As is true of many other brightly colored tropical birds of which the sexes are alike, the species of *Tangara* that I know best remain mated through the year. The pairs often roam through the treetops in company with other small birds. Unlike certain other members of their family, these elegant tanagers are poorly endowed with song. None that I know well would rank as even a second-rate songster. From some I have heard only series of sharp *ticks*, or dry, insectlike notes. Theorists of an earlier generation reasoned that nature, economical despite her prodigal diversity, parsimoniously withheld song from birds that she had lavishly adorned with color. Modern ornithologists have noticed that birds of various kinds sing most profusely when they lack mates, or are separated from them. Although constantly paired, tropical wrens are among the most gifted and persistent of songsters, doubtless because these little birds of subdued coloration commonly forage amid such dense vegetation that they would lose contact with their partners if they did not keep in touch by voice. Brilliant tanagers, which forage and fly more visibly, have less need of voice; a few notes are adequate to inform their partners that they are about to fly. Apparently, their songs have degenerated, in the course of evolution, because they have little need of them.

The four species of *Tangara* at Los Cusingos come to the feeder to eat bananas, but not with equal frequency. The least constant attendants are Bay-headed Tanagers, who prefer wild fruits and arillate seeds to bananas. Indeed, all the tanagers come more seldom to the feeder when such native foods are abundant in the vicinity. While at the board, the males of all these tanagers may sometimes be seen, especially as the nesting season approaches, passing billsful of banana to their mates, who have been helping themselves freely to the same fruit.

Three of our four species of *Tangara* (the Bay-headed, Golden-masked, and Silver-throated tanagers) have color patterns typical of their genus, with solid patches of bright color. The fourth is unusual not only in its genus but in the tanager family as a whole. The well-named Speckled Tanager is heavily spotted with black over most of its bright yellowish-green upper plumage and its whitish underparts. Its curious appearance is increased by a heavy black mark between the base of its short, thick, black bill and its dark eye, above which is the yellow streak that formerly caused it to be called the Yellow-browed Tanager. In some pairs, the male is more heavily spotted than the female, but this may be related to age as well as to sex, as young birds are more lightly spotted than adults.

Family bonds are strong in Speckled Tanagers, who between breeding seasons often fly in groups of three or four, rarely more, evidently parents with full-grown offspring. Their call is a short, clear, somewhat bell-like note. Their song, if song it may be called, consists of a series of similar, weak, clear notes, repeated with increasing frequency until they form a sort of trill, which seems to taper off

to a sharp point as the hurrying notes diminish in volume. One morning, a family of four, impatient for their breakfast, came right up on the porch, to peck at bananas I had laid on a table, intending to take them to the shelf in the garden. When bananas become scarce, we place halved oranges on the feeder. Most of the attendants find them an acceptable substitute for the more solid fruit. Speckled Tanagers are particularly fond of orange juice, pecking into the orange again and again and lifting up their heads to make the juice flow into their throats.

Last October, I watched a pair of Speckled Tanagers approach one of the silken nests that the small, black Spinning Ants weave, by means of their thread-secreting larvae, among the clustered green foliage of trees. The tanagers plucked ant after ant from the surface of the nest or the surrounding twigs and leaves. Raising a wing, each bird rubbed an ant along its lower or inner surface, then seemed to eat the insect. Sometimes a tanager appeared to put the ant under its forward-tilted tail, and sometimes to swallow it immediately without touching it to the plumage. However, the swiftness of the birds' movements, the height of the ants' nest, and interfering foliage prevented my seeing this well enough to be certain. For several minutes, both tanagers continued uninterruptedly to treat ant after ant in this fashion, while the poor little ants stood upright on their nest, as is their habit when disturbed, and probably, by striking their abdomens against it, made a rattling sound that I was too far away to hear. Then, with their little trilled call, the pair of birds flew away, leaving me perplexed, as I always am when I watch this curious practice, widespread among birds, called "anting." Despite many more or less ingenious explanations, we are still not sure why birds treat ants, or some substitute for them, in this curious fashion.

I have found eggs of the Speckled Tanager from April to June, but chiefly in May. The breeding season is evidently much longer than this, for in several years

I have seen parents feed fledglings in October and even early November. The dozen nests that I have found were in trees and shrubs, from four to fifty feet above the ground, but only two were below ten feet. Although the few nests that I have seen were in shady clearings near the forest, I suspect that many are built high in forest trees, where they escape detection.

As in all species of *Tangara* for which I have information, the nest of the Speckled Tanager is a compact open cup. It differs, however, from that of its three relatives in this valley in the absence of living moss, liverworts, or diminutive epiphytic ferns, which give their green color to the outsides of the nests of the Silver-throated and Bay-headed species. The Speckled Tanager's nest is composed of such dry materials as the fine, curling secondary rachises of the twice-compound leaves of the Climbing Mimosa, with a middle layer of small leaves or strips torn from larger ones, and a lining of horsehairs or the black fungal filaments that resemble them, sometimes called "vegetable horsehair." The nest is bound together and attached to its support by cobweb, and in the bottom are usually a few pieces of gray foliaceous lichens that grow on the bark of trees.

Both sexes of the Speckled Tanager cooperate in building the nest, as is usual, though not invariable, in the genus *Tangara*. As a rule, they arrive together with material in their bills, and each in turn enters the nest to place what it has brought and shape the structure. Occasionally, one passes its contribution to the other who is already sitting there. During intermissions in the work, the male may feed his mate.

In May, some years ago, I found a pair of Speckled Tanagers building a nest amid clustering foliage, far out on a horizontal limb of a Red Poró tree in our garden. The female's right foot had somehow been so severely injured that it was quite useless, and she always held it up when she perched. Probably because of her impediment, she and her mate worked slowly and built an exceptionally shallow structure, which appeared unfinished when it received eggs at the end of the month. The set consisted of two, the number of eggs I have always found in nests of this and other species of *Tangara*. The shells were dull white, heavily mottled with brown, especially on the broader end.

I did not watch the female incubate, but doubtless she carried on this task alone, as at other nests of the Speckled Tanager that I have studied, and as appears to be true throughout the tanager family. Probably, while attending her nest, she was fed by her mate; one male Speckled Tanager fed his incubating partner ten times in a day, and another seven times in a day; but the females needed more food than this and had to forage for the rest. After a few days, one egg vanished from the nest in the poró tree, probably having fallen from the shallow structure. The other egg required at least fifteen days to hatch, which is a day or two longer than normal. Evidently, the crippled female, unable to forage with full efficiency, prolonged her absences from the nest while she hunted for food. A sound Speckled Tanager leaves her nest about fifteen times each day, for intervals that rarely exceed twenty minutes, and she keeps her eggs covered for 75 to 80 percent of the daytime.

The nestling was a typical newly hatched tanager, with pink skin shaded by sparse gray down, tightly closed eyes, and a mouth that revealed a red interior when lifted up, gaping widely, for food. After it hatched, I devoted more time to watching the nest. Its mother's right leg, which had not improved while she incubated, was prominently swollen at the ankle joint and twisted inward. From her stance when resting on a twig, one would hardly suspect that she perched on one leg, holding up the useless limb. Sometimes while standing beside the nest, however, she rested her half-spread right wing against the rim to help support herself.

Her movements at the nest often appeared slightly clumsy, suggesting her impediment; yet, on the whole, she carried on her parental activities remarkably well.

The severity of the female tanager's handicap was more evident when she visited the feeding shelf, which had recently received a coat of asphalt paint for cleanliness and preservation. When wet from the showers frequent at this season, the board was so slippery that the lame tanager found it hard to stand. To support herself, she sometimes rested on her whole sound foreleg, also putting down her bad leg, which I never saw her do while she perched on a twig. In this unnatural posture, it was difficult for her to push her bill into the firm fruit and remove a bite. While trying to do so, she slid around pathetically, and, after taking a few nibbles of banana, she flew off. Other birds were hardly troubled by the glossy black surface of the board. Planting both feet firmly on it, they easily removed pieces of the banana; or else they stood on the fruit while they ate it.

I applauded the indomitable spirit of the female tanager, faithfully attending her nestling despite her severe impediment. On the morning when it was a week old, she brooded it two-thirds of the time, with sessions that lasted about a half hour. She fed the nestling only two or three times in three and a half hours, while her mate brought food twelve times. When he arrived with a billful while she brooded, he might pass it to her for delivery to the nestling, or he might give part of the food to her and the rest directly to the nestling. Once, while the female was giving the nestling food that he had brought to her, he reached over her back and fed it at the same time—a charming sight.

As the nestling grew older, it became evident that it had *three* attendants. The helper was a Speckled Tanager in adult plumage, indistinguishable from the lame female's mate. Sometimes the three arrived or flew off together; but, more often, the two parents came to the nest together, while their voluntary assistant, of unknown sex, went its own way. During nine hours of watching when the nestling was twelve to fifteen days of age, its father and the helper fed it a total of 62 times, while the crippled mother, who was certainly doing her share, fed it 52 times. Doubtless, the father was bringing food more often than the helper. In all, the nestling was fed 114 times in nine hours, or at the rate of 12.7 meals per hour. The food was carried largely in the attendant's bulging throat or inside its bill, only partly protruding, so that it was difficult to identify. Often I distinguished black berries, and sometimes the fleshy red arils that enclosed the seeds from nearby *Clusia* trees.

It is not unusual for parent tanagers of the genus *Tangara* to receive help while caring for their offspring. In the Golden-masked Tanager, the helper may be either a juvenile from an earlier brood of the same season, readily distinguished by its dull plumage, or an older bird indistinguishable from the parents. I once watched four Plain-colored Tanagers—Cinderellas of their brilliant genus—attend two nestlings. In Trinidad, four or five adult Turquoise Tanagers sometimes feed the young of a single brood.

The lame tanager brooded her nestling in the poró tree nightly until it was twelve days old. On its last three nights in the nest, it slept alone, and it left at the normal age of fifteen days. Soon after its departure, I found it perching on a neighboring fence wire. As I approached the fledgling, its three attendants ventured almost within my reach, voicing sharp notes. Although well feathered, the youngster flew weakly, and I easily caught it in the high grass, where it tried to escape me. After examining it, I set it in a shrub for greater safety.

During the next two weeks, I often saw the crippled tanager carry billsful of banana from the feeder, sometimes with two companions, who also flew off with full bills. Then, sixteen days after it left the nest, I for the first time noticed the juvenile in the Guava tree that held the shelf. It rested above the board, while its lame mother carried up billsful of fruit, which it received in dignified silence, instead of with the importunate clamor of some other young birds whose parents brought them there to be fed. For a full month after it left the nest, or until it was forty-five days old, the young Speckled Tanager was fed by its mother and other attendants; but, a few days before the end of this interval, I noticed that it also helped itself.

After mid-September, I looked in vain for the crippled mother. All the Speckled Tanagers that now came to the board for bananas, sometimes five together, had two good legs. I hoped that one of them was the valiant lame female, now enjoying the use of two sound feet; but, in view of the severity of her injury, this seemed unlikely.

Three years later, I noticed that four Speckled Tanagers were interested in a nest in a Muñeco tree in view of my study window. When I held up the mirror to see the two eggs, all four came close, protesting. Unfortunately, after I set up a blind, to watch the nest from a more advantageous position, the birds deserted it. Neighboring shrubbery had forced me to place the blind closer than I wished, but I never dreamed that these generally so confiding birds would be so touchy. This happened in mid-April. During the following months, the four tanagers continued to come together to the feeder. Then, one day in August, they arrived with two fledglings. Although the young birds already helped themselves to the fruit, at least three of the older birds were feeding them.

Until the following year, these six tanagers were often on the table together. I never noticed any discord among them; but, one afternoon in January, when nine Speckled Tanagers were present, uplifted heads and harsh notes revealed mutual antagonism. Finally, two clutched together and fell to the ground, where they promptly separated. This inconsequential tiff was one of the few displays of violence that I have seen among tanagers, which are among the most peaceable of birds.

As late as February, the six Speckled Tanagers came to the shelf in the Guava tree as a flock. The breeding season was approaching, and I wondered whether all would attend the same nest. But, before building began, I went up into the highlands for a season with different kinds of birds, and, when I returned in July, the six no longer visited us together.

10. *Quadruped Partners*

 A FEW years ago, the road that skirts Los Cusingos was roughly ballasted with river stones. Now the bus to San Isidro passes our gate three times daily. Horses have nearly disappeared from the highways and are hardly ever seen on the streets of the town, which lacks places to tie them. Although, since the petroleum crisis, the price of gasoline has risen to nearly two dollars a gallon, the valley has become thoroughly motorized.

It was not thus when I came here. Even the poorest barefoot farmer rode his horse, with never a motorcar to push him from the middle of the road. Many of the horses were so small that elsewhere they would have been called ponies; when I mounted some of them, my feet almost touched the ground. During my first year in the valley, I bought a bay gelding for a journey over El Cerro de la Muerte—"the Mountain of Death"—to Cartago and San José. Having come by air, I wished to know this long, rough trail, about which I heard so much. Although far from being an equine giant, my new horse was so much bigger than most of those in the valley that neighbors referred to him as El Caballón—"the Big Horse." Shortened and anglicized, this designation became his name, Bayon.

On the long, steep trail up El Cerro de la Muerte, through unbroken forest teeming with black flies and deer flies that persecuted the poor animal mercilessly, Bayon behaved so badly that I sent him back and continued for four days on foot,

carrying on my shoulders the blanket roll, provisions, and other impedimenta that he should have borne.

Despite this unpromising start, Bayon and I finally became friends. He served me well on botanical collecting trips about the valley and, five years after I bought him, carried me around while I searched for the farm that became my home and his. Here he had lush pastures, a stream of clear water to drink, and umbrageous trees to provide a cool retreat from the hot midday sun. Until buses displaced horses, he was my preferred mount on my infrequent trips to town.

Bayon was a horse of strong character. His ability to read his master's mind was amazing. He would come running when his name was called, lick salt from my hand, and, as a rule, permit me to caress him or put my arms around his neck, while he stood free in the pasture. Even when lying down, he allowed me to pat him—an unusual display of confidence. But, if I wished to saddle him for a ride, he seemed to divine my intention, and kept just beyond reach. With a rope hidden in my pocket, I would saunter up to him in the most casual manner, as though only to pat his neck; but he would suspect my motive and move away. My most successful ruse was to talk first to the other horses and gradually approach him. Unlike some horses, even bananas, corn, or salt would not lure him within reach when he feared he would have to work. Yet a rope thrown loosely over his back would stop his flight, making him stand quietly and obediently until I put a loop around his neck and led him to be saddled.

At opening gates, Bayon displayed genius. Many gates in this valley are of barbed wire, attached at the open side to a stick that is fastened to the gate post by two wire loops. Bayon soon learned to seize the top of the stick between his strong teeth and tug until it came loose and the gate fell open. The only way to prevent

◀ COWS RESTING

his opening such a gate was to tie the stick to the gate post with a rope. Wooden gates were often more difficult to open; but I watched with amazement while he discovered the secret of a lever that closed an unfamiliar gate. Only when the gate was secured by a padlock did I feel confident that Bayon would remain in the pasture.

The purpose of all this annoying opening of gates was to reach the sweeter grass on the other side of the fence, or, if on a journey, to run home. Once, while I visited a distant farm, Bayon escaped from the pasture and took the road up the valley. He would have left me horseless, twenty-five rough and hilly miles from home, had not the policeman seen him as he ran through the next village and pursued him on another horse, finally catching the runaway and returning him to me, for which service the man received due reward. When I married and was bringing home my bride, we found it necessary to spend the night in San Isidro. The three horses that had been brought from Los Cusingos for us were turned out in a pasture with a flimsy gate, which I was sure Bayon would open, so in the evening I tied it securely with a cord. Next morning, the cord was cut, as though with a knife, the gate open, and the horses gone. After searching for hours in the vicinity without finding the truants, I hired two horses. On our way home, we learned that our three had preceded us at a trot to the farm. This was an embarrassing beginning to my married life.

Bayon's long, steady legs served well for fording the many unbridged streams of the valley. Returning one afternoon from San Isidro, we were caught in a heavy downpour. On reaching the Quebrada Hermosa, two miles from home, we found it swollen with dark, rushing water, carrying logs and other flotsam. Several horsemen were waiting for the river to subside. Beside the ford was a narrow footbridge, suspended by cables, over which children crossed on their way to and from the little thatched schoolhouse. Removing saddlebags, saddle, and bridle, I carried these over the bridge, while Bayon easily crossed the ford alone. Then I resaddled and rode off, leaving the other men, with smaller horses, patiently waiting for the current to subside.

Bayon was not always consistent. The next time, when returning home, I found the Hermosa in flood, I tried to cross in the same manner; but Bayon resisted all my efforts to drive him over the ford. A swollen mountain stream is much less dangerous to a horse than to the rider. If the horse stumbles and the man loses his seat, he is often swept away by the current and drowned; the animal, with four legs and a higher center of gravity, usually manages to regain his feet and wade ashore.

While I stood struggling with Bayon, a man I knew rode up, swaying as though he had taken a cup too many; a farmer who had accumulated enough money to relax, he filled his idle days gossiping in the country stores and drinking strong liquor. After a single glance at the rushing water, he dismounted, cut a big switch, then remounted and drove his little mare into the swirling flood. As I watched them struggling in midstream, with water above the girth of the perilously swaying horse, I recalled the old saying "Fools rush in. . . ." Nevertheless, the man safely gained the farther shore, then turned to watch me, still trying to persuade Bayon to cross the ford alone. Returning by the footbridge, he offered to ride my horse across the river, for a price higher than I cared to pay.

When I tried again to make Bayon enter the water, the recalcitrant horse ran up along the shore. The more I thought about my watch, wallet, mail, and purchases I was taking home, the more I hesitated to risk wetting them by riding across the swollen stream, the more determined I was that Bayon should obey me. Daylight was fast fading. When the slightly inebriated farmer, who had continued to watch, came again to offer his services, he reduced his fee to two *colones*, for which he rode Bayon through the water.

When colts came, Bayon would race around and frolic with them more than would their mother, staid Rosilla. His relations with them were always most friendly; he endured a surprising amount of playful nipping of his legs by mischievous youngsters. Although his work ranged from long journeys with a rider to carrying sacks of grain and loads of miscellaneous household chattels, it was, on the whole, light and did not wear him out. Even in his early twenties—a horse's middle age—he still occasionally raced around the pasture like a colt. The first drops of an approaching shower were often the stimulus that released these tremendous outbursts of energy. After a brief, undiagnosed illness, Bayon died, eighteen years after I bought him, when he was about twenty-three years old. His passing left a void on the farm.

After the Second World War ruined the market for my botanical specimens, I had to think about deriving an income from Los Cusingos. Since it already had extensive pastures and I liked horses, I decided to raise them for sale. As told at the beginning of chapter three, soon after I acquired the farm, I bought, in San José, a young bay stallion named Cañero, and the roan mare whom I named Rosilla. When I first saw the mare, she was a sorry sight, covered with fat ticks and large areas from which all the hair had been rubbed. But she was young, with a good figure and a soft pace. I believed that with proper care she would make a good horse, and, at two hundred *colones*, she seemed a safe investment.

I took these two horses over El Cerro de la Muerte, riding them alternately, and reaching the farm in four days. After our arrival, connoisseurs of horses persuaded me that Cañero was not fine enough to serve as a stud, for his trot was hard.

The local farmers cared little about the size and color of a horse but were most critical of its pace, preferring a soft amble. Accordingly, I sold Cañero for a small profit. He was finally acquired by a man who almost killed him by hard riding. When I learned this, I decided not to raise horses for people who might mistreat them.

With sulphur, red lead, kerosene, and cart grease, I cured Rosilla's mange. After a few months on good pasture, she became a handsome mare, for whom I had several offers, but I would not sell her. Her chief defect was an insuperable aversion to bridges, especially covered ones. This led to great conflicts of will, some of which she might have won but for the timely arrival of some traveler who would apply pressure at the rear, while I pulled the reins in front. Perhaps she remembered a terrifying experience with one of the rotten wooden bridges all too common in remote rural areas. Her muzzle bore permanent scars, which, I was told, indicated that she had been "broken" with a headstall equipped with an iron band. Apparently, most of the spirit and intelligence had been knocked out of her while a filly, for she was not half as bright as Bayon and her two colts.

When the horses were called to receive bananas or salt, Rosilla was always the last to respond. She followed where the others led. She never learned, like Bayon and her colts, to push her head through the dining-room window, where I sat like Robinson Crusoe at my solitary meals, and beg for tortillas and other delicacies from the table. Nearly all the misfortunes that befell the horses came to poor Rosilla. She was bitten by spiders, bled by vampire bats. She became lame more easily and was always the leanest. For ten months, I nursed an ugly running sore in her ear, which apparently resulted from a bite by one of the great, hairy "bird spiders." Finally, it healed, but left her permanently disfigured with a fallen ear.

Yet she had the same care as the other horses, and less work, scarcely any while she was pregnant or nursing a foal.

A year and a half after I bought Rosilla, she gave me a filly, whom I named Atalanta, for the Calydonian maiden famed for fleetness. I have since learned that to give a child or an animal a name suggestive of a quality that one hopes the new-born creature will eventually possess is to invite disillusion. As she grew up, my Atalanta developed certain good qualities, but swiftness was not among them. Black at birth, Lanta, as we came to call her, became lighter through the years. At four, she was prettily dappled; at eight, wholly light gray; in later years, plain white. When, at the age of a month or two, she began to race over the pasture with Bayon, staid Rosilla would trot along, trying to interpose her body between the big horse and her offspring. But Rosilla's participation in the frolic was prompted by maternal solicitude rather than playfulness; soon she gave up and left Lanta and Bayon to romp alone.

Like other colts, Lanta had a propensity to chew cloth, so that drying garments had to be hung beyond her reach. Once she ruined a pair of trousers that Abel's wife had hung over a fence to dry. One day, I set my cloth blind before a Buff-throated Saltator's nest in a bushy pasture. Arriving at the following dawn to enter it for a morning's watching, I found, to my dismay, that the naughty colt had ripped the brown wigwam from top to bottom. The blind and my study of the saltator's nest were spoiled. As she matured, Lanta outgrew this bad habit.

Lanta would lick salt from my hand before she would permit herself to be touched or caught. When about five months old, she foolishly tried to pass through a barbed wire fence with a loose strand, was caught in the wire, and, in her frightened struggle to break free, scratched herself badly. This one lesson was enough; she never again tried to squeeze through a fence. It became necessary to catch and tie Lanta in order to treat her wounds, and this was the beginning of her education. By the time they healed, she had lost her shyness and no longer ran away when I wished to catch her. But she pulled back when I tried to lead her with a rope around her neck, and her first lesson was in following when she was led. After she had learned to follow, I put a saddle on her, which frightened her with its swinging stirrups. Soon, however, she became accustomed to walking with a saddle, and perhaps saddlebags for additional weight. Not until she had passed her second birthday did we mount her. She accepted her first rider calmly. Then her training consisted in making journeys of increasing length, with a rider and in company with one or more older horses, until she was ready to be ridden alone.

I have read of feral horses of the Asiatic steppes that were caught, thrown, saddled, and ridden until exhausted, thus being "broken" in a single day. Lanta's training was spread over several years, with a minimum of force and compulsion. As a result, she became a calm, sweet-tempered mare, who would come when called and not, like Bayon, run away when wanted for work rather than to receive food. But she grew too fat to be fleet, and she inherited her mother's aversion to crossing wooden bridges. Most of our disagreements were caused by this unfortunate trait. Lanta lived to be thirty-one years old. During her last year, she wasted away to a shadow of her former self. Then she fell, could not rise again, and was mercifully shot—a decision simple to execute but very hard to make.

Five years after Lanta was born, Rosilla foaled again. Her new colt was bay and would not change color as he grew older. I called him Rocalpe, an invented name without antecedents that might raise false expectations. Before he was six months old, Rocalpe would lick salt from my hand along with the grown horses, and he soon showed his masterful spirit by nipping them gently when they pushed ahead of him. Although he would eat from my hand, he was too alert to be caught by arms flung around his neck. Months passed, and he grew no tamer. I could pat him and catch him by the tail, but not by the neck, as was necessary for putting on a rope. Finally, he was lassoed. Then, for several weeks, he roamed the pasture trailing a rope, by which he could be caught and brought to hand. As he became less skittish, the rope was shortened, until it hung only a foot below his neck. Soon he would permit me to embrace his neck, and the rope was removed. Then followed lessons in being led and, finally, in carrying a rider. After he could be caught easily, he was hardly more difficult to train than Lanta had been.

As he matured, the young stallion turned against his former playmate, Bayon, and tried to drive him from the pasture and the mares, so that the two had to be separated. Now, in his thirtieth year, Rocalpe is wasting away, as his mother and half-sister did, despite good pasture and extra rations. He stands for hours with a pathetically wistful look, as though dreaming of the exuberant vitality that once was his but can never be his again.

In this valley, horses live the year around in the open pasture. Ours have always had a shed, open at the sides, where they can take shelter from rain, a comfort that some of the neighbors' horses have lacked. Grass has always been their main food, with a weekly ration of salt, and every evening a special treat, in the form of bananas or corn, to vary the monotony of their diet. When Guavas fall from the trees scattered through the pastures, horses eat them eagerly. The small, hard seeds pass through them undigested, to germinate and start more trees. Cleaner than many animals, our horses have never, except in extreme old age, fouled their shelter or its surroundings, nor the lawn around the house, which they keep cropped short, as well as any lawn mower. To relieve themselves, they seek a patch of weeds or high, coarse grass, away from the lower and sweeter grass where they prefer to graze.

For years, I was more closely associated with Bayon than with any other living being. We traveled together, fell together on rough and slippery trails, then picked ourselves up to continue the march. I entrusted my life to his sureness of foot while fording swollen mountain torrents, where a fallen horse often meant a drowned rider. He would come to my call, eat from my hand, and often seemed to know my intentions. Yet a vast gulf separated his mind from mine. I often wondered what he thought, what he felt, what was the quality of his inner life.

We speculate about the presence of living things on distant planets; we ask whether, somewhere in the solar system, or in the wider universe, beings akin to ourselves may exist. Every mind, of every sentient being of every sort, is in a sense a planet, pursuing its distant and lonely course through the vastitude of space, far beyond the reach of every other planet. We humans are planets of a special kind, which send meaningful signals across the interplanetary void by means of spoken or written words, gestures and facial expressions, or the symbolism of music and the visual arts. From these intercepted signals, we draw inferences about the spiritual atmosphere of those other planets that we call human minds, but we can never prove that these inferences are exact.

The minds of animals of other species are planets separated from us by distances greater than those that intervene between us and other people. The signals that reach us from them are less articulate, more difficult to interpret. As differences in the density and composition of the atmosphere, in the intensity of solar radiation, in the strength of the gravitational field, in the lengths of the day and the year—as all these differences are certain to cause the living beings on other planets, if such beings exist, to differ profoundly from those on Earth, so the different bodily organization of other animals must give their psychic life a quality different from our own.

Not only did Bayon and I differ enormously in heredity and personal history, we examined our environment with sensory organs that differed greatly in acuity and relative importance. Scent revealed more to him than to me. He seemed to see better by night, but I distinguished objects more clearly by day. Sometimes he shied at a big banana leaf lying a few yards ahead in the roadway, which someone had used as an umbrella and dropped when the rain stopped. After sniffing at the leaf, he would eat it. My eyes did not leave me so long in doubt about the object in the roadway.

I do not pretend to know how much horses think and feel or to be able to assess the quality of their psychic life. But whatever satisfactions they are capable of experiencing, whatever values they may realize in their lives, I wish to facilitate. If their lives are shorter and poorer in depth and variety of feeling than mine—and if, as has been alleged, my spiritual existence will continue into an unknown beyond, whereas theirs will end with bodily death—then it seems so much more urgent that in their briefer and narrower span they enjoy whatever felicity is possible for the equine nature. I wish them to have good food, sleek coats, and not too much work.

For a while, I asked myself how I could justify driving my horses around and forcing them to work for me, when they showed no spontaneous inclination to do so. Had my authority any sanction other than that of might, which ethics does not admit as valid? Finally, it occurred to me that my association with my horses was a mutually beneficial symbiosis, of which the living world provides many examples. As fungi and algae combine to form lichens—which, by means of the cooperation of these two so different forms of vegetation, thrive on barren rocks and in other spots where neither fungus nor alga could flourish alone—so horse and man form an association that helps both to survive.

In this valley, formerly covered with heavy forest, horses could not long exist without men to make pastures for them, and to keep these pastures free from swiftly springing weeds and woody plants, which, if unopposed, would soon shade out the grass. This hard, costly work deserves some remuneration. And, while our roads were too rough for wheeled vehicles, other than slow, jolting ox-carts, we would have found living here difficult and uncomfortable without horses to carry us, our supplies, and possessions. The work that horses did for us was our remuneration for the grass and salt and care we gave them; these things were their reward for the services they rendered us. By mutual cooperation, we both lived more comfortably and securely than either horse or man could have lived without the other.

I was careful not to demand of the horses an amount of work disproportionate to the benefits that I provided for them, for this would have been robbery and the rule of might. I did not wish to make existence burdensome to them, in order that I might live at ease, for this would have affronted justice and love. And since, by virtue of my greater experience and intelligence, I was sole judge of the fairness of the transactions between us, and they lacked a defender, I felt more comfortable when I gave them the benefit of all the uncertainties in our situation. Who, after all, is to assess the relative values of the work of a man and that of a horse, who is to say which effort, if either, ranks higher? I preferred to charge the horses too little rather than too much for the benefits I provided for them, to maintain a credit balance with them rather than be in debt to them. If I am, in any sense, nobler than some other creature, it is because of what I give, not of what I take.

I became a cattle owner almost by accident. Abel wanted me to buy a cow so that his children would have milk. I was not in the habit of drinking milk, and I hesitated to undertake the responsibility for cattle, which require so much care.

However, on a sunny morning in my first October on the farm, a lean, grizzled stranger, with a white patch over a blind eye, arrived at my home. Did I wish to buy a cow? He had left her tied at the entrance to the farm, and would sell her cheaply. I walked out to the gate with him to see her. The cow was black and white, with small, neat horns; she had borne her first calf, and would have another in a few months. She looked rather scrubby; but, after some bargaining, we agreed on a price of a hundred and thirty *colones*; and I decided to risk the investment. She turned out to be a fence jumper, and I soon suspected that I had bought a box of troubles. Accordingly, I called her Pandora.

After three months, Pandora gave birth to a fawn-colored female calf, whom I called Io, which, if written I°, is Spanish for *primero*, or "first." As she grew up, Io became so pretty that one might have imagined her to be the Argus-guarded heifer into which Zeus had metamorphosed the maiden who, by catching his roving fancy, had aroused Hera's ire. As the first-born of my farm animals, I became attached to her. But, when sixteen months old, she died miserably, of a disease that a veterinarian, who gave a long-distance diagnosis, thought was hemorrhagic septicemia. She was buried where she died, under the Guava trees by the house.

Six weeks later, Pandora succumbed to the same malady, orphaning a female calf four months old. I called Pandora's second calf Polygala, after the milkwort, and hoped that the name would be the earnest of full and generous udders. Escaping from an enclosure, the little calf sucked her mother only a few hours before the latter's death. We were sure that we would lose her, too; but she surprised us by living to become the mother of several calves. A beautiful, deep chestnut and white at birth, she became black and white as she grew older, and she proved to be a fence jumper like her mother. Finally, this last gift from Pandora's box was sold

to a neighbor, after her master had wearied of her fence-jumping antics and of curing the teats that she tore as she skimmed too low over barbed wire.

Although between May and August or September we had no lack of fruits and
vegetables, during the last months of the rainy season and through most of the dry
season our diet became monotonous, and I came to depend upon milk to improve
it. After Pandora's death, I bought Galactia, a higher-priced and better cow, who,
with her children and grandchildren, soon built up our small dairy herd. For a
while, I owned a pair of black, white-spotted oxen, Diamond and Carbon, who
pulled a cart and earned a little money for the farm; but, during a period of labor
troubles, I sold them.

Here, on small farms, it is customary to rear all the calves. The women of the
farm are, as a rule, responsible for milking. I assigned this duty to my cook, who
always performed it in the local fashion, as she had been taught at home to do. The
calf is caught in the afternoon and tied up for the night under a roof. Next morning, the cow is brought from the pasture, tied by the horns, and hobbled to prevent a kick. Her calf is led up, eager and hungry, and permitted to take a few sucks
at each teat, "to start the flow of milk." Then it is tied just beyond reach of the
coveted liquid; while the girl, stooping beside the cow's flank without a stool,
wipes the teats with a damp cloth, then milks with one hand into a vessel that she
holds in the other. After the first flow has been drained from three of the teats, the
calf is given a few more sucks at each, the wiping is repeated, and the last of the
milk is drawn out into a separate vessel, as it is believed to have a special quality
and is esteemed for coffee. Finally, the calf is released, to empty the teat that has
been reserved for it, and to pass the greater part of the day with its mother, sucking
and munching grass as it lists. In the afternoon, it is caught again, and kept apart

from the cow until the following morning. This schedule continues until the calf is weaned, after it has become so big that, at milking time, it jostles its mother with rude vigor. The milk is promptly boiled, so that, without refrigeration, it will keep at least throughout the day.

The Hindus call the cow "man's second mother," for she gives us milk after our human mother's breasts have dried. From this, it follows that the calves who share the cow's milk with us are our foster brothers and sisters; we and they are nourished at the same fount. As such, they have a claim to our fraternal protection, to considerate treatment at our hands. To deprive the cow of her offspring and take all her milk for ourselves selfishly violates this relationship. But to claim part of her milk, in return for all the food and care we give her, seems fair enough, especially since, with good treatment, she yields more milk than her calf needs for healthy growth. The cow repays the attention we give her with milk, as the horse does with work—a mutually advantageous exchange. We make a partner of the cow and a commensal of her calf.

When a female calf grows up, she becomes a milch cow, like her mother. Until the recent shift to motorization, a large proportion of the male calves in Costa Rica became draft oxen, who stood in much the same relation to ourselves as the horses did, paying with work for the food they received. The oxen, too, are entitled to such satisfactions as they may experience in the monotonous round of their bovine existence, in gulping down great mouthfuls of dewy herbage as the sun rises, then lying in the shade to ruminate, or standing ankle-deep in cool water at the river's edge, to escape the midday heat. Who would begrudge them their well-earned rest from pulling a cart or heavy log, with their horns strapped to the ponderous yoke? Who would needlessly abbreviate their hours of leisure?

When I bought Los Cusingos, it had fairly extensive pastures, but was inadequately fenced for cattle, with only two strands of barbed wire between the fields, and none at all between the pastures and the forest. Such was the usual practice of the neighborhood, where poor farmers tried to save labor and money by small economies. The horses, who could be held by a single strand of wire, usually stayed out of the forest; but the cattle were continually jumping over the fences or roaming off through the woodland, perhaps to find a field of luscious young maize or tender rice sprouts on the farther side. Much of the time, the horses stayed in the enclosure around the house, where they kept the lawn neatly trimmed and rarely touched the shrubbery. Cattle eat a much wider variety of plants; and, whenever a cow invaded the garden, she would go straight to my finest hibiscus bush, or tear away the red foliage of the dracaena. Gradually, the fencing was improved, but not before straying cattle had led us many a chase, often in drenching rain.

The cattle were far more susceptible to diseases and parasites than the horses that shared the pastures with them. Although a horse in fair condition was rarely attacked by ticks, except in the ears, my cattle became periodically covered with them and had to be bathed with an insecticide. The horses were almost never troubled by *Tórsalos*—fly larvae that burrow under the skin of various animals, including man, and raise great lumps. Although various chemicals were recommended for the control of these larvae, I found nothing so effective as squeezing and pulling them out, one by one, with special toothed forceps, through the hole in the skin through which they respire and, at maturity, escape to pupate in the ground. Each fat, white larva is covered, from end to end, with transverse rows of little, sharp, black spines, with an outward curvature that makes its removal difficult and painful.

At certain seasons, removing the *Tórsalos* was a fortnightly task. Sometimes a fat *Tórsalo* popped into my face when I pressed, or the bloody pus that replaced one which had died under the cow's skin spurted into the mouth or eye of an unwary operator. Often I finished the task of removing scores of these troublesome larvae with bloody hands, a blood-spattered face, and a ruffled temper. The cattle, held by horns and nose by an assistant, struggled and bucked as each fat grub was extracted; but, as soon as released, they resumed their placid grazing, apparently little the worse for their experience. A curious fact about the *Tórsalo* is that the fly does not lay its eggs directly upon the host animal, but upon some other insect, such as a mosquito, from which emerging larvae pass to the mammal that the insect carrier bites.

Each break in a cow's skin that failed to receive prompt attention became a nest of squirming larvae of another kind of fly, which had to be plucked out with tweezers or killed with a disinfectant, or removed by the combination of both methods, which was most effective. Another affliction was warts, which on one heifer appeared in hundreds, until her neck was covered with them and her ears drooped with the weight of great foliaceous excrescences. As each wart dropped off, it left a raw spot where flies laid their eggs and maggots bred. For six months, I attended poor Garza almost daily, until, at last, most of the growths fell away and she was clean again. Spider bites made the skin of a cow's tongue peel off in thick, pale flakes. Mastitis attacked the udders and dried up the springs of milk. More virulent diseases carried off the cow altogether, as happened to Pandora and Io. All these troubles, and more, I experienced, not in the course of a veterinarian's extensive practice, but on my own farm, in a few years, with cows that gave milk for only two houses. The cattle seemed to be born to suffer, and their owner suffered with them. No wonder that I periodically proclaimed that I would sell the whole horned family—a threat that always brought protests from those who would miss the milk!

For over a dozen years, I struggled with the cattle, who often seemed to give more trouble than milk. Then, one day in March, a prosperous-looking stranger arrived on horseback, with a thick roll of bank notes in his pocket. He was starting a farm and wanted cows for breeding, not for slaughter. Would I sell him some? At about the same time, my cows, who had strayed, were brought back with a note from a neighbor, claiming recompense for damage that they had done to his sugarcane. The stranger could not have arrived at a more opportune moment. I sold him Galactia, the matriarch of the herd, and three other cows. Not without a pang, I watched them being driven away. In spite of or, more probably, because of all the burdensome care I had given them, I had grown attached to them. Later, I sold the two remaining heifers to neighbors. The few bull calves born to my cows had already been sold to other neighbors who needed oxen. For several years, we bought milk from a farmer who had bought a heifer, then from another neighbor. Finally, these sources failing, we came to depend on powdered milk brought from afar. For a while, the pastures seemed sadly deserted without the cows. Yet, it was fortunate that we no longer had them, for, a few years after their departure, when the river cut through the farm, the best of our pastures became difficult to reach. And, without the cattle, I had much more time for other things.

11. *Chickens with Personality*

WHEN I acquired Los Cusingos, I regarded it as my poultry yard, the nearly three hundred species of birds found here—as permanent residents or migrants—as the chickens that I had taken under my protection. I wished to become intimate with these feathered inhabitants of the forests and thickets and watercourses, to learn all that I could about their lives. With so many free birds to occupy my attention, I had no time for domesticated fowls brought by man from distant regions and surviving here only under his care. With their instincts and patterns of life distorted by countless generations in unnatural conditions, they seem to have fallen from the level of their untamed progenitors. Often they lack the brightness and alertness that give charm to free creatures. In short, I regarded domesticated fowls as inferior birds and did not want them to interfere with my studies of the native birds.

Although I never ate chicken or other flesh, for breakfast I enjoyed an egg, which helped me to get through the morning without feeling hungry. When I first came to El General, I bought eggs at twenty for a *colon*, which was less than one cent apiece in the currency of the United States. But, with the Second World War, local highway construction, and inflation, the price crept up and up, until today one cannot buy two for a *colon*. Long before eggs reached their present high price, a neighbor offered me her flock of ten hens and a cock for thirty-three *colones*, and I bought them in order to economize.

The acquisition of a flock of chickens did not involve elaborate preparations for their accommodation. A safe roost was prepared by encircling the trunk of a Guava tree with a broad band of metal, obtained by flattening an empty five-gallon kerosene tin. This guard prevented opossums, Coatimundis, and other quadrupeds from climbing the trunk because the hard, slippery metal afforded no toehold. The chickens went to roost by walking up a long, inclined pole, which was removed from the tree after they had settled for the night. Nearly all the chickens in the neighborhood slept in this fashion, apparently none the worse for the occasional nocturnal rains.

A few neighbors had provided covered roosts for their chickens, which seemed a more considerate arrangement. After a while, I made a roost of this sort: a thatched gable roof, supported on two high posts, each with its metal guard, and beneath the roof horizontal poles for the birds to perch upon. But they preferred the treetops, open to the night breezes, the dew, and the rain. From the roof of their shelter, they flew up into the surrounding trees, abandoning their cote, which was then used to shelter the calves. Years later, I made a different kind of shelter, away from trees, which our chickens deigned to occupy.

In rural Central America, hens often lay their eggs in such nooks and corners of the owner's dwelling as take their fancy. In a small country hotel, I once returned to my room to find a newly laid egg on my bed. One day, while I was out in the forest collecting plants, a neighbor's hen entered the solitary cabin I then occupied, to lay her egg on top of my plant drier, after digging a hollow in the corrugated cardboards softened by moisture from the plants, thereby damaging equipment that becomes so precious in remote places. In rural homes, it is not unusual to find a biddy quietly hatching her eggs in a corner of the kitchen or a box beneath a bed. To keep my hens out of the house, I made nest boxes for them on

the broad back porch and soon trained them to lay there. Some pullets made the nest for their first eggs on the ground, amid a clump of weeds or tall grass; but when this nest was found and the eggs removed, all except a few stubborn hens learned to use the boxes.

Although I cared for my chickens much as neighbors did, the women had one habit that I refused to follow. They often plucked the tail feathers from their squawking, protesting hens, thinking that this mutilation made them lay more eggs. I have seen no evidence in favor of this belief. If the removal of the tail influences egg production, the effect should be adverse; for the hen must use to form new feathers materials that might otherwise go into her eggs. Moreover, the practice is cruel; and it destroys the graceful appearance of the hens, whose tails seem to balance their long necks as they walk over the ground with bobbing heads.

My chickens were of no special breed. The "creole" stock, which for centuries has been naturalized in the country, with little selection beyond that exercised by the natural environment, is hardier than recently imported, named breeds. They are also better able to scratch for themselves, and they survive with less feeding and care. With no effort by breeders to obtain uniform appearance, they have varied enormously. Such oddities as congenitally bare necks, which give the hens a repulsive, vulturine aspect, and frizzled plumage all turned the wrong way are frequent in the local flocks. Fasciated combs are also common. But the greatest variation is in coloration. My chickens ranged from white to black, with endless intermediate colors, both singly and in combination. The hens with a single color were buff, yellow, red, brown, and gray, in many shades, although never in pure brilliant tones, such as other birds display. Some of the hens were barred, or else intricately penciled and spotted, beautiful as hen pheasants. A few of the cocks were most elegantly attired, leaving no doubt in my mind that our common barn-yard fowl is rightly classified in the aristocratic pheasant family. I treated them all as partners in the endeavor to live well, rather than as expendable machinery for producing eggs.

In temperament, the chickens varied almost as much as in appearance. Before I became intimate with them, I did not know that chickens could have so much personality. With this discovery, my respect for them increased. It seems to be generally true that the more one studies almost any kind of living creature, the more reasons he finds to admire and even to love it. Among themselves, some of my hens were aggressive and domineering, others placid and demure. With people, some were friendly and confiding; others, reared in the same brood, were aloof and resentful, pecking the hand that would caress them.

One of my favorites was Cercomacra, so named because she reminded me of a female Tyrannine or Dusky Antbird, *Cercomacra tyrannina*. She was a lovely hen, deep coppery red on head and throat. The feathers on the back and sides of her neck and on her shoulders were golden, with an arrow-shaped black mark along the middle of each. Her back and wings were deep gray in general tone, but when examined attentively they revealed fine vermiculations of buff and black, with a narrow golden margin on each feather. Her foreneck was deep rufous-chestnut, which paled to rufous-cinnamon on her breast.

When ready to lay an egg, Cercomacra would come, clucking softly, to look for me in my study. If she found me there, she would fly up on the table if I happened to be writing, or on the arm of my chair if I sat reading. Here she would rest, uttering low, conversational notes, until I caressed her and carried her to a nest box. After she entered, I would drape a sack over the front, so that she could lay her egg in the privacy that she preferred. Sometimes she would seek me long before she was ready to lay. Then she refused to stay in the nest, but jumped out and came to me again. When she opened her mouth and panted, I was sure that her egg was about ready to emerge, and she would sit in her box until she came forth cackling, to announce that it had been left there.

Another favorite hen was Corvina, everywhere as black as a crow. Although not beautiful in plumage like Cercomacra, she won our affection by her placid ways, and the soft, low notes she uttered whenever we lifted her up. Little Mab endeared herself by her tameness and the quiet persistence of her begging for bananas. Thamnophilus, all barred with black and white like the male antshrike for which she was named, had a personality to match her salt-and-pepper plumage. Calpurnia, whom my English wife renamed "Glamour" because of her big, dreamy, film-star eyes, was remarkable for her appetite. She was nearly always the first to arrive when the chickens were fed. She seemed exceptionally greedy, but she used what she ate to give us the biggest eggs.

Many birds have a definite time for laying. Our abundant tanagers and hummingbirds lay early, before sunrise or a little after, the tanagers with an interval of twenty-four hours between their first and second eggs, the hummingbirds with an interval of forty-eight hours. Some of the finches deposit their first egg around sunrise and the second somewhat later on the following morning, with an interval of twenty-five or twenty-six hours between the two. Flycatchers and thrushes commonly lay later, often around the middle of the forenoon, but the hour is quite variable. Manakins and anis usually deposit their eggs around midday. The Pauraque, a crepuscular nightjar, lays in the afternoon.

When Darwin and Barbara Norby were studying with me after the revolution of 1948, I suggested that records of the times when our hens laid would be interesting. Barbara made a long series of observations, which showed that the intervals between successive layings varied widely from hen to hen, and more narrowly with the same hen. Hens who rarely laid on consecutive days laid with an interval only exceptionally less than forty-eight hours. Other hens laid, on consecutive days, a series of eggs, the length of which depended chiefly on the interval between layings. The egg that started off the series was usually deposited early in the morning, and each following egg at a somewhat later hour, until the laying occurred at midday or in the early afternoon. Then the hen would miss a day, and begin a new series, usually early on the second day.

It follows from this that the shorter the interval between layings, the more closely it approximated twenty-four hours, the more eggs the hen could lay without bringing her time of laying past noon and having to skip a day and begin a new series. Thus, Thamnophilus, whose interval between layings ranged from twenty-four to twenty-four and a half hours (rarely as much as twenty-six hours) laid eleven eggs in as many days, establishing the best record in Barbara's study. Another barred hen, whose interval ranged from twenty-five to twenty-eight hours, would lay from two to four eggs in a series, then rest for two or three days. Races of chickens highly selected for egg production do much better than these two; one hen laid sixty-nine eggs in as many days.

Some hens, our best layers, never became broody. Doubtless it would be advantageous to have only hens of this kind, if one used a mechanical incubator and brooders to hatch and rear the chicks. One pullet hid her first eggs in the tall grass, where they were not found until she had a nestful and began to incubate them. Her failure to appear at feeding time led us to search, until she was discovered sitting amid the grass, and her eggs taken. After this, she never again became broody, although she lived for over three years. Most of the hens became broody after laying a variable number of eggs, and some seemed to spend about half their adult lives sitting as though incubating, with not an egg beneath them. The hens' propensity to "incubate" on empty nests is probably a result of many generations of domestication. Such useless sitting is so rare among free birds that I have found only one instance of it, a female Gray-headed Tanager who attended an empty nest as assiduously as though it had eggs; and a few examples of such behavior have been reported by others.

Among our neighbors, some housewives tie broody hens beneath a bush or tree, with a string around a leg, until the "fever" passes, when they soon resume laying. A few drenching showers accelerate the cure. Some people confine their broody hens in a little coop or cage, which seems to be the kindest way. Others douse them in the river, a drastic treatment. A rapid immersion has little effect, as I proved experimentally. When released, the hens shook the water from their plumage, then ran, clucking, back to the nest boxes, to resume their useless sitting. But, apparently, if held in the water until half drowned, they will be shocked out of their broodiness.

I have often noticed that when lifted from the nest and placed on the ground, a broody hen picks up straws, leaves, or feathers in her bill and throws them over her back. Similarly, as a female Marbled Wood-Quail walked away from her nest to begin her single, long, daily recess, she picked up leaves from the forest floor and tossed them backward toward her covered nest. Some of these leaves fell on the roof and increased the nest's already excellent concealment. The wood-quail belongs to the New World branch of the pheasant family, the domestic hen to its

Old World branch; and these two branches have been separated for a long age. Yet they preserve the same behavior, which in the domestic hen has become useless. So conservative are birds in their ways!

Once I gave white Blanche sixteen eggs to incubate. One of these eggs was still unhatched when fifteen chicks were dry and ready to follow their mother from the nest. This last egg was placed beneath black Josepha, who happened to be broody; and from it, by coincidence, a black chick hatched a day or two later. When this chick could walk, it was given to Blanche, who each day was enclosed in a cage, through the bars of which the chicks could pass and run over the grass, while their mother served as a fixed center of attraction that prevented their wandering too far. Now Josepha claimed a proprietary right to the black chick that had hatched beneath her. At every opportunity, she would lead it away, clucking contentedly while she scratched diligently for it. She could not distinguish her own dusky chick from others of the same hue, and often had three or four black ones following her. But she would have nothing to do with any of the lighter members of the brood, and pecked them away whenever they tried to join her and profit by the food exposed by her busy feet.

Hens, and birds of many other species, lack an innate image of the newly hatched young of their own kind. Accordingly, they will accept and care for the young of other species that hatch beneath them. Small birds of many kinds diligently attend baby cuckoos or cowbirds whose parents have dropped an egg into their nests; and domestic hens serve as foster parents for ducklings, turkeys, and other nidifugous chicks that they have hatched. After a few days, the parent learns to recognize individually the chicks in her brood, be they of her own or a different species, and she may repulse with pecks strange chicks that attempt to join the family. Josepha's partiality for black chicks was evidently not because this was her own color, but because she happened to hatch a chick of this hue. Since the chick had not been left with her long enough for her to become familiar with it as an individual, she satisfied her maternal impulses by taking under her wing all of Blanche's black chicks that would respond to her clucking and follow her. Blanche cared equally for all the little ones in her brood, white, buff, or black.

Like other species of pheasants, the domestic chicken is naturally polygamous, each cock attempting to gather a harem of several hens. Yet the two sexes are hatched in approximately equal numbers, a situation that leads to competition among the males. Many birds have developed complex, ritualized patterns of courtship, which include distinctive calls, "dancing," and odd antics, but exclude lethal struggles between competing males. The courtship of the Red Jungle Fowl of India, southeastern Asia, and western Indonesia (the wild ancestor of domestic chickens) is less complex than that of numerous other birds, and fights between cocks in their native jungles have been reported by Nicholas E. and Elsie C. Collias[1] and other observers. Nevertheless, the fiercely fighting cocks that gamesters pit against each other are products of man's selection, not nature's. The distressing strife that often arises between rival cocks of breeds kept for egg production appears to result largely from the artificial conditions in which they live; concentrated in a dooryard or poultry run, mature males cannot separate as they would in the wild. In India and Thailand, young cockerels and yearlings of the Red Jungle Fowl flock with a few others of the same age and sex; or they follow at a respectful distance an older cock and his hens, until they are mature enough to win females. In the San Diego Zoo, Allen W. Stokes found that hens of the Red Jungle Fowl who had not yet laid follow mature roosters, but hens with chicks are often accompa-

1. Nicholas E. Collias and Elsie C. Collias, "A field study of the Red Jungle Fowl in north-central India," *Condor*, 69 (1967): 360–386.

nied by yearlings who help to feed them.[2] If a mother hen is lost, a yearling may take full charge of the orphaned chicks.

After the revolution of 1948, as though we had not already had enough troubles, a plague of cholera attacked the chickens throughout the neighborhood and depleted most of the flocks. When the disease was at its height, I procured vaccine from San José and inoculated all the survivors. Probably because of this treatment, my flock came through better than most. After the plague ended, I had seventeen hens and four cocks. The oldest of the cocks was Memnon, whose age was about six months. He was a big, black bird with hackles beautifully penciled with silver and buff. The other three were of another brood, several weeks younger. Sandy was also a big cock, golden and buffy yellow. Tommy was equally big but much more variegated; his upper parts golden brown and maroon, his breast black with big white spots, his wings and tail black and white. Regulus, smallest of the four, was black, with hackles, back, and breast closely streaked and penciled with silver, buff, and other light shades.

As the oldest rooster in the flock, Memnon, on coming of age, made himself leader. When Regulus grew up, he took second place, dominating Sandy and Tommy, in spite of his considerably lighter weight. Sandy suffered from a slight lameness, which put him at a disadvantage against light-footed Regulus, but he managed to dominate mild-mannered Tommy. The order of leadership was then Memnon, Regulus, Sandy, Tommy; and this was maintained for several months.

Then, one day in August, Regulus challenged Memnon for first place. Fairly evenly matched, the two continued to fight for a long while, until blood oozed from torn combs and wattles and their handsome plumage was all disheveled and clotted with gore. They were most tenacious, continuing to chase one another

2. Allen W. Stokes, "Parental and courtship feeding in Red Jungle Fowl," *Auk*, 88 (1971): 21–29.

alternately, panting heavily, and so weary that they could hardly run anymore. When the pursuer overtook the fugitive, the two flew against each other, striking with their spurs; or else one jumped nimbly over his adversary. Finally, tired of seeing them fight, I told the boys in my employ to catch whomever they could. Memnon was captured, torn, bleeding, panting like a tired dog, and confined for several hours; while Regulus, despite his woebegone aspect, strutted around with the hens, crowing defiantly. After a while, I released Memnon; and soon he and Regulus were struggling fiercely again. This time, I permitted them to fight it out. Memnon retained his supremacy.

Then, during two or three months of relative peace, each of the cocks fled from those above him in rank; so that Memnon chased all and fled from none, while poor Tommy ran from all and pursued none. In November, Regulus again challenged Memnon. They dueled for several hours, becoming as sorry-looking as last time; but, again, Memnon kept his supremacy. When Regulus was weary, torn, and panting from his long bout with Memnon, Tommy and Sandy decided that it was time to settle the long arrears in their respective accounts. Tommy fought a long while with Regulus. It was useless to separate them; if chased by me or the boys, they would meet somewhere else and resume hostilities. At last, Tommy was victorious. Sandy engaged Regulus separately, but could not defeat him.

These conflicts left a strange situation among the four roosters. Memnon remained master of them all. Regulus still dominated Sandy but was in turn dominated by Tommy, whose status in relation to Sandy remained unchanged. Thus, Sandy chased Tommy, who chased Regulus, who chased Sandy—a circular arrangement, although I never saw the three running in circles. Tommy delighted to pursue Regulus, as though to settle old accounts, and crowed most vaingloriously to celebrate his prowess. However, his victory was short-lived; after a week or so,

Regulus confronted him again and started a fierce battle. They fought much of the afternoon, until at nightfall Tommy was too exhausted to climb into the Guava tree to roost. He fell asleep on the pole up which the chickens walked to the lowest branches of the tree. Here I caught him after nightfall—a terrified, raucous squawk!—and carried him to the house for safekeeping until dawn. He was smelly with clotted gore, his handsome plumage a wreck, although no worse than that of his rival, Regulus. After a few weeks, Tommy recovered his beauty but not his pride, for he was again subordinate to Regulus and the last of the four.

Finally, disgusted with so much fighting, I sold belligerent Regulus to a neighbor who had no cock for his hens. Several days later, Memnon failed to come to roost in the evening. I could find no trace of him in the pastures; possibly some animal caught him in the neighboring forest, which he often entered to scratch. This left only Sandy and Tommy, with fourteen surviving hens. Sandy still dominated Tommy. Often they started to fight; but after flying against each other a few times, they suddenly discovered that they were hungry, and with an embarrassed air began assiduously to look for food on the ground where they stood, a few feet apart. Thus the fight ended before it was well begun. Both Sandy and Tommy ate from my hand, although the more pugnacious black cocks, Memnon and Regulus, would never do so.

After nearly a year of leadership, mild Sandy, of whom I had grown fond, did not come to roost one evening, and was never seen again. This left Tommy, who had been the least aggressive of the cocks, as the sole, unchallenged leader of the flock. Soon younger cocks, potential rivals, grew up; but they never contested Tommy's lordship. Indeed, after the sale of Regulus and Memnon's disappearance, years passed with hardly any fighting, although at times ten grown cocks were present. Gradually they became accustomed to living peaceably with others of their own sex, as I wished them to do. Probably, with careful selection, a breeder could develop a pacific, monogamous race of chickens.

King Tommy became an impressive rooster, portly, resplendent in his richly variegated plumage, and most of the hens followed him. The younger cocks hung on the outskirts of the flock, or loitered around the house, hopefully waiting for some morsel to be thrown out to them, in sharp contrast to Tommy's group, which scratched diligently for their own food. Tommy was, on the whole, a mild sovereign. When out with the hens, he was usually satisfied if his rivals preserved a respectful distance and did not approach too near his harem—behavior that has been reported of the Red Jungle Fowl. With the hens, Tommy was not aggressive or domineering but their protector. The younger cocks, more eager to tread the hens, molested some of the more timid ones more than was good for them. When pursued by the too ardent youngsters, the biddies ran to Tommy for protection. As the hens approached the master, he impressively waved his black-and-white wings, whereupon the subordinate cocks desisted from the pursuit. He rarely himself covered a hen, unless she invited it by crouching. Thus he served as policeman of the flock.

An interesting friendship arose between Admetus and Balder, two cockerels hatched by Cercomacra. Balder was golden, orange, and buff; he much resembled Sandy, who was probably his father. Admetus was at first everywhere barred with light gray and black. As he approached maturity, golden and orange hackles appeared on his neck, back, and wing coverts, at first mixing with the barred feathers, finally concealing them. All his upper parts, from his crown to his rump, were covered with shining feathers; he appeared to wear a golden cloak, left open in front to reveal a vest barred with black and gray, and pantaloons to match the vest. He was broad-chested and corpulent, pompous as an alderman, and withal a pampered pet. Tamest of all the roosters, when I sat on the porch to shell the maize from the cobs, he often jumped on my lap to help himself from the basket.

When Balder and Admetus were hopeful young cockerels essaying their first ludicrous crows, Tommy did not permit them to accompany his flock. To solace their exclusion from the group, they kept one another company and were nearly always together. After they became mature cocks with well-developed spurs, they continued this habit, but were perhaps slightly less chummy than when younger. Sometimes one would approach and sidle around the other with the wing on the far side spread downward, as though displaying to a hen; but, as a rule, the display was suggested rather than fully performed, as when addressed to a hen. Although these two were so friendly, they were not exactly equals. Admetus was dominant over Balder.

Raising chickens beside a large tract of forest, into which they often wandered a short way to scratch, exposed them to many dangers. Of the one hundred and fifteen whose life span I recorded, only fifteen survived as long as seven years. Eleven of these lived for eight or more years; eight for nine or more years; but only three passed their tenth birthday, soon after which they died from the infirmities of age. Many, even of those that survived long enough to start laying when about six months old, had short lives. A few succumbed to disease; still fewer to accidents, such as flying against a barbed wire fence. Most, like Cercomacra, Corvina, and Calpurnia, simply disappeared; at daybreak, they came for corn; in the evening, they failed to go to roost. The animal that we most often discovered carrying off chickens was the Tayra, a big, black member of the weasel family that lives in the forest. Suddenly sallying forth from the woods, it would seize a chicken, sometimes a large rooster, in the pasture or even in the garden near the house. Apprised by the agonized squawks of the poor victim and the excited cackles of its companions, we would rush to its aid, sometimes in time to rescue it, perhaps with injuries to which it would eventually succumb. More often, I would follow, far into the forest, a trail of feathers that never led me to the spot where the culprit was devouring its victim.

Other enemies of the chickens were hawks, including the Collared Forest-Falcon, and probably opossums, although we never caught one of the latter in *flagrante delicto*. If we had kept the fowls penned in a poultry yard, we might have lost fewer to marauding animals; but, from all I have heard, they would have been more subject to diseases. At the price of their freedom to wander where they would, and probably also of being treated with more disinfectants and medicines, our chickens might have lived more securely, but perhaps not more contentedly. Is it not the same with ourselves? Can we increase our security, economic and otherwise, without abridging our freedom? Can we expect a paternal government to take care of us, however unfortunate or shiftless or profligate we may be, without sooner or later discovering that we have bartered our freedom for security?

Even the few of our chickens that died peacefully of old age were short-lived as birds go. Pelicans, parrots, owls, eagles, and other large birds have survived in captivity for half a century or more. Small songbirds have shorter potential life spans; but even a pair of tiny Blue Honeycreepers lived at least twenty-four years in an aviary, where they evidently received excellent care.[3] In the wild, where they are exposed to many perils, few small birds escape death even half that long. With them, as with our chickens, freedom is incompatible with security.

Had our chickens been as exceedingly wary as free-living Red Jungle Fowls are reported to be, fewer might have fallen into the clutches of Tayras and other quadrupeds. Far from fleeing from them, they often seemed to be curious about

3. D. M. Schumacher, "Age of some captive wild birds," *Condor*, 66 (1964): 309.

them, stretching up their necks to look and following for a few steps when a small terrestrial animal approached. Their fearlessness in the presence of mammals is understandable when we recall that, for thousands of years, domestic fowls have been raised in close association with a variety of farm and household animals— dogs, cats, pigs, goats, and cattle, of all sizes and shapes and colors. If they had not lost all innate fear of quadrupeds in general, they would have lived in a frenzy of excitement. Indeed, calm acceptance of four-footed associates was evidently an essential part of their domestication. Now they are unable to discriminate between animals, such as dogs, that have been trained not to harm them, and dangerous wild animals. Our chickens still sound the alarm note when large birds fly overhead; but here, too, they are undiscriminating, for the birds that excite this cry are nearly always harmless pigeons, parrots, and vultures.

I have sometimes wondered why the domestic fowl has never, to my knowledge, become feral in the New World, where for nearly five centuries it has lived, often close to the wilderness, in the most varied regions, some of which seem not to differ greatly from the habitats of its ancestor, the Red Jungle Fowl, in southern Asia and western Indonesia. The hens often lay their eggs on the ground amid dense, concealing vegetation, just as the jungle fowl does. Domestic chickens roost in trees, and appear to suffer no ill effects from tropical downpours. Apparently, it is not the habitat, but their loss of wariness, especially in the presence of mammalian predators, along with diminished power of flight and probably some reduction of hardiness, that prevent them from surviving in tropical and subtropical America without protection by man.

Once a neighbor brought me a half-grown pullet with a broken leg. Apparently, she had been plucking insects from a horse's hind leg and received a kick. The bone was so badly shattered that I doubted it would mend; but I made a little

L-shaped splint and, with my wife's help, bound up the leg. After keeping it in the splint for a week or two, the bone knit so well that the pullet grew to be a hen who hardly limped. Small animals appear to have much less resistance to infectious diseases than large ones do, but their wounds and fractures may heal with surprising speed.

Psychic shocks may leave more lasting traumas. When Marcus was a half-grown cockerel, a hawk seized him by the head but released him promptly when one of us rushed to his aid. Marcus suffered apparently superficial head wounds that soon healed, but he never quite recovered from the shock. He became exceptionally timid, not only of hawks and other large birds but of us who attended him and even of other chickens. He became lowest in the social scale, constantly fleeing from all the others, afraid to go near them, ready to scamper at the slightest movement that chicken or human made toward him. His physical development was retarded; he remained gangling and cockerel-like long after his brood mates had become well-developed, mature cocks. He crowed far less than the others. Only when well over a year old did he at last appear "grown up." Because he stayed close to the house while the other cocks wandered widely with the hens, he finally became more confiding with us and would eat from our hands, as most of the hens but few of the roosters would do.

While still a pullet, Bluebell was seized by a Collared Forest-Falcon that tried to drag her back into the forest. Alerted by her agonized squawks, I raced up in time to rescue her. She lost many feathers but had no visible lesions. Although she became an exceptionally big hen, she was the last of her brood to begin to lay, and she never laid regularly. She went almost daily to sit in a nest box, but she rarely left an egg.

These experiences have made me speculate about the effects of trapping and banding upon free birds. To be caught, especially to become badly entangled in a mist net, as frequently happens, and then seized and manipulated by human hands, can be hardly less terrifying than to be pounced upon by a raptor. Some birds evidently recover rapidly from the shock; others may suffer an enduring trauma. Probably the more intelligent they are, the more their subsequent behavior is affected by their experience. Just as our repeated visits to nests to learn whether they succeed in producing fledglings may influence their rate of success, so the banding of birds to study their behavior may more or less subtly alter this behavior.

12. An Appraisal

Horses, cows, and chickens have been our only dependent animals at Los Cusingos. The birds that come to the feeder are not dependents, for they are well able to nourish themselves without our aid. They enjoy the oranges and bananas that we offer them; we enjoy watching and learning about them; and this seems a fair exchange. For a short while after I married, we had my wife's dog, for whom another home was found after he chased and bit a cow. As a boy, I had a succession of canine pets, loved in life and mourned in death. As I grew older and took greater interest in wild nature, the companionship of a dog on my walks through fields and woods became intolerable. The free animals that I wished to watch were disturbed by his presence more than by mine. A barbarian in the woodland, he could hardly be restrained from chasing every small creature that he saw on or near the ground. The dog, a fit companion for man in his rude hunting stage, seems unable to accompany us into the higher ranges of human experience. Although it pleased Maeterlinck to believe that his dog regarded him as a god, I would not feel flattered by the adulation of an animal so undiscriminating of human character and conduct, save as they affect himself. After all, many of the gods that men have worshipped had far from admirable characters.

To dwell among contented domestic animals that we treat as sensitive living creatures rather than as unfeeling machines to do our work, produce our food, or

increase our wealth, and that mingle peaceably with the free animals that surround us, calms and uplifts the spirit. We approach, even if we cannot fully attain, that delightful harmony with nature that, in *Sakuntala*, the poet Kalidasa so beautifully portrayed in his doubtless idealized picture of an ancient Indian hermitage. If to live in harmony with our fellow men is the goal of morality, to achieve harmony with animals of other species is a still higher accomplishment, the aspiration of a nobler, more inclusive ethic than has commonly been cultivated, especially in the West. To truly generous spirits, an ethic tightly closed around the human species is still a tribal ethic, as stifling as an unventilated dungeon. We desire an ethic that embraces all creatures, such as that which grew up in the ancient East. Although to achieve a moral relationship with all animate creatures is an ideal that we may never realize, and that may, indeed, involve us in untenable situations if too stubbornly followed, if we cultivate it with intelligence, forbearance, and absence of greed, we can come much closer to its realization than if we never try.

Although it is pleasant to dwell among domestic animals that we treat as partners in the effort to live well and try to make happy, the relationship is not without shortcomings and perils. Since, at best, we communicate most imperfectly, we cannot reason with them to resolve conflicts of will, as we can sometimes do with human associates. For their good as well as our own, we must often compel them to obey. Such exercise of power becomes increasingly distasteful as we grow more thoughtful, and it can, like all unregulated authority and unchecked power, prove morally corrosive. If we treat our animals indulgently, they may become annoyingly importunate in their demands for food or attention. When injured or sick, they sometimes become exasperatingly difficult, obliging us to force down their medicine or use our ingenuity to disguise it in their food. Not understanding our

◀ HEN WITH CHICKS, AGOUTI, BANANA PLANT

intentions, they persist in struggling while we try to cure their wounds, until even a saint might lose his patience, as I did with a cow who kicked every time I tried to extract maggots from a sore just above her foot. If our animals could only tell us as soon as they feel unwell, or come for treatment as soon as they cut or scratch themselves, they would be so much easier to keep well and sound.

Then there is the problem of too many males among cattle that we raise for milk or among chickens raised for eggs. If we keep all the male calves that are born or male chickens that hatch, they grow up to fight among themselves, molest the females, and, moreover, they may consume more food than we can well spare for them. Yet to destroy them, or sell them for slaughter, violates the relationship that we try to establish with our animals. With cows, the difficulty is acute, because they do not continue to yield milk unless they continue to bear calves, many of which turn out to be of the undesired sex. With chickens, the problem may be solved if methods are perfected for determining the sex of a fresh or slightly incubated egg. With horses, fortunately, the difficulty need not arise; because both sexes are equally serviceable for riding or hauling, their usefulness does not depend upon their reproduction, and it is easy to control the number of foals that they bear. With them it is easier to achieve the reciprocal exchange of benefits (mentioned in chapter ten) that is the foundation of a sound morality, more wholesome and beneficial to all concerned than unilateral charity or almsgiving.

I am aware that animal husbandry with a conscience, such as we have practiced on a small scale at Los Cusingos, would be wholly inadequate to supply the demands of huge urban populations. Even the callous methods of our ancestors are proving inadequate to satisfy the market, and animals are increasingly raised by methods that approximate as nearly as possible to the assembly-line production of a large factory. The chemicals and unnatural foods used to make them yield more flesh or eggs pose a largely unassessed risk to the health of their human consumers. Moreover, the operation of these animal factories can hardly avoid brutalizing those engaged in it.

Accordingly, although I am convinced that, with patience and kindness, we can cultivate a much more pleasant and ethically acceptable relationship with domestic animals than is commonly achieved, I am sure that it would be much better, from every point of view, if we could learn to live without them—except possibly horses. This is becoming increasingly feasible as dietetics and food processing improve and well-balanced, appetizing meals can be prepared with vegetable foods alone. If we could avoid the wasteful conversion of vegetable products into animal products for human consumption and depend directly upon the primary producers, green plants, for all our food, we could support a given population on a much smaller acreage than is now exploited. Then, if we could hold the number of people within reasonable limits, we could allow much greater areas to remain in, or revert to, their natural state, where animals of many kinds could lead their lives without persecution by man, to the immense benefit of the beauty, healthfulness, and ecological soundness of our planet.

Although I have loved our farm animals, and treated them as kindly as I could, I sometimes feel sorry for them. Domestication has distorted or disrupted the innate patterns of behavior that are the foundation of an animal's integrity, without giving them an adequate substitute. Even after thousands of generations of intimate association with man, they have not become well adjusted to living with us. They have not learned to refrain from eating the growing crops upon which a farmer's prosperity and, ultimately, their own depends. With few exceptions, they do not freely perform the work that is a fair return for the food and care they receive, with the result that we must often resort to the disagreeable necessity of compelling them. When we must dose or doctor them, they misunderstand our benevolent intentions; they are often as refractory as young children, and the larger of them are much stronger to resist. They commonly ignore our need of cleanliness and order. We have deprived them of their ancestral ways, without adapting them well to our ways.

When I compare my experiences with domestic and with free animals, I find deeper values in the latter. Naturally, my relations with the animals dependent upon me have been far more intimate, frequently involving bodily contact, whereas I have only rarely been touched by free animals, and then usually in a hostile context, as by birds defending their nests. I am gratified when a horse nuzzles my shoulder, a chicken jumps upon my knee, or a cow reclining in the pasture permits me to rest upon her. Perhaps, instead of expressing friendship, the horse or chicken only desires food. Nevertheless, these intimate contacts are manifestations of confidence, which in the living world is too rare to be disdained. When we recall that the struggle for food has been the chief source of enmity and fear among animals, it seems fitting that food, freely given, can help to overcome fear and establish mutual confidence.

Although free animals remain aloof from me, with patience I can often disclose the details of their integrated patterns of behavior, which are often beautiful, and almost always admirably adjusted to the circumstances in which they live. (A few of these patterns are outlined in chapters six, nine, thirteen, and twenty.) Although we commonly treat our domestic animals as inferior dependents, in the presence of the smallest and weakest of free creatures, one that I might enclose in my hand and crush with its pressure, I feel that I stand before an equal, free as I strive to be, self-reliant as a civilized man can rarely become. I need never impose my will upon free creatures, as I must often do with my domestic animals. They seem to know what is best for themselves, as I try to learn what is best for me. I must treat them with perfect courtesy, for abrupt movements or unrestrained familiarity may cause their instantaneous flight. When dealing with free animals, I am on my good behavior, as it is not always necessary to be with dependent animals. The contemplation of creatures so adequately equipped to meet the difficult demands of living enlarges my conception of life's immeasurable potentialities and enhances my self-respect as a member of the living world.

13. Family Life of the Golden-naped Woodpecker

FOR studying hole-nesting birds, there is no place like a new clearing in tropical forest. Forty years ago, when I first came to the Valley of El General, I spent many hours watching birds in such a clearing, high on a ridge overlooking a broad mountain torrent. To save work while preparing the *milpa*, the axeman had left a few big trees standing in the midst of desolation. Now, killed by the fire that had raged through the prostrate woodland, they stood, charred and gaunt, high above the dense weedy growth that sprang up after the maize was harvested. Woodpeckers of six species carved their holes in the decaying trunks. Toucans, tityras, martins, and other hole-nesters unable to carve, watched eagerly for a chance to seize cavities made by the industrious woodpeckers.

In December, when the wet season passed into the dry and the weedy clearing was bright with flowers, I found a pair of big Lineated Woodpeckers digging a nest cavity high in one of these dead trees. While studying these woodpeckers with flaming crests, I learned that a much smaller woodpecker, of a kind new to me, slept in an old, weathered hole above their unfinished one. At dawn, one of the big woodpeckers arrived, clung to the trunk below the new hole, and cautiously peered into it from every angle, to make sure that no snake or other animal had intruded there. Then it drummed a loud tattoo that brought its mate from the neighboring forest. Next, it climbed up toward the hole from which the smaller woodpecker was gazing out at the brightening landscape. The smaller bird at first drew back into her bedroom, but, as her neighbor continued to approach, she slipped out and fled. The big woodpecker chased the little one, who nimbly dodged from tree to tree, until at last she sought refuge in the forest. Here I found her breakfasting on the fruit of a tree with glossy leaves.

The strange woodpecker was largely black on the upper parts, wings, tail, and sides of the head. A wide white band extended down the middle of the back and broadened over the rump. The throat and breast were yellowish gray; the abdomen was scarlet; and the sides of the body were irregularly barred with black and off-white. The top of the head and the nape were yellow, with a transverse band of black on the crown. This was the mark of the female; males are similar in plumage, except that the top of the head is bright red, leaving only the forehead and nape golden yellow. Months later, when I could visit a museum, I learned that this beautiful bird is called the Golden-naped Woodpecker, and that it occurs only on the Pacific side of southern Costa Rica and the adjacent part of Panama. A similar form inhabits northern Colombia.

At the end of the dry month of February, when the early brood of the Lineated Woodpecker had flown, I found a pair of Golden-napes sleeping together in an old, weathered hole in the top of a branchless trunk, at the head of the same clearing. This was an exciting discovery, because most adult woodpeckers lodge alone, the male in one cavity and his mate in another.

These Golden-napes were excavating a new hole lower in the barkless trunk where they slept. Male and female shared rather equally the task of carving into the hard wood. Their spells of work rarely exceeded half an hour. When one tired of

the task, it stuck its head through the round doorway and called its partner with a resonant *churr*. The mate, foraging at a distance, often responded promptly to the summons to take over the work. At intervals, the tapping inside the trunk ceased, and the carver stuck its head through the doorway to release a billful of fine wood particles, which looked like powdered gold as they drifted downward in the bright morning sunshine. Other billsful followed, once forty-eight in succession.

After the new hole was large enough, the mated pair slept in it. By the last week of March, I nearly always found the cavity occupied, evidence that they were incubating, although I could not reach the high nest to see the eggs. The two partners replaced each other frequently; at this and other nests of Golden-napes, I never saw one continue incubation for more than fifty-one minutes in the daytime. Other woodpeckers, including some smaller than the Golden-napes, may sit uninterruptedly for hours. Probably the Golden-napes' frequent change-overs are a consequence of their strong attachment to their home, which brings the free partner back to it after a short absence.

By April 7, when the dry season was ending, the parent Golden-napes were carrying food into their high hole. Although years passed before I found an accessible nest in which I could examine the nestlings, I had no doubt that the newly hatched young were, like other woodpeckers, weak and sightless, with pink skin wholly devoid of natal down, the lower mandible longer and broader than the upper mandible, and the heels covered by a callous pad studded with little projections, to prevent abrasion on their nursery's unlined wooden floor. The parents carried the nestlings' food, consisting of both insects and fruits, visibly in their bills, instead of regurgitating it in the manner of Lineated Woodpeckers, flickers, and certain other members of the family, especially species that subsist largely

◀ GOLDEN-NAPED WOODPECKER, MALE

upon ants. They brought meals much more frequently than do woodpeckers that regurgitate. In the early morning, their nestlings might receive as many as ten meals in a half hour.

At intervals, the parents emerged from the hole with heaping billsful of waste, which they usually carried to a distant tree to drop. In this pair, both parents attended to the sanitation of the nest, but in other pairs I saw only the male perform this duty. Among woodpeckers, he is often the more domestic member of the pair.

Both parents continued to sleep with the nestlings, as they had done with the eggs. Usually the female left at daybreak a few minutes before her mate; more rarely, they emerged together. The nestlings were no less than twenty-five days old before they climbed up the foot-high wooden wall of their nursery to look through their lofty doorway. They were now well feathered, with red crowns like their father. On May 10, I first saw one clinging to the outside of the trunk, near the doorway, through which another youngster was gazing. Soon the one outside climbed back into the sheltering hole.

On the following day, I waited long without seeing a head in the doorway. Looking around, I found the Golden-nape family high among the trees at the forest's edge. With the parents were three male fledglings, who could already fly for considerable distances, although not so swiftly and confidently as the adults. Their call was a weaker version of the adult's vibrant *krrr*. They had left the nest thirty-four days after I first saw the parents carry in food, when they may already have been a few days old. At a number of other nests, some of which I could look into, the nestling period of the Golden-naped Woodpecker varied from thirty-three to thirty-seven days. In their first plumage, the young resemble their parent of the same sex. Of thirty-five young raised in fifteen nests, twenty were red-crowned males and fifteen black-crowned females.

Each evening found the whole family, parents and young together, safely ensconced within the solid wooden walls of their lofty home. During their first days abroad, the three young woodpeckers retired early. Sometimes I found them all inside soon after three o'clock, even if no rain fell, as it often did those May afternoons. But they had no fixed time for going to rest, and sometimes one would delay in the open long after his brothers had entered the hole. If there were no shower, their homecoming seemed to depend upon how soon they tired of climbing over the trees.

Even on the first day when I noticed these young woodpeckers at a distance from the home trunk, one of them found his way home without parental guidance. At other nests, however, the adults led the fledglings back after their first outing. The parents may cling on opposite sides of the doorway, or one may rest beside it while the other enters, and the young promptly do the same. After the fledglings return early to the nest, the parents feed them there, just as though they were nestlings who had never flown. The sight of its siblings receiving food in the hole may prompt a laggard fledgling to come hurrying home. Sometimes, after retiring early, a youngster flies out again. Then the call of a parent, or an exemplary visit to the hole, brings it back.

Golden-nape parents differ greatly in the care they take to keep their fledglings dry. I have known families in which, when rain fell hard, one or both parents sought shelter in their hole, leaving their recently emerged young exposed to the downpour. Perhaps because they lived at a higher altitude, where showers were colder, my first pair was more careful to keep their young out of the rain. In this region, rain in the forenoon is rare; but once I saw the father lead one of his sons back to the hole to escape a light shower that began around seven o'clock in the morning. The rest of the family stayed outside; and the lone fledgling, preferring

companionship to dryness, soon came forth to join the others. In the rainy afternoons, however, the young woodpeckers regularly took shelter. If the rain were
light, the parents flew through it bringing food to their young in the hole; but a
heavy downpour might drive the whole family into the chamber long before dark.
If the rain abated early, the parents would come out to seek food for their offspring; but if it continued to fall hard into the dusk, all would remain within from
about four o'clock until the following morning, the fledglings going hungry to
sleep.

One of the young males vanished before he had been out of the nest for a fortnight. In October, another young male disappeared. But the third young woodpecker continued to lodge with his parents until the following March, when they
were preparing to raise another brood. He had dwelt in the parental home for ten
months after he first flew.

In later years, I have followed the fortunes of a number of other Golden-nape
families, finding that, on the whole, they behaved much as my first pair had done,
with some interesting and instructive variations. Although, when I first arrived in
the Valley of El General, I found Golden-napes nesting only in the forest or near
its edge, with increasing human settlement and deforestation they adapted to the
changed conditions and ventured farther from the heavy woodland. My longest
association was with a pair, or succession of pairs, that for seven years resided in
the small coffee plantation at Los Cusingos. They became regular attendants at the
feeder beside the house, sharing bananas with a colorful crowd of tanagers, honeycreepers, finches, orioles, and barbets.

This pair carved their holes in the old, dying Inga trees that shaded the coffee
bushes. As the higher branches decayed and broke off, the woodpeckers made
their holes lower, until at last I had nests that I could reach with a long ladder. The

lowest in which eggs were laid was only seventeen and a half feet up. My earlier Golden-nape nests, in dead trees of the original forest, were inaccessibly situated from forty to one hundred or more feet high.

At these lower nests, I learned that Golden-napes lay sets of four eggs about as often as they lay three, although I have never known them to raise more than three nestlings. These eggs, which have the lovely, glossy, pure white shells typical of woodpeckers, are laid early in the morning, on consecutive days, and they hatch after twelve days of incubation, or a little less. Thus, the nestling period is three times as long as the incubation period, which is unusual among small birds.

One year, the Golden-napes in the coffee plantation had an exceptionally shallow hole, only eight inches deep, with the bottom narrowly oblong instead of rounded. It had been carved rather hastily in a dying avocado tree whose wood seemed hard for the woodpeckers. Although by day the two parents shared incubation in the normal way, at night they separated, the male attending the eggs, while the female slept alone in a hole higher in the same tree. This was most unusual for Golden-napes, who prefer to sleep together at all seasons. However, in the majority of woodpeckers for which we have information, the male alone stays with the eggs and nestlings through the night.

A few days after the eggs hatched in this low, shallow nest, the nestlings vanished. The parents then carved another hole higher in the same trunk and hatched another brood, which also disappeared within ten days. The bereaved parents then acted most strangely. Again and again, they took food into the desolated nest. After a little, they would appear in the doorway, still holding the food, then take it down inside once more. They might do this three times in succession, before they finally ate what they held. The male would stay in the nest for minutes together, as though brooding. This behavior continued for at least six days after the nestlings vanished. I have known birds of other kinds, including trogons, vireos, and tanagers, to persist in bringing food to nests from which they had lost young, but never for so long as these woodpeckers did. They seemed unable to accept the reality of their loss.

Even when their last year's nest hole came through the long wet season in a fairly sound state, the parent Golden-napes would move into a newly carved one as the next breeding season approached. Frequently, the young hatched in April or May remained with their parents until the following March or April, when the latter were about to resume breeding. Usually these young birds continued to sleep in their old home when, two or three weeks before the female began to lay, the parents moved into the neighboring new cavity; but one young male followed his parents to the new chamber and roosted with them until laying began. In any case, the last of the preceding year's brood always vanished from the vicinity before incubation started. I do not know what sends the yearlings off at this season. Sometimes I have noticed antagonism toward them on the part of the parents, but it has never been violent. Perhaps the young depart spontaneously. I doubt whether these woodpeckers, still without territories or mates in March or early April when the breeding season begins, will nest in the same year. Possibly they do not become sexually mature until the following year.

Here in El General, Golden-naped Woodpeckers usually raise only one brood a year; but twice the pair in the coffee plantation undertook to produce second broods, as did one other pair. The first time that this occurred, they had raised a single female fledgling, who slept with her two parents while they incubated their second set of eggs. This nest was prematurely destroyed, apparently by ants. Three years later, the woodpeckers in the coffee plantation brought forth three female fledglings on May 3. This was the earliest brood that I have recorded, and the only one consisting of three females. Although I noticed mild antagonism on the part of the father, these juveniles were permitted to occupy the second nest while it held eggs and nestlings.

As far as I could learn, these three young females took no share in incubating the second set of eggs, with which they were so closely associated; but they were definitely interested in the nestlings that hatched from these eggs. On the first morning when I saw the parents carry in food for the newly hatched young, one of these adolescents tried repeatedly to enter with her brooding mother, only to be repulsed at the doorway. Later, while her father was brooding, she went in without visible opposition and stayed. Possibly he pecked her within the hole, for presently he appeared in the doorway with a downy feather sticking to his bill. It adhered so stubbornly that he climbed out to remove it, leaving his daughter within, perhaps brooding the nestlings. Later, this young woodpecker, or one of her sisters, stayed in the cavity for a long while, to the parents' great annoyance. How I wished for a window in the wall of the high nest chamber, so that I could see what was happening inside!

During the nestlings' final week in the hole, their elder sisters from time to time brought them food. At least two of the adolescents, now nearly four months old, were so engaged, and probably all three were. Instead of encouraging their young helpers, the parents, particularly the mother, sometimes chased them mildly; but often she made no hostile move when she saw them approaching the nest.

These juveniles were far from expert in their self-appointed parental role. They always came with very small particles, as though for newly hatched nestlings instead of vigorous feathered ones. Moreover, they did not know how to deliver what they brought. The parents were now feeding at the doorway, inclining their heads sideward to facilitate the transfer of the food to the nestlings' grasping mouths. The young helpers, who had not learned this trick, hesitated to approach those rudely snapping bills. Sometimes they carried the food away again. More often, after several timid advances and retreats, they gathered courage to push past the importunate nestling in the doorway. They entered with head drawn in, and probably also closed eyes, in the attitude of a man trying to shield his face from blows. Apparently, the sisters delivered the food inside the hole, as the parents no longer did.

These woodpeckers are not the only juvenile birds that I have known to attend siblings a few months younger than themselves. I have watched Groove-billed Anis, Southern House-Wrens, and Golden-masked Tanagers feed their parents' later broods. Other naturalists have recorded such precocious parental activity in birds as diverse as gallinules, pigeons, swallows, bluebirds, cardinals, and many others.

In this late nest of the Golden-napes, one male and one female were raised. After they began to fly, the whole family lodged in the nest chamber, which, accordingly, sheltered the two parents, three females of the first brood hatched late in March, and one male and one female of the second brood hatched late in June. These seven formed the largest family of woodpeckers of any kind that I have found sleeping in the same hole.

Two weeks after the second brood left the nest, the branch containing it broke off, and the seven woodpeckers went to roost in the long-neglected hole where the first brood had been reared. But they promptly started to carve two new chambers in the stub of the branch that had held the fallen cavity. In this task, the parents were assisted by their offspring. Not only one or more young females, but even the male of the second brood, who had been out of the nest only three weeks and was about two months old, lent their bills to the work. He remained at his task after all the rest of the family flew away. I could not see what he did inside the hole, but I watched him throw out ten billsful of chips. This young male continued to receive food from his father until he was at least ninety-four days old.

Soon after this, the Golden-napes abandoned the coffee plantation, where the dying Inga trees no longer offered adequate sites for their nests. Sixteen years passed before I again found a pair of these woodpeckers raising a second brood. Curiously, only three of the thirteen first broods that I have watched consisted of females alone, and each of these was followed by a second brood. The ten first broods with one or more males were not followed by second broods. Apparently, Golden-napes are not satisfied until they have reared at least one male fledgling; or, the presence of a second male in the family inhibits further breeding until the following year. However, three cases are hardly enough for firm conclusions.

This third pair that raised two broods in a season occupied a tall, slender, dead Cecropia tree on the hillside behind the house. After failing to complete a new hole in this trunk, the female laid in the old one in which her mate had long been sleeping, while she lodged in an older, dilapidated cavity above him. They raised two young females, who left the nest on June 3. As usual, these juveniles returned in the evenings to sleep with their parents; but, with two neighboring holes available to them, they did not consistently follow the usual practice of sleeping all together. On the contrary, the four members of the family occupied their two bedrooms in various combinations, with different groupings on different nights. Thus, on one night one juvenile slept with both parents, while the other young female slept alone. On another night, the mother slept with her two daughters, while their father slept alone. By the end of June, the parents were incubating again, and the whole family of four passed the night in the cavity with the eggs, an arrangement that they continued after the nestlings hatched.

Now I watched carefully to learn whether the two juvenile females would help to attend their younger siblings, whose number I could not learn in this high nest in a decaying trunk of uncertain stability. One of the juveniles was more closely associated with the nest than the other, who on some nights did not come to sleep in the Cecropia tree, evidently because she had found lodging elsewhere. The other young female formed the habit of returning late in the morning, entering the nest cavity, and taking food that her father had brought for the nestlings. Instead of passing it on to them, she always, as far as I could see, ate it herself, no more than one insect in a forenoon. Her mother, less complaisant, usually avoided her entreaties for food and was mildly antagonistic to her, but never hostile enough to disrupt the family. Although they were about three and a half months old when the second brood left the nest, the young females of the first brood never, as far as I could learn, fed the nestlings. After these nestlings were older, their two elder sisters sometimes slept with them, while the parents retired at nightfall into a nearby hole. Apparently, juvenile Golden-naped Woodpeckers only exceptionally serve as nest helpers on the rare occasions when their parents raise a second brood.

Golden-napes stand about midway on the scale of sociality in the woodpecker family. At about the same level are the Olivaceous Piculets and related species, which lead newly fledged young back to the nest hole, where they sleep with both parents, an arrangement that is continued for months. Sometimes young piculets sleep in the cavity where their parents are incubating eggs or raising nestlings of their second brood, but I have not known juveniles to feed their younger siblings.

More social than Golden-napes are the Red-cockaded Woodpeckers of the southeastern United States, whose families remain together from year to year. Parents give food to their young up to the age of five or six months; and, as yearlings, the latter diligently feed their siblings, both in the nest and after they fledge, although they are not known to brood them. In one respect, however, Red-cockaded Woodpeckers are less social than Golden-napes. Adult males and females sleep in different holes; the male alone occupies the breeding nest at night while it holds eggs and nestlings; and newly emerged young, instead of being led back to lodge with their parents, roost clinging to trees in the open until they can find or make holes for themselves.[1]

Most social of all the woodpeckers that have been studied in some detail are the Acorn Woodpeckers, who live permanently in family groups on defended territories. Unfortunately, the latest available information does not definitely settle the question of whether they breed communally, with two or more females laying in the same nest, like anis, or whether a single breeding pair is assisted in parental duties by other members of the group. However, the number of eggs in Acorn Woodpeckers' nests suggests that usually a single female lays. Only one adult, probably a male, stays in the nest at night, while the other attendants sleep together in a different hole, or perhaps several together in each of two or three neighboring cavities. In California, as many as twelve have been found sharing a roost hole. Occasionally, Acorn Woodpeckers continue to feed their young up to the age of one year.[2]

Of the many species of woodpeckers that are less social than the Golden-napes, the Red-crowned is typical. The first nest of this woodpecker that I studied was situated in the same clearing that contained my first Golden-napes' nest; and

1. J. D. Ligon, "Behavior and breeding biology of the Red-cockaded Woodpecker," *Auk*, 87 (1970): 255–278.

2. M. H. MacRoberts and B. R. MacRoberts, "Social organization and behavior of the Acorn Woodpecker in central coastal California," *American Ornithologists' Union. Ornith. Monogr.* no. 21 (1976): 1–115.

I was impressed by the contrasts in the family life of these related species, which occasionally occupy different holes in the same high trunk. Before the breeding season, the male and female Red-crowns always slept in separate holes. Since the male is the more diligent carver and usually has the newer and sounder chamber, his mate lays her eggs in his dormitory rather than in her own. He continues to occupy it by night while it holds eggs and nestlings, while she sleeps elsewhere, although by day she alternates with him in incubating the eggs and brooding the nestlings. When, at the age of a month, the young begin to fly, they are not led back to sleep in the nest, as fledgling Golden-napes are. Quite the contrary—if, as night approaches, they try to join one of the parents in its dormitory, they are firmly repulsed; if they steal a march on a parent and enter its hole first, they are unceremoniously evicted. They must roost clinging to a trunk in the open until they can find an unoccupied hole, or carve one for themselves. However, if a trunk contains enough holes for each individual to sleep alone, young Red-crowned Woodpeckers may remain closely associated with their parents until the following breeding season. What a contrast between the Spartan treatment of Red-crowned fledglings and the solicitous care that young Golden-napes receive!

14. *Which Should I Protect?*

 OUR planet's generous hospitality to teeming life in innumerable forms imposes upon us annoyances, problems, and difficult decisions from which a more barren planet, only sparsely populated with living things, should be relatively free. Years ago, on Barro Colorado Island in the Panama Canal Zone, I was suddenly confronted by one of these troublesome dilemmas. I had been studying a nest that a pair of tiny, yellow-breasted Bananaquits had built in an orange tree, close beside the biological station's main building, which stood in a narrow clearing in the tropical forest and looked over a wide expanse of Gatún Lake to the wooded hills of eastern Panama. One evening in the dusk, a long, black-and-yellow Mica climbed into the orange tree and slid outward along a branch toward the little covered nest, in which two nestlings rested. Knowing this snake to be an insatiable robber of birds' nests, I found a stick and killed it.

"I thought you protected wild things," remonstrated Dr. Frank M. Chapman, one of the best-known ornithologists of his day, author of *My Tropical Air Castle* and many other books.

"I protected the Bananaquits," was my reply.

A few years later, when I built my house at the forest's edge in Costa Rica, I faced the same dilemma. By planting fruit trees and shrubbery around the house

and supplying food on a board, I soon had, nesting in my dooryard, a remarkable concentration of birds, mostly inhabitants of the clearings but some primarily forest dwellers. In one year, at least fifty-two pairs of thirty-two species nested in slightly less than four acres of garden and shady pasture surrounding my dwelling. Soon two kinds of toucans from the neighboring forest discovered that this was a rich hunting ground, and with huge, colorful bills that menaced the distressed parents, plucked their eggs and young from the nests. Then snakes and squirrels entered my dooryard and systematically plundered the nests that escaped the toucans. Which should I protect, the smaller nesting birds or the toucans, snakes, and squirrels? Did I not owe some protection to the birds that I had encouraged to nest around my home, and that I wished to study?

In one way or another, most of us who go through the woods and fields with open eyes, and are not wholly indifferent to the consequences of our acts, are brought face to face with the same riddle. Sometimes, walking along an unfrequented woodland path, we find our way blocked by a beautiful orb web that some laborious spider took much of the night to weave, and on which she depends to ensnare the insects necessary to keep her alive. We pause to admire her work, its marvelous geometric regularity, its delicacy and strength, the use of two kinds of silk, smooth for the supporting framework, sticky for the transverse strands that serve to entangle the prey. It seems a pity to push heedlessly by, destroying in a moment the careful work of hours.

But no! If we spare the spider's web it will be fatal to some unfortunate moth or bee. Would it not be better to walk on, just as though we had not noticed the orb, so the result would be the same as if we had not paused to admire a spider's web and get caught in an ethical tangle? Unhappily, it is now too late to follow

◀ SCARLET-RUMPED BLACK TANAGER, MALE (LEFT) AND FEMALE; GREEN TREE SNAKE

this blissfully innocent course; the dilemma has been thrust upon us, and we cannot escape it. Whether we follow the straight path or make a detour to avoid the web, we do so with at least a general knowledge of the consequences of our decision. However carelessly or hurriedly we make the choice, it is an ethical choice, bearing in its train momentous consequences for living creatures.

Or sometimes in the forest we find a tree whose soaring trunk is encircled by a thick woody vine spiraling upward to the spreading crown. Each year the coils of the liana bite more deeply into the expanding bole, while its leaves spread a smothering blanket over the tree's own foliage. Eventually, either the tree or the vine will succumb in this lethal struggle. Probably the victim will be the tree. With a stroke of the machete, we can sever the liana and release the tree. Should we give the decisive blow?

Problems like these confront every thoughtful person who lives somewhat intimately with nature. When we see one creature menacing another, which should we aid? Or should we leave them to work out their own destinies without human interference? Too often we decide the question on the spur of the moment, without any guiding principle. Sometimes we destroy one animal to save another that we hold to be prettier, or that has happened to engage our interest. Nearly always, when we take sides, it is to defend the creature to which we have devoted most attention. This makes it appear that if the circumstances had been reversed, that if we were more familiar with B, which we now attack, than with A, which we now defend, we would favor B at A's expense. Clearly this is not moral conduct. The first principle of morality is to act by rule rather than on impulse; to treat the beings that surround us according to considered judgments instead of permitting our conduct to be influenced by the shifting winds of personal preferences and aversions. Immanuel Kant, the great German philosopher, taught that we should always act in accordance with a rule that we could wish to become a general law of nature.

To answer the question "Which should we protect?" we must search for guiding principles. The following five seem worthy of our consideration.

1. *Regard for human interests only.* — This is the principle — or perhaps, lack of principle — that has most often regulated man's treatment of other living things in the West. Philosophically, it was clearly propounded by Spinoza, who based man's unlimited right to exploit animals simply upon his power to do so, and upon the difference between their nature and ours. Those who accept this doctrine commonly hold that all nonhuman creatures may be used for human ends, regardless of their suffering, destruction, or even the extermination of whole species. Even if we admit this as a valid principle, it fails to give adequate guidance. Most often it is interpreted to mean economic interests, with a liberal provision for the "sporting" or amusement interests; instead of demanding "Bread and the Circus!" from the Roman emperor, people expect nature to fill their stomachs and provide an outlet for savage impulses. But in addition to economic and sporting interests, we have aesthetic, scientific, and ethical interests, which strongly influence the decisions of people not wholly brutalized. The principle of exclusive concern for mankind must certainly try to reconcile these diverse and often conflicting motives.

Even if we give this principle the narrowest interpretation, limiting it to mean that our relations with nonhuman creatures should be regulated by the single consideration of providing people with food, shelter, clothing, and other material necessities, we may find its application perplexing. Immediate profit is in perpetual conflict with long-term advantage. Although the ruthless exploitation of all nonhuman life may satisfy man's immediate economic interest, some alternative principle may be more compatible with his continuing welfare.

2. *The Principle of* laissez-faire.—This is the principle expressed by W. H. Hudson's maxim, "Neither persecute nor pet." Our pampering of free animals, well meant but often ill considered, may be almost as disastrous to them as deliberate persecution. Therefore Hudson, who loved wild nature, believed that we should permit free creatures to work out their own destinies, with a minimum of human interference, while we watch and try to understand, never favoring one more than another of the antagonists in nature's fierce and frequent struggles for survival. Evidently, to feed free animals is not strictly consistent with this principle. Thereby we make life easier for them; they may become less self-reliant than nature forces them to be, less able to shift for themselves when not under our protection. Our "petting" may be, in effect, an inverted form of "persecution." Doubtless Hudson, no less than Chapman, would have rebuked me for killing the snake that was about to swallow the nestling Bananaquits. I might have defended my action by pointing out that I had devoted much time to studying this nest and was eager to complete my observations. This would have been an application of the principle of human interests only—the interest, in this particular case, being scientific curiosity tinged with feeling.

3. *The principle of* ahimsa.—Since this principle for the regulation of our relations with nonhuman creatures has been applied chiefly in India, we may fittingly use the ancient Sanskrit word, which means "without harm." From the *Bhagavad Gita* and other ancient writings, we learn that to refrain from harming all creatures was held to be indispensable for the attainment of spiritual enlightenment and holiness. The doctrine has persisted down to our own time, and for a modern view we may turn to a conversation reported by Paramhansa Yogananda in his *Autobiography of a Yogi.* The Yogi was visiting Gandhi at his hermitage at Wardha, India:

"Mahatmaji," I said as I squatted beside him on the uncushioned mat, "please tell me your definition of *ahimsa*."

"The avoidance of harm to any living creature in thought or deed."

"Beautiful ideal! But the world will always ask: May one not kill a cobra to protect a child, or one's self?"

"I could not kill a cobra without violating two of my vows—fearlessness, and non-killing. I would rather try inwardly to calm the snake by vibrations of love. I cannot possibly lower my standards to suit my circumstances." With his amazing candor, Gandhi added, "I must confess that I could not carry on this conversation were I faced by a cobra!"

Gandhi, one of the great men of the twentieth century, and politically one of the most important, believed that his long quest of truth would be adversely affected by deviating from the strict practice of *ahimsa*. Certainly, this is the noblest ideal to guide our treatment of all living things; but, as with the two foregoing principles, its practice in an active life involves us in perplexities. Gandhi himself was obliged to relax the practice of *ahimsa* to protect the people at his convent from venomous snakes.

4. *The principle of favoring the highest.*—According to this principle, which is implicitly followed by many who perhaps do not explicitly profess it, we take the part of those creatures that we believe to be "higher" against those that we hold to be "lower" in the scale of life. The "highness" may consist in greater similarity to ourselves, which, on evolutionary theory, implies closer genetic relationship. In accord with this interpretation, we would defend mammals against fishes, reptiles, or even birds, for the first are obviously closer kin. Although it is doubtful whether birds are genealogically nearer to ourselves than snakes, we might recognize a closer kinship to them because of their greater similarity to ourselves: they are warm-blooded, have family ties, carefully attend their offspring as we do, are tune-

ful and communicate by voice; whereas snakes are in each respect the reverse. On this ground, we might deem it proper to protect birds from serpents.

Or we might adopt the great principle of Utilitarian ethics, which taught that the fundamental rule of moral conduct is to choose that course, of all those open to us, which promises to promote the maximum of pleasure or happiness among all sentient beings, regardless of species, social class, or kinship to ourselves. In this case, we shall favor the creatures that we believe to be most highly conscious, therefore most capable of feeling pleasure or happiness. But, as the critics of Utilitarianism pointed out, in the absence of a numerical measure of happiness, we cannot know when, or how, it reaches a maximum. In the strictest sense, we cannot prove that happiness, or consciousness itself, exists anywhere except in our individual selves, where we are immediately aware of it. Doubtless warm-blooded birds and mammals feel more keenly than cold-blooded reptiles, fishes, insects, and mollusks; but we cannot prove this.

Alternatively, we might adopt a more Stoic interpretation and favor the animals whose behavior appears noblest or most admirable. We see many birds and mammals cooperating together, toiling to nourish and protect their young, at times risking or even sacrificing their lives to protect their progeny; and these activities suggest moral or quasi-moral attributes that set the warm-blooded animals above the majority of reptiles, amphibians, and fishes, for in these classes of vertebrates true cooperation and the nurture of offspring are exceptional. Similarly, we see ants, bees, wasps, termites, and a few beetles working together and attending their young, in a manner unknown among butterflies, mosquitos, dragonflies, and most other insects. Some will hold that the moral value of these activities, which objectively so closely resemble commendable human behavior, depends upon their motivation, which is invariably hidden from us. Despite this uncertainty, spontaneous sympathies often impel us to ally ourselves with the creatures whose be-havior most resembles that which we most admire in man.

Finally, we might believe that the most intelligent animals most deserve our protection. Here we are on more solid ground. Intelligence reveals itself by ability to adapt to novel situations, and it can be measured, at least roughly, by the time needed to solve the puzzles that students of animal behavior set before their sub-jects, whereas these investigators hesitate to commit themselves upon such ques-tions as the consciousness and ethical motives of the creatures they study. Unhap-pily, some of the most intelligent animals, such as coyotes and crows, are often man's chief competitors for food; so that the adoption of this interpretation of the principle of favoring the highest would bring us into sharpest conflict with man's economic interest.

5. *The principle of harmonious association.*—We can best illustrate this principle by a concrete example. We build a house, plant a garden around it, and attract a variety of birds, which on the whole live peaceably together and with ourselves. If we keep a horse and a cow in adjoining pastures, they fit harmoniously into the association, never deliberately harming the birds, although they may accidentally trample a ground nest, as we sometimes do. We offer the birds food and sites for their nests; they repay us with beauty in sound and color and protect our shade trees from the ravages of insects. We give the cow and horse pasturage and other food, care, and shelter; one provides us with milk and the other with transporta-tion. Every member of the little community is compatible with every other, and there is a mutual exchange of benefits. We are, of course, the center of this har-monious company, the nucleus about which it is built. Accordingly, harmony with ourselves is a prime requisite for admission to it; we cannot admit a rat that might severely damage our home or its contents. We dwell in a little islet of peace

and goodwill amid the stormy seas of nature and of man; we enjoy a small measure of Messianic concord in a far from peaceful world.

But peace is rarely perfect or long-continued on a planet overcrowded with hungry creatures of many kinds. Before long, a hawk arrives to pounce upon the birds that delight us with their songs, terrorizing those it cannot catch. A snake or squirrel surreptitiously invades our garden, plundering the birds' nests one by one, or a maurading cat disturbs the peace. Are we not morally obligated to protect, as well as we can, the creatures that we encouraged to live near us? Are we not justified in removing the one or two that disrupt the harmony of the many? Need we perplex ourselves about superiority or inferiority, noble or ignoble attributes, before we remove the hawk, the cat, the squirrel, the snake, or whatever other unwelcome intruder disturbs the atmosphere of peace and mutual trust that we had painstakingly built up around ourselves?

Whether we remove the culprit by death or deportation will depend largely upon our ability to catch it and our feeling toward it. If we decide upon deportation, we should remember that the deportee may disrupt another fairly harmonious association in the locality where we release it. Yet we should always employ the mildest remedial action consistent with the end in view.

When we forcibly remove the creature that disrupts the concord of the little community occupying our dooryard or garden, we follow approved principles of modern jurisprudence. Our treatment of the swindler, the burglar, and even the murderer tends to become independent of vindictive feeling and judgments of moral turpitude. After all, these lawbreakers follow their nature, just as the snake and the hawk do; they are trying to live in their own fashion. Society attempts to preserve such harmony as it has painfully achieved, by the removal, temporary or permanent, of disruptive elements; and modern nations tend increasingly to adopt the mildest measures consistent with this end. May we not follow the same principle in the little society over which we rule in our dooryard?

To apply the principle of harmonious association requires the close control that it is possible to exercise only around our homes, and with difficulty there. For an extensive wilderness, the best policy is that of *laissez-faire*, or "hands off." This is not because the remote wilderness is the abode of perfect harmony that man's interference would only upset. Perhaps it appears peaceable to the superficial observer, but beneath its calm surface is endless strife. Nevertheless, a precarious balance of opposing forces tends to preserve an unstable equilibrium that permits a wide diversity of organisms to flourish from generation to generation.

To find ultimate harmony, we must look not to nature but beyond or above it. Nevertheless, when dealing with nature on a large scale, it is prudent to respect whatever semblance of harmony we find there, for the simple reason that, in our prevailing ignorance, our interference might only make matters worse. If, however, we have foolishly begun to meddle, as by short-sighted "game management," we may find it necessary to continue our intervention, striving to substitute a blunt man-made balance for the more subtle natural equilibrium that we have upset—as when the removal of large predators from the Kaibab Forest in Arizona made it necessary to reduce the numbers of the deer that were multiplying beyond the habitat's capacity to support them. In applying *laissez-faire* to wilderness areas, we also safeguard human interests; by this policy, whatever values for man the wilderness contains are most likely to be preserved for man's future benefit.

Where, as in my own case, one's dooryard borders a large tract of old forest, deciding what principle to follow is more perplexing. It may be necessary to compromise between harmonious association and *laissez-faire*. The forest animals have a stronger tendency to invade the clearings than the creatures of open country have to venture far into the forest. Prowling into one's dooryard and garden, they create problems difficult to handle.

In advocating one principle for our immediate surroundings and another for the remote wilderness, I follow a criterion that I believe would be generally admitted in the more narrowly human sphere of ethics. Personal contact appears to authorize acts of charity and kindness that might be indefensible on a large scale, or in situations where the personal element is lacking. For example, to undertake general measures to reduce infant mortality in a greatly overpopulated country with a stubbornly high birthrate is misapplied charity, which will ultimately produce much more misery than it alleviates; the resulting increase in population will intensify poverty and crime and perhaps bring on ever more disastrous famines. Yet, if we live in such a country, we can hardly turn a deaf ear to a neighbor's plea to save her baby, when we are able to help her. The unyielding application of general principles in such intimate situations might be so inhumanly harsh that the loss in common kindness and goodwill would outweigh any increase in the difficulty of living that our generous deed might eventually produce. Similarly, when dealing with the free creatures around our homes, where the little community centers about ourselves and is daily influenced by our activities, it seems permissible to follow our strong desire to preserve a harmonious association, when necessary having recourse to remedial measures such as would be indefensible if applied on a large scale in the wilderness, where they might have unforeseen effects upon the natural balance.

In view of the great diversity of the situations that we encounter, it is hardly possible to find a single practical principle sufficiently general to guide our relations with all the diverse forms of animal and vegetable life. For large tracts of wilderness, the principle of *laissez-faire* appears soundest; but even here, if we have begun to meddle, it may be necessary to continue our interference in order to forestall a worse disaster. In the intimate surroundings of our homes, harmonious association seems to be the most satisfactory principle; indeed, to safeguard ourselves and our property, we can hardly avoid applying it to a certain degree. The principle of favoring the highest will continue, for all the baffling uncertainties attending its interpretation, to fascinate those who yearn to penetrate the outer husk of living creatures and glimpse their psychic life. As long as we, like every other animal, must wrest a living from a competitive world, we cannot lose sight of human interests; but we should remember that our interests are aesthetic, intellectual, and ethical no less than economic, and that by pushing to the limit the tremendous practical advantages that we enjoy over other animals, we may irreparably damage our own long-term interests no less than theirs.

Of the guiding principles that we have examined, that of *ahimsa*, or harmlessness to all creatures, appears to be the oldest as an expressed maxim, and it is spiritually the most satisfying. Like certain others of our highest, noblest ideals, its perfect realization may be intrinsically impossible in the circumstances of human life, but that is not an adequate reason for rejecting it. In addition to rules of conduct that we try to follow unconditionally, such as not cheating or not wantonly inflicting pain, we should cultivate ideals that we know to be unrealizable yet to which we can approach ever more closely by strenuous perseverance as we grow in insight and moral stature. Such is the ideal of harming no living thing, which appeals the more strongly the more we become aware of the marvelous organization of even the least of them, the more we suspect that every form of life is the outcome of an effort to achieve satisfying existence, or, as Wordsworth expressed it poetically, "every flower enjoys the air it breathes."

My own practice, as a dweller amid exuberant tropical nature, has necessarily been a compromise between the principle of *ahimsa* and that of harmonious association, not uninfluenced by a tendency to favor the creatures that appear to be higher in the scale of animate life, not anatomically or physiologically but psychically. As with any high ideal that we strive to realize in a perplexing world, the effort to reconcile *ahimsa* with harmonious association has involved me in many a distressing dilemma. The very principle of harmlessness has led me reluctantly to oppose with force some animal that has become too harmful.

I have consistently destroyed snakes that, especially in the nesting season, enter the garden in numbers and empty every bird's nest they find. We set traps for rats that, in spite of all precautions, slip into our rooms and work havoc with books, fabrics, and woodwork. Once I reluctantly shot a squirrel that I caught plundering nests, but, perhaps inconsistently, I have been most lenient with these rodents, although they have destroyed a number of rarely-found nests that I greatly desired to study. Aside from a cherished horse who fell, never to rise again, and trespassing pigs, the squirrel was the only warm-blooded animal I have ever shot. I would not have killed the pigs that were making themselves obnoxious if their owners had heeded repeated pleas to remove them, or if the law had permitted me to catch and give them away. For this I could have been prosecuted for theft.

Although, since ancient times, devout Jains and Taoists have refrained from harming insects and worms as well as larger creatures, modern humanitarians, conservationists, and other protectors of animal life commonly give them scant consideration. Yet, how can we claim to have reverence for life if we have none for the most abundant macroscopic creatures on all the continents and islands? Because a small minority of the nearly one million species of insects and their allies are annoying or harmful to man, his crops, or his property, we too often regard the whole immense assemblage as "vermin" unworthy of our forbearance, possibly excluding from this damning category only the beautiful butterflies and the useful bees. Insects, whose psychic life is for us a tightly sealed book, should be as deserving of our clemency as larger creatures.

Although I confess that I swat the mosquitos, little black flies, and other insects that hunger for my blood, and destroy the ticks that attach themselves to my family and domestic animals, I have been most reluctant to spread poison for insects. I have still not used all of the pound of DDT that I bought, soon after it came on the market, to combat termites that were invading the house. In the next chapter I tell how I managed for a long while to cooperate with leaf-cutting ants instead of destroying them. Probably because we plant our crops in small fields amid native vegetation, we have never found it necessary to spread pesticides. I rarely crush some tiny creature that jeopardizes what I must protect without reflecting upon the wonderful intricacy of the structures that I annihilate in an instant. If nature were not so prodigal in the multiplication of such structures, we would be spared the painful necessity of destroying them so often, and might experience the serenity and innocence that the perfect realization of harmlessness would bring us.

15. *Cooperation with Ants*

As predation, parasitism, and every form of ruthless exploitation of one organism by another are proof of evolution's tragic failure to create a harmonious community of living things, so every instance of fruitful cooperation is evolution's triumph, a sample of what it might have achieved with a different sequence of mutations over the ages, or better, if it had been guided by a wise, compassionate Intelligence—a sample, too, of what the living world may be on some far-distant planet happier than our own.

Of the modes of cooperation that have arisen in this world of strife, none is more widespread and beneficent than that between plants and the animals of many kinds that transfer their pollen or disseminate their seeds. To the insects and birds that cross-fertilize their flowers, plants give sweet nectar or nutritious excess pollen as payment for their services. For the animals, chiefly birds, that carry their seeds far and wide, the plants provide fruits that help to nourish them and in some cases comprise their whole diet. These are not, like many instances of symbiosis, defensive or exploitative alliances against other organisms, but wholly peaceful associations that injure nothing. Doubtless it is no accident that the beneficent cooperation between plants and their pollinators and disseminators is responsible for a substantial share of Earth's beauty: the loveliness of flowers and colorful fruits, and of such nectar-drinking or fruit-eating birds as hummingbirds, sunbirds, tanagers, and birds of paradise. Probably it is because our remote ancestors were arboreal fruit-eaters that we, like other primates, enjoy the color vision that so enriches our lives, although many of our fellow mammals lack this enhancement of vision.

A quite different mode of cooperation is that between certain plants and the ants that dwell within them. These plants, known as myrmecophytes or myrmecophilous plants, are scattered through many diverse families, including the ferns, and nearly all are tropical. The ants establish their colonies in hollows in stems, leaves, thorns, or special gall-like swellings. One of the most carefully studied examples of the symbiosis of plants and ants is that of certain acacias and ants of the genus *Pseudomyrmex*. Because these shrubby or arborescent acacias, which thrive in the drier parts of Mexico and Central America, are distinguished by paired, swollen, hollow thorns that resemble the horns of an ox or bull, they are commonly known as the bull's-horn acacias.

Near the apex of one thorn of each pair is a narrow orifice through which the long, slender ants that live inside go in and out. Each of the small leaflets of the twice-compound leaves produces at its tip a tiny, white protein corpuscle, which is the special food of the ants. In return for board and lodging, the ants defend the acacia trees against leaf-eating animals large and small, and even destroy competing vegetation, as Daniel H. Janzen has shown.[1] One can hardly touch these acacias without receiving painful stings from the ants. Although the rather sparse foliage of the bull's-horn acacias offers poor concealment, birds of many kinds raise their families in them, taking advantage of the garrison of ants that in defending their tree repel nest robbers.

In other cases, the advantage that the plant derives from the ants regularly associated with it is more doubtful. This is true of the Cecropias, which are among

1. Daniel H. Janzen, "Birds and the ant × acacia interaction in Central America, with notes on birds and other myrmecophytes," *Condor*, 71 (1969): 240–256.

the most widespread, characteristic trees of tropical America, where their tall, slender, coarsely branched form is a familiar sight in clearings and second-growth thickets. The Cecropia appears to make special provision for its ants in the form of an exceptionally wide central hollow in trunk and boughs, where the insects dwell; pits in the enclosing walls that make it easy for them to open doorways; and a constantly renewed food supply in the tiny, white protein corpuscles produced on a brown, furry cushion at the base of each long leaf stalk. Although the little Azteca ants that regularly inhabit the Cecropia trees undoubtedly benefit from the association, they do not sting but bite, so weakly that, despite their multitude, they fail to protect the tree from the monkeys, sloths, and insects that devour its foliage and immature inflorescences.[2]

As seems inevitable, the prevailing relationship between ants, the most abundant and aggressive of insects, and man, the most aggressive mammal, is one of conflict rather than cooperation. To defend our homes, our food, and our crops against the depredations of ants demands constant struggle, especially in warm tropical lowlands, where ants thrive in immense variety and numbers. Of late we have heard much about the costly campaigns, destructive of much wildlife and not very effective, waged against Fire Ants in southeastern United States, where they arrived not long ago. In tropical America, where these small, dark ants are widespread and well established, they are never, to my knowledge, a serious threat to agriculture (although they are undeniably troublesome, above all if one carelessly stands on their low mounds in the lawn and they swarm up his legs, stinging painfully).

2. The Azteca–Cecropia association is discussed in detail in the present writer's *A bird watcher's adventures in tropical America* (Austin: University of Texas Press, 1977).

◀ LEAF-CUTTING ANTS

Competition is often keenest between organisms of similar habits. Accordingly, it is not surprising that, in tropical America, agricultural man is often at war with agricultural ants. These ants, of the genus *Atta*, are often known as leaf-cutting or parasol ants, because one often sees them marching in long columns, each homeward-bound brown ant bearing above its back, like a parasol or banner, a tiny piece of green leaf that it has cut with its mandibles from a living plant. Often several ants attach themselves to the same bit of leaf, possibly in an effort to carry it; but the smaller ants are hoisted aloft and borne along by the strongest of them.

If one follows the column of leaf-bearing ants marching along their narrow, clean, well-trodden trail, he eventually arrives at a low mound of excavated earth that may be as much as four or five yards wide. Into one of the several openings in the top of the mound the endless column pours, to reach a labyrinth of subterranean galleries and chambers. Here the leaves are cut into tiny fragments that resemble coarse sawdust. They are heaped up to make a compost on which the ants sow a special kind of fungus, the filaments of which produce tiny, knoblike bodies, each resembling a miniature kohlrabi, that the ants eat. On her nuptial flight, the female ant carries, in a special buccal pocket, pieces of fungus that she will sow in the new colony she establishes. Thereby the Attas' special food plant is preserved from generation to generation, as men transport and preserve the seeds, bulbs, or cuttings that propagate their edible plants.

In natural woodlands with a large variety of trees, shrubs, vines, and herbs, the leaf-cutters seldom seem to do great harm. On plantations where the variety of leaves available to them is limited, they may substantially reduce the yield of man's agricultural operations in order to support their own. Not long ago, great coffee plantations employed special squads of men to dig out the leaf-cutters' nests, often leaving a gaping hole in which an ox could be buried. Now that so many highly effective insecticides are available, chemical warfare against the ants has largely replaced the more laborious older methods of combatting them.

At Los Cusingos, the leaf-cutters have rarely been troublesome. I hesitate to kill any creature, no matter how small and apparently insignificant, because in my dense ignorance of the quality of its psychic life, which may be more intense than we commonly suppose, I do not know what a pleasant existence I may terminate. I am especially reluctant to harm these ants, which work so hard to produce their food instead of preying on other small creatures, in the manner of many other kinds of ants. As a vegetarian and agriculturist, I feel a bond of fellowship with these vegetarian agriculturists, as though we were members of the same club or guild—even if what with me has been a deliberately chosen mode of life with them may be an innate pattern of behavior devoid of thought. What a man or any creature does is certainly no less important than the often obscure motives for doing it.

One year, after we had chopped down a large patch of low, lush second growth where we sowed beans, we discovered a populous city of the leaf-cutters close beside it. Although ready to combat them if they attacked the beans, I was deeply thankful that they left the sprouting bean plants wholly untouched.

Leaf-cutters often prefer cultivated plants introduced from the Old World, such as coffee, banana, citrus trees, and common Privet. Years ago, I planted around the enclosure where the house stands, and beside a pasture, about a thousand feet of privet, which makes a prosaic but easily managed hedge. For many years, the laborer who lived on the farm, with his family, pruned the hedge when farm work permitted. Finally, soaring wages, combined with obligatory additional payments and troublesome labor laws that sometimes seemed to poison the relationship between employer and employee, made keeping a permanent farm hand too costly. Now, depending upon occasional labor from outside the farm, I usually pruned the hedges myself. In the long rainy season, the privet grew rapidly and required frequent attention.

About this time, the leaf-cutters established a large colony between two of the hedges and, extending their narrow, well-cleaned pathways through the pasture grass, began to harvest privet leaves. Reluctant to attack their city, I waited to see the outcome. It soon appeared that the vigorous privet could stand a good deal of defoliation, which slowed but did not stop its growth, so that now it did not need to be pruned so often and left me more time for other things. Grateful to these little helpers who made no exorbitant demands, I permitted them freely to enjoy the usufruct of my privet hedges. Moreover, I often gave them a bonus. When I pruned hedges that they did not reach, I deposited fresh leafy cuttings over their trail near their nest, thereby lightening their labor at the same time that I reduced their pressure on parts of the hedge that they might have been exploiting too freely. The toiling ants soon removed all the leaves from the twigs piled near their entrance and carried them piecemeal into their subterranean chambers. Although they dropped many bits of leaf along the few feet of pathway between the pile and the burrow, later they retrieved most of these fragments. Finally, I removed the bare twigs.

In fairly stable tropical environments, such as rain forest and clearings in its midst, birds tend to hold their populations stable from year to year. With insects, the situation is different. At intervals such conspicuous insects as butterflies and the larger beetles inexplicably become very abundant, then for months or years the same species may remain rare, perhaps vanish, to reappear in force at some unpredictable time.

Atta ants undergo such puzzling fluctuations in abundance. After four years of mutually advantageous cooperation, they began to get out of control. New colonies sprang up everywhere, including one right in the privet hedge. Soon it became apparent that, by too frequent defoliation, the ants were killing a long stretch of hedge. Knowing that if they exhausted their supply of privet leaves they would attack fruit trees and ornamental shrubs in the garden, I reluctantly dropped poison into the mouths of their burrow—almost the only insecticide that in nearly four decades I have used on this farm, where we have never sprayed fungicides or weed killers. Then, the following year, leaf-cutters became so rare, even where I had not disturbed them, that I lost all my small helpers. Now, with more work for my wife and me to do, we missed them.

Doubtless, if we could have understood each other, the ants and I might have continued indefinitely to cooperate, to our mutual benefit. One of life's greatest tragedies is the difficulty of communication, with free creatures, with our domestic animals, and often, too, with our fellow humans. If only we could understand each other's nature and needs, situations that lead to strife and death might be transformed into helpful cooperation.

Here a main enemy of the leaf-cutters is the raiding army ant, especially *Eciton burchelli*. In *A Naturalist in Costa Rica*, I told of one invasion of a leaf-cutters' nest by a ravaging horde of Ecitons. Since that raid, I have witnessed several others, one upon a colony of leaf-cutters that were helping me to keep the hedge pruned. When I came upon the scene, the corpses of many Atta soldiers lay around the entrance to their galleries, and hundreds more were scattered, for a distance of several yards, along the path that the leaf-cutters had made and which was now serving the invaders. Some of the dead and dying soldiers had lost one or both antennae, or a leg or two; a few were cut in half. Many more that had no evident injuries could have been killed by stings, or may have struggled until exhausted. I noticed very few Atta workers, and wondered what had happened to the rest of them.

For hours the invaders continued to pass in a steady stream along the path to the leaf-cutters' city, in and out of its portals. Many Ecitons bore beneath their bodies white immature Attas. Strangely, some of the plunderers were carrying their victims away from the nest, while others were taking them back inside. They transported no adult leaf-cutters to their bivouac, evidently because the hard brown bodies were not a suitable food. Their treatment of the Atta soldiers and workers was curiously different; although they ruthlessly slaughtered the former, they merely snatched from the smaller workers the white larvae and pupae they were trying to save, leaving the poor nurse ants wandering about desolate but uninjured. After some of these raids, the Atta colony was gradually repopulated and continued to thrive. Just as, in the early stages of human history, roving hunters and herdsmen from the hills raided the settled agriculturists in the valleys, so, among ants, the nomadic warriors periodically pillage the cities of the peaceful fungus growers.

16. *The Rocky Channel*

FROM the southeastern corner of the pasture in front of the house, a rough cart road ran down beside the Río Peñas Blancas. It passed a gap in the high, stony bank, evidently made by the former owner to permit horses and cows to drink at a tiny sandy beach. Here, after a long horseback trip through the forest to the farm that was not yet mine, I took my first refreshing bath in this torrent that flowed cool and clear from high, wooded mountains.

Not far below this point, the road dipped to cross a depression where a branch of the river had once flowed, then continued through light, second-growth woods along a strip of land between the river and its long-abandoned side channel, now overgrown with shrubs and small trees. Soon it reached an open pasture of sticky, strong-scented Calinguero grass, on rough, rocky land where the river had passed, possibly when glaciers scooped out shallow lakes and piled up moraines on the high, craggy summits of Cerro Chirripó to the north. Beside this pasture, the river flowed along one of its most enchanting reaches, now with high, verdure-covered banks, now with low, stony shores.

At the foot of the pasture, where a tributary brook fell into it, the river turned sharply to the right and entered our best swimming pool. On our side, the short stretch of deep, swift water was bordered by a little sandy beach shaded by the wide-spreading boughs of an ancient, epiphyte-laden Riverwood tree, beneath whose dense, cool shade the cows took refuge from midday heat. On the farther side rose a cliff covered with luxuriant tropical vegetation. Here we came to swim, then eat a picnic lunch while we sat on rounded streamside boulders. Often, while we ate, we watched a pair of charming little Torrent Flycatchers flit from rock to rock above the rushing torrent, or an Amazon Kingfisher or a Green Kingfisher fly swiftly past, following every turn of the channel, perhaps on its way to a nesting burrow it had dug into a narrow vein of soil in a high, stony bank. A short distance below the swimming pool, the old, long-abandoned side channel met the main river.

For twenty years after I came to Los Cusingos, to walk beside the clamorous river down into the lower pastures was a delight when life was untroubled and a solace when things went wrong. Sometimes I watched otters play in the cold water, or a large, crested Gray Basilisk lizard scuttle over it, so swiftly that its long hind toes failed to break through the surface, while its small, idle front legs were held aloof. Or a Neotropic Cormorant that had come up from the coast, in the olive plumage of juveniles, might rise from a midstream boulder, where it had been spreading its wings to the morning sunshine. For a while, lovely Sunbitterns foraged along this river, but, perhaps persecuted by neighbors, they did not stay.

As more and more heavy forest was shorn from steep slopes higher on the watershed, the river became more destructive when in flood. One October it rose so high that it carried away the covered wooden bridge that spanned it a short distance above Los Cusingos. For a long way downstream, sheets of heavy corrugated iron roofing, crumpled like paper, were strewn along the shore; here and there a huge squared beam lodged against a tree trunk, to remain for years, until it rotted away. The luxuriant growth of ferns, aroids, orchids, bromeliads, and other epiphytes

LINEATED CICHLIDS ▶

was scoured from streamside rocks and trunks that they had adorned for years. Even some of the Riverwood trees, so firmly anchored by roots that twisted through the boulders in the banks and clasped them in a firm embrace, yielded to the pounding of the flood waters. At the same time, the wider Río General, into which our river flows, went upon a more disastrous rampage, carrying away bridges, houses, and cattle, leaving a few families homeless.

A few years later, the Peñas Blancas gnawed into the high bank where the horses descended to the little sandy beach to drink. Perhaps foolishly, I cut another ramp into the bank, for this was the best watering place for the animals in the upper pastures. This warning that the river had become wilder should have made me more cautious.

Although our heaviest rains come toward the end of the year (with the peak usually in October), May, early in the wet season, can be a very rainy month. Beginning in the evening of May 9, 1960, rain continued far into the night, until the swollen river roared and boomed as it shifted huge boulders in its bed and battered them with floating tree trunks. By daybreak the sky had cleared and the torrent was subsiding, leaving signs that the river had risen as high as I had ever seen it. I had not walked far down the riverside path before I was halted by a swirling, muddy deluge, twenty yards wide. The flood had reopened the side channel, abandoned so many years before, tearing away the trees and shrubs that had flourished in its bed. Now much of the river's current flowed for a quarter of a mile through the farm, to rejoin the main channel below the swimming pool.

I became, unwillingly, the proprietor of an island of five or six acres, where we had recently planted a field of corn, bananas, Cassava, Taro, and a small vegetable garden. Even after the flood subsided, it was difficult to reach the crops; we had to wade through the rocky stream bed or jump precariously from projecting boulder to projecting boulder. Fortunately, to harvest the corn in August we found an intrepid young man who was not afraid to take his ox-cart through swift water that reached above the hubs of the high wooden wheels.

For years the island lay idle, while dense, impenetrable thickets overgrew the pasture, the corn field, and the banana plantation. Amid this riotous growth, leaf-cutting ants established their subterranean cities beneath low mounds of nearly bare earth, five or six yards across. The swimming pool at the bend of the river was now rarely visited.

As though to prove that it treated foreign residents and native Costa Ricans impartially, the Peñas Blancas now began to cut into my neighbor's farm across the river, intersecting his land with several side streams that fell back into the main channel in foaming cascades. At the same time, it started to pile rocks at the mouth of the branch that it had opened through Los Cusingos. The process of occlusion was slow. After each raging torrent that audibly shifted boulders, I would go to see whether it had built an effective dam, only to be greeted by a voluminous current still flowing through the side channel.

Nevertheless, by the thirteenth year after its incursion into the farm, the river had deposited so many rocks at the channel's mouth that it flowed through only when in high flood. Most of the time, this branch was now an avenue of bare rocks of all sizes, from huge, rounded masses of andesite to shingle and pebbles, all tumbled in vast disorder between high banks. At last we could farm the abandoned fields—now on an island only when the river was swollen. We cut down several acres of dense second growth that included tall, spreading trees, burned it off so that we could reach the ground, and sowed maize, pumpkins, Taro, and vegetables. In this soil that had rested for so many years, they yielded well.

After the river abandoned the rocky channel, it remained a rough passage between tangled thickets difficult to traverse. Sometimes, when the rocks are not wet and slippery from recent rains, I follow the channel from end to end, laboriously stepping or hopping from rock to rock, with staff in hand for greater security against a disastrous fall, and clambering around the margins of the deeper pools that at intervals block my way.

Near its upper end, where the channel is shaded by tall second-growth woods, its high banks are profusely covered with beautiful plants. Between great projecting boulders green with moss grow a variety of shrubs that, each in its season and some throughout the year, display white, pink, red, yellow, or violet flowers. Among them stand wild plantains with broad leaves two yards long and spreading, orange floral bracts. Early in the dry season, tall begonias hold panicles of whitish flowers above glossy leaves. In June and July, an anthurium with great, heart-shaped leaves invites birds to eat little, pale yellow, two-seeded berries, displayed on long, fleshy, bright red spikes that catch the eye from afar. Ferns in great variety grow upon the rocks or in the soil between them. Sometimes I have found plants sprung from seeds that the river has carried down from higher altitudes, including the scrambling composite *Hidalgoa ternata*, with attractive, bright orange, rayed floral heads. To my regret, these strays from cooler life zones have not persisted with us.

Where more sunshine reaches the channel, Job's-tears flourish in pockets of sandy soil between the rocks, to display in nodding clusters their hard-shelled seeds, like big, glossy, white beads. Along the banks, many young Riverwood trees have sprung up from waterborne seeds, perhaps—if they continue to thrive —to mark the course of this channel with umbrageous crowns through many future years.

Birds are not numerous along the channel. Most in evidence are Riverside

Wrens, elegant birds with bright chestnut upper plumage, underparts finely cross-barred with black and white, and white faces curiously marked with black. Lurking in dense marginal thickets, they scold harshly as I pass, or sing back and forth to each other with ringing notes. Once I found one of their nests in a shrub overhanging the channel. A globular structure of fibrous materials and green moss, it was entered by a wide doorway that faced downward and inward and gave access to an antechamber, or vestibule, in front of the brood chamber. In the latter lay two downless nestlings, the largest number I have found in this species.

In the surrounding thickets, Orange-billed Nightingale-Thrushes repeat their quaint little songs through much of the year, rarely exposing their bright brown bodies with long orange legs and eye rings of the same vivid color. In the lusher thickets Black-hooded Antshrikes call. One morning I watched a male catch an insect in his strong, hooked bill, then repeat his dry rattle until his mate came and received it from him—another record of nuptial feeding to add to the many I had already gathered for antbirds. Once I watched a pair of Pale-billed Woodpeckers with high red crests peck over trees along the bank. Rarely, Buff-rumped Warblers cross the rocky channel; they prefer the main river. In the months of the dry season, the most abundant birds in the surrounding trees are Chestnut-sided Warblers, now all in the subdued plumage that males acquire after the nesting season and females wear throughout the year. In these months the loud, insistent sizzling of big cicadas is the most frequent sound along this channel where water no longer babbles.

During the early months of the year, the uppermost reach of the channel is dry. Continuing downward, I detect a tiny trickle, seepage from surrounding higher ground. Following a devious course through tumbled rocks, the water collects at intervals in pockets among them, forming limpid pools usually no more than four or five yards across and a foot or two deep—although the largest, below an immense rock, is ten yards long by more than a yard in depth.

In these sunny pools lives an attractive fish that I call the Lineated Cichlid. In nuptial attire, its pale gray or blue-gray head contrasts strongly with its much darker olive body. A sharply defined black line arches across the forehead from golden eye to golden eye, and another narrow black line crosses the head between this and the blunt nose. The sides of the body are marked with broad, vertically elongated, blackish patches, usually ill-defined, and on some individuals well developed only toward the tail, which is more or less tinged with iridescent blue at the end. After the breeding season, the head darkens to the color of the body, or only a little paler, and its black stripes become faint or vanish. Even the dark patches along the sides of the body tend to disappear, but the eyes remain bright yellow. I have estimated adults with young to be from about three to five or six inches long.

I have not been able to measure these fishes more accurately because it seems impossible to catch one without a trap, which I do not possess. They pass most of their lives hiding beneath the big rocks that surround the pools and cover their bottoms, exposing themselves, except when attending young, chiefly as they dash rapidly across open water from one sheltering boulder to another. The least disturbance sends even parents back to a stony refuge. When not breeding, grown individuals may live in loose companies of three to five.

One morning in late January, I watched one large cichlid, still without head stripes, swim persistently around a slightly smaller one, sometimes circling it, and repeatedly touching it with its head, perhaps "kissing," gently biting, or butting it. Soon the pair retired beneath a rock, thereby terminating my view of what was evidently courtship. On another occasion, I saw two in nuptial colors, apparently a pair still without young, swim together beneath a rock and remain as long as I watched. I have never found eggs in the pools. From these few observations, I infer that courtship, laying, and hatching take place beneath rocks too heavy to lift.

After the eggs hatch, the parents emerge with their tiny young, much less than an inch long. I have not been able to count them as they move through the water in a shifting swarm, but I have estimated the larger broods to contain thirty or forty. While the little school drifts slowly, apparently gathering invisibly small items of food from the water and the surface of the rocks, one or both parents accompany it. Whenever any other fish comes near the brood, a parent darts swiftly at it, puts it to flight, then returns to its family. In these pools that contain no fishes bigger than the largest cichlids themselves, I never saw an intruder, except another parent, resist a parent's charge, or wait for physical contact—not even when the individual so threatened was much larger than the attacker; and I never saw one fish prey upon another, of whatever size.

After a while, the whole family retires beneath a stone, where it may remain out of sight for many minutes. Nevertheless, one can be sure it is still there, for any other fish that seeks shelter in the same little cavern is promptly evicted. Often it appears to be the hungry young, rather than the parent, who initiate the exit from the cave and the resumption of foraging through open water. If the parent does not follow them, they wander only a foot or so from the sheltering rock and soon rejoin their guardian beneath it.

I have watched some broods for a long while without discovering more than one attendant parent, doubtless the female. Many, however, are guarded by both parents. In every case, one guardian is slightly larger than the other and has its tail tipped with blue, a color that its partner may lack. The larger member of the pair is evidently the male, as in other species of *Cichlasoma*, such as the Midas Cichlid of the Nicaraguan lakes. The smaller member of the pair is always the more faithful guardian, remaining more constantly with the little ones, more often chasing intruders. At intervals, the larger parent leaves the family to swim across the pool alone, or to rest beneath a rock, while the smaller parent guards the brood in the open. If I move conspicuously beside the pool, he may retreat beneath a sheltering stone while she remains faithfully with their young. Occasionally a brood is divided, each parent taking part of it; but, as far as I have seen, this arrangement does not continue long, and the family is soon reunited. The cichlids recognize each other individually. A female may repel one male and accept as coguardian of her brood another who to me looks much the same.

Although slightly gregarious when without dependents, Lineated Cichlids are strongly territorial while breeding. Usually I find only a single brood in a pool, rarely two, and only once have I seen three pairs and one lone parent with broods. These four families were in a middle-sized pool, about four or five yards long and broad and one foot in greatest depth.

Although fishes without young flee immediately when a guardian darts toward them, two parents often confront each other. One day I watched a single parent, without blue on her tail and evidently a female, who shared a pool with a pair of smaller fishes with a brood less numerous than her own. Sometimes the lone female left her family to swim as much as two yards across the pool and threaten her neighbors. Usually she withdrew immediately, without, as far as I could see, physical contact; but once this parent and one member of the pair whirled around together for a second or two before they separated, apparently without having hurt each other. On other occasions the two swam toward each other, faced one another from a distance, then turned around and rejoined their broods without having come close together. Nearly always it was the smaller member of the pair, with no blue on her tail, who confronted the belligerent neighbor.

On the following day, in this same pool, I watched the interactions between the solitary female and a third family, consisting of a fairly big male, a very small female, and young so tiny that they appeared to have been newly hatched. Although the three families now in the pool remained aloof from each other most of the time, once the solitary female accompanied her brood to the corner where the tiny hatchlings lived. When she was there, the little resident female kept her brood behind a rock, in very shallow water at the pool's edge, while her larger partner lurked continuously beneath a sheltering stone. After the lone female and her brood drifted toward the center of the pool, the paired female moved farther in, and her mate, emerging from his retreat, rejoined her. Now the adults darted threateningly toward each other; once both members of the pair confronted the solitary parent; but I saw no actual fighting.

This strong territoriality doubtless explains why, at a time when some cichlids had broods, I so often found, in the same pool, a number of others, of about the same size, that had none. Some of these fishes without progeny wore the nuptial colors, while others, equally large, might lack them. It seems that individuals who soonest come into breeding condition and dominate a small pool, or a section of a large one, inhibit reproduction by others, possibly even the acquisition of the black stripes on a pale gray head. Among birds, individuals who cannot secure territories fail to breed.

The young of certain other cichlids nibble the sides of their parents, evidently deriving nourishment from a secretion—the primitive forerunner of mammalian milk! I looked in vain for the Lineated Cichlids to do so. They seem to subsist wholly on minute organisms that they find in the water and on the rocks.[1]

The Lineated Cichlids breed only in the drier weather, when the water in the sunny pools is perfectly clear and only a little current flows into them. When December has few or no hard downpours that send a strong current through the rocky channel, I may find the cichlids breeding freely by the end of the month, or in the first week of January. In 1975, when in late February and early March hard rains up on the mountains made the river rise so high that a strong, muddy current rushed down the side channel and through the rock pools, I found no parents with broods during March. In April of that year, the river remained lower, and, toward the month's end, I found a brood of young already as big as any that I have seen still attended by a parent and apparently on the point of becoming independent, as they did not stay close to their guardians.

Through the rainy months from May to December, when the swollen river frequently overflows into the side channel, depositing in the rock pools much silt, which rises in muddy clouds when the water is stirred, I have found no cichlids with broods. At the other extreme, if, in a very dry year, so little water flows into a pool that a scum covers its surface, probably reducing the supply of oxygen, the cichlids also fail to breed. They raise their broods in water so pure and calm that every detail of the bottom, every decaying leaf and twig, is clearly visible from above, while the surface mirrors all the surrounding vegetation.

After breeding stops, even the largest cichlids lose their nuptial colors. A few may retain their head stripes into May, but by early June only traces of these markings remain. Through the long rainy months, little fishes up to an inch or two long,

---

1. D. L. G. Noakes and G. W. Barlow, "Ontogeny of parent-contacting in young *Cichlasoma citrinellum* (Pisces, Cichlidae)," *Behaviour*, 46 (1973): 221–255.

and devoid of distinguishing marks, are much more prominent in the rock pools than grown individuals, in part because they swim about freely, seeking food, while the bigger ones stay much of the time beneath the rocks. Although invisible to me, they may keep a watchful eye upon what is happening in the pool. If I throw a scrap of wood or a small green fruit upon the surface, one or more may promptly dart out and up to seize it. After being deceived a few times, they fail to respond to such inedible objects.

Sometimes I wonder how the fishes survive the flood waters that at intervals rush through the channel, carrying trunks and driftwood, shifting the rocks beneath which they doubtless seek shelter. Probably some are crushed when the boulders roll, a disaster that must occur more frequently in the main river, where the current is stronger. Nevertheless, many of the tiny cichlids live to grow up, acquire nuptial colors, mate, and lay eggs when the dry season returns.

A rarer inhabitant of the rock pools is a slender fish, up to about five inches long, with a narrow golden stripe along the ridge of its back. This stripe has thin dusky margins, and at each end is a conspicuous patch of black. The tail is tinged with red. I watched two of these Golden-backs, alike in coloration but differing slightly in size, keep close company as they swam through a pool, as though they were a mated pair. They stayed together for at least three weeks, but I have never found this species with young.

One morning, while I sat motionless beside a rock pool watching the fishes, a half-grown Gray Basilisk lizard ran through the tangled vegetation along the bank and climbed far up the trunk of a slender, vine-draped tree. Following the lizard more slowly came a shiny black Zopilota snake,[2] about seven feet long. The pur-

2. The name "Zopilota" is also applied to the yellow-and-black *Spilotes pullatus*, but I have more often heard the latter called "Mica."

suer started up the tree through the vines, sensing the trunk with its long, thin, forked tongue. When the snake was halfway up, the lizard jumped, falling into the bushes on the bank, amid which it promptly vanished. Thereupon, the serpent slowly turned around and slid out upon a leafy bough on the side from which the basilisk had leapt. Here it delayed a good while, before it descended almost to the ground and slid away through low bushes in the direction the fugitive had taken. I hoped that the basilisk was already out of danger.

Once, as I walked along a forest path, a smaller lizard scurried across in front of me, pursued by a Zopilota that almost bumped into me. On another occasion, I rescued a squealing frog from a Zopilota's jaws. These big snakes are reputed to prey largely upon other reptiles, including venomous serpents, for which reason they receive legal protection in Brazil, where the species is known as the *mussurana*. Although other nonvenomous snakes flee when threatened by man, the Zopilota holds its ground and may even turn upon its assailant with open mouth.

I have nearly always found black Zopilotas upon the ground. But one day, when I followed the rocky channel down to its meeting with the river and walked upward along the latter, past the swimming pool, something shiny on a high bough that extended horizontally above the channel caught my eye. Until I focused my binoculars upon the shiny object, I could not make out what it was. A large black Zopilota was stretched along the branch in the sunshine! I had never seen one of these snakes half so high. As I stood watching it, an involuntary shiver ran along my spine, although I was certain that I was in no danger.

I began to reflect upon the snake's powerful grip upon the human mind and emotions. Why have serpents been deified by some races and regarded as the embodiment of evil by others? Why, when people who frequent tropical forests

GRAY BASILISK LIZARD ▶

meet, does their conversation so often turn to snakes, when the forests contain many more amiable creatures? Why do some people, especially daring youngsters, make pets of snakes, while others can hardly force themselves to touch them? Why did I shiver so irrationally as I stood looking up at that Zopilota sunning itself and doubtless unaware of my presence?

The reason can hardly be that some snakes are dangerous, able suddenly to inflict death in a peculiarly painful form. Other things equally or more dangerous fail to affect us so powerfully. Is it because a snake has so few attributes of animality that it hardly seems to be an animal, but rather a creature of a unique category, as though a length of vine became able to creep rapidly through the herbage and slither up trees? It is the only large, widespread terrestrial animal that moves without limbs. It has no evident ears and cannot close its lidless eyes. Its only sound is a hiss, and, although sometimes gregarious, as when many mass together in winter torpidity, it is never really social. With few exceptions, including certain pythons, it is devoid of parental solicitude, never caring for its young.

Many mammals and birds are likewise inveterate predators; but, by attachment to their mates, devotion to their young, a more or less developed social life, and often, too, certain indications of playfulness and joy in living, they may stir our sympathy. The serpent is stark predation, the predatory existence in its baldest, least mitigated form. It might be characterized as an elongated, distensible stomach, with the minimum of accessories needed to fill and propagate this maw—not even teeth that can tear its food. It crams itself with animal life that is often warm and vibrant, to prolong an existence in which we detect no joy and no emotion. It reveals the depths to which evolution can sink when it takes the downward path and strips animals to the irreducible minimum able to perpetuate a predatory life in its naked horror. The contemplation of such an existence has a horrid fascination for the human mind and distresses a sensitive spirit.

In the wet season, when more water flows through the lower pools, even on days when the river does not enter the head of the rocky channel, I can rarely see the fishes as clearly as I do in the dry season when the surface is smooth, for now the stronger current ruffles the water with irregular patterns of little waves that distort objects viewed through them. Sometimes I sit on a poolside rock, fascinated by the patterns of light and shadow that sunshine throws upon the shallow bottom, especially by dark round patches, each narrowly margined by a bright yellow rim. From the size of a small coin up to an inch or two in diameter, these dark circles rimmed with light glide downstream a short way before they vanish. Often they can be seen to revolve, and sometimes two fuse into one.

These figures puzzled me, until I noticed that they are formed by tiny whirlpools that develop where gently flowing water slips past the edge of a projecting stone or one very shallowly submerged. By their centrifugal action, these whirlpools dimple the water surface with slight concavities, which, bending the sun's rays outward, make bright rings around dark shadows. Strange that I had never before noticed this phenomenon, which must be common enough!

Nature, even in her destructive moods, sometimes gives more than she takes. By sending a raging torrent through the farm, she deprived us for years of easy access to several of our most fertile acres, and to our best swimming pool. But, as compensation, the rocky channel that was finally left almost dry furnished the opportunity to learn things that otherwise I would have missed. It offered me wholesome exercise clambering over the rocks, and many hours of quiet contemplation in the sunshine. Nature's bounty is inexhaustible.

17. The Singing Wood-Rail

On my first visit to Central America, I dwelt for half a year in a house set amid beautiful shrubbery and trees, close by a broad lagoon that wound with many a turn down to the Caribbean Sea. The lagoon, an old channel of the Changuinola River in western Panama, was bordered by tall wild canes, huge-leafed herbs, and vine-draped trees. Behind this fringing vegetation stretched great plantations of cacao and bananas. Multitudes of birds of many kinds swam in the still water, flew above it, or lurked in the dense marginal thickets. Sometimes, especially in late afternoons of April and May, my attention was held by a series of ringing notes, floating up to the house from the shores of the lagoon. Clear and loud, *tick tock, tock tick, tick tock tock tock tock tick* sounded in the distance—at least that is how I heard it then. At times an answering refrain seemed to come from the mate of the first bird. The effectiveness of this remarkable performance, the sense of mystery that it evoked, was increased by its sudden beginning and equally abrupt ending. I waited in vain for its repetition.

On my last day in this fascinating region, I went for a farewell voyage on the lagoon, paddled in a dugout canoe by the black man who took care of the garden. Pointing out a large rail that foraged beneath a spreading tree on the shore, he assured me that this bird was the author of the sounds that had so impressed me. Since he was a keen observer of nature, I had no doubt that he was right; but a decade passed before I succeeded in confirming this information.

It was not until I came to live in El General, some years later, that I became familiar with this elusive rail, a slow process that has taken a long while. One morning, on my way to collect plants, I met along the road a man with a pair of the woven saddlebags used by Costa Rican country people slung over a shoulder. From one of the pouches protruded the head of a bird, whose body was stuffed inside. Noticing my interest, the wayfarer stopped and offered to sell it to me, explaining that it was a *chirincoco* (pronounced with all the syllables almost equally stressed), which he had caught in a drop-trap. After some bargaining, he reduced his price to two *colones* (then about thirty cents), and I bought the bird.

It was a Gray-necked Wood-Rail, a long-legged, short-tailed bird about thirteen inches in length. Its back was brownish olive, deepening to black on the rump and tail. Its head and neck were largely gray, with a white patch on the throat. The breast, sides, and upper abdomen were a lovely orange-chestnut. But what chiefly impressed me was my captive's beautiful, bright red eyes. After carefully examining the bird's plumage, I untied its legs and released it in the next woodland through which we passed. I was delighted by the alacrity it displayed in jumping from my hands and running into the neighboring undergrowth.

Not long after this, while I sat in a blind watching a burrow of the Buff-throated Automolus in the low bank of a stream that meandered through second-growth woodland, I heard a deep, hollow note emanating from the thicket on the farther shore. Presently, a wood-rail came into view, walking with slow, measured steps over the level ground at the top of the bank. It pushed aside fallen leaves with its short, green-and-yellow bill, searching for food, then stood erect and repeated the sounds that I had just heard. They reminded me of the plunking noise made by the entry of air into a very large, nearly empty bottle from which water is being poured, or the striking of some hollow, yielding, nonmetallic body. The bird's throat swelled with each repetition of the peculiar note, but its bill was kept closed.

Soon the rail was joined by its lagging mate, and the two proceeded silently with long, deliberate strides of their bright red legs, until they passed from view around the bend of the stream. Soon after they vanished, I heard another call—the long-continued song, of which the bird's local name, *chir-in-co-co*, is an excellent rendering. This was, so far, my most intimate encounter with a free wood-rail, and the best evidence I had yet obtained that it is, in fact, the author of the far-carrying notes that made such a lasting impression on my mind during my first visit to Central America.

Two years after this meeting, I came to Los Cusingos, where wood-rails live amid tall, tangled, second-growth woods beside the creek that flows into the Río Peñas Blancas in front of the house, and in other areas of low, light woodland. Occasionally I have seen them on the hill behind the house, a hundred feet above a rivulet, but I have never met them in heavy forest with light undergrowth. Of late years, they have been entering the shady garden, to eat fallen fruits of an African Oil Palm; and sometimes they venture close to the house, evidently to pick up scraps thrown out for the chickens. The moment they find themselves observed, they run with long strides back toward the tangled vegetation along the creek. Here in Costa Rica, I have never had six wood-rails in view at one time, as I did on the bare muddy shore of a sluggish stream on the llanos of Venezuela.

With few exceptions, all of my most revealing meetings with the retiring wood-rail have come while I sat in a blind, watching the nest of some other bird. Once, when the blind was set in a field densely overgrown with head-high weeds, in view of a nest of Pale-billed Woodpeckers, a wood-rail approached along the narrow path that led to it. When the bird came in view of the strange object that

GRAY-NECKED WOOD-RAIL, OPOSSUM ▶

concealed me, it hesitated, as though doubting whether it would be safe to pass. Finally, it made a detour around the blind. As it passed through the dense growth around me, I heard a sort of resonant moan, a deep, full note, such as I could make in my throat with closed lips.

Wood-rails sing through much of the year, from January into October, but they are most vocal in April, May, and June, the first three months of the long rainy season, when the majority of our birds of many kinds sing and nest most freely. They perform more in wet, cloudy weather than on bright, dry days. They may be heard at almost any hour of the day, and also at night, not only while the moon shines but even in the dense darkness of a clouded, starless night. As the famous ornithologist Frank M. Chapman long ago pointed out, their performance is, at least at times, a duet; and the two performers are often decidedly unequal in musical ability. This became clear to me one day in July, while I sat in a blind in the coffee plantation watching a Blue-black Grosbeak's nest. One rail sang at the edge of the thicket in front of me, another along the stream to my right. The notes reaching me from widely separated points left no doubt that they emanated from two throats. The duetists, doubtless mated birds, kept perfect time; and the voices of both sounded somewhat strained or cracked.

With other pairs, however, it has appeared to me that one member delivers a loud, clear, resonant *chirin co chirin co chirin co co co co chirin co*, while a weak, cracked voice tries to accompany the first, forming a bizarre contrast. Accordingly, the rails' song is more pleasing and effective when the birds are so far away that only the clear, ringing notes reach the hearer, than when they are nearby and the performance is marred by an undercurrent of cackling. I was impressed with this one April morning when the *chirincocos* sang alternately from the thicket beside the garden and from the streamside about a hundred yards away. From the stream, only the melodious notes reached and delighted me by their long-continued flow. But soon the rails would come closer, and the cracked notes intruded most annoyingly. Then, after a while, the rails returned to the lower level, and the song recovered its arresting beauty. This continued for almost a quarter of an hour. A single song may last a minute or two, with hardly a pause. I have heard this *chirincoco* song up to nearly four thousand feet in Costa Rica, and near Valencia in northern Venezuela, where it sounded much the same as at Los Cusingos.

In addition to the booming sound, which I have rarely heard, and the loud, long-continued duet, the rails have a third utterance, an extremely harsh, stentorian cackle, suggestive of intense excitement or alarm. I have repeatedly heard this arresting cackle issue from the thicket across the creek and hurried down, only to have it cease before I could come in view of its source. But soon after sunrise, on another day in April, I cautiously approached in time to see a large opossum chasing a rail along the rocky stream shore, beneath spreading Riverwood trees. The bird ran or walked ahead, while the marsupial lumbered clumsily in pursuit. Twice I clearly saw that one member of the pair of rails was following the opossum while the latter pursued its mate. They turned off into the bushes on the farther side of the stream, then, after a while, emerged again on the shore. Thus the pursuit ran in circles, at the same time moving slowly upstream, until all three participants vanished amid dense vegetation. Once, while the chase continued, I heard the rails deliver a few notes of their *chirin co co* song; and they also cackled a little more.

The only explanation of these strange proceedings that occurred to me was that the rails had eggs or chicks hidden nearby, and that one was luring the opossum from them, while the other followed to watch, or to deflect the animal if it turned back. In somewhat similar fashion, domestic chickens sometimes walk slowly, with upstretched necks, toward a small animal that alarms or perplexes them.

In chapter four, I told how the rails visited the thatched shed, to pick up grains of maize that fell from the raised storage bin to the dusty ground where the horses stood, but were always so shy that I could watch them only from a distance, through field glasses. One September morning soon after sunrise, on the opposite side of the pasture where the shed stood, I saw a wood-rail emerge from dense shrubbery at the foot of a wooded slope. With elegant steps, it walked over the open ground, at intervals picking up and eating some small object. From time to time, it moved a fallen leaf by flicking it toward itself with its strong bill. Once the rail jumped high to break a cluster of bright blue berries from a shrub of the coffee family at the edge of the woods. Dropping the cluster to the ground, it picked off and swallowed the berries, one by one.

Then it resumed its sedate walk over the close-cropped grass, constantly twitching its short, uptilted, black tail. Sometimes a ripple began in its slender neck and flowed along the body to the tail. It never ventured more than a yard or two from the thicket; and when a pigeon flew by, it slipped inside the bushes, to emerge a few seconds later. When the rail walked into bright sunshine, it spread its lovely chestnut wings and held both almost horizontally, with its little black tail and under-tail coverts sticking up between them, where they did not seem to belong. For a minute or two, the rail stood this way, its back toward the sun. Then it folded its wings, resumed its walk, and soon vanished into the thicket. This was my most prolonged view of a wood-rail while I stood unconcealed.

Beside the coffee grove grow some Pejibaye palms, whose tall, slender trunks, bristling with long, needlelike, black thorns, bear spreading crowns of graceful, plumy fronds. The fruits, about the size of plums, are borne in heavy, compact clusters just below the leaves. When they begin to ripen in June or July, tanagers, finches, woodpeckers, and other birds flock to feast on them, dropping to the ground many fragments and half-eaten fruits, and some that are whole.

The wood-rails come from the neighboring streamside thicket to devour these fragments made available to them by smaller birds, but they are so wary that I have been able to see them do so only while hidden in a blind. In the course of one morning, I witnessed four visits by a rail, whether always the same individual, I could not tell. It never stayed in the open long enough to swallow what it found, but each time it hurried off holding the whitish fragment of unripe fruit in its bill. On the first three occasions it carried the morsel right back into the thicket beyond the palms, but on the fourth visit, it walked through the edge of the plantation, between the coffee bushes, taking long strides and looking cautiously from side to side, then breaking into a run as it neared the bank of the stream, where it vanished into dense shrubbery. With its long red legs, orange-chestnut breast, big red eyes, and green-and-yellow bill, how bright the rail appeared as it crossed the open spaces of the plantation!

Pejibayes are edible by humans only after they have been well cooked, which is usually done with salt; when raw, they sting the mouth. But birds appear not to be troubled by the stinging sensation, if indeed they feel it. Dry maize, juicy berries, and palm fruits are the only foods that I have distinctly seen the rails eat, although doubtless their diet includes a variety of insects, worms, frogs, lizards, small snakes, and other creatures that they find beneath fallen leaves that they push aside with their bills. One day, while I watched a Royal Flycatcher, a wood-rail jumped with a noisy splash into the shallow rivulet above which the flycatcher's long nest hung, frightening her from her eggs. Apparently, the rail was trying to catch a small fish or tadpole. Gray-necked Wood-Rails that live at the edges of mangrove swamps are reported to eat crabs.

The wood-rail's nest is a large, compact mass of dead leaves and twigs, measuring from twelve to fourteen inches across the top and, in the bulkier examples, about nine inches in height. In the top, lined with twigs, is a shallow depression, in depth sometimes less than the thickness of the eggs it holds. Unlike the nests of some of the smaller members of the rail family, it is open rather than roofed. It resembles the masses of dead leaves and branchlets that often accumulate in tangles of vines, and I would not have paid much attention to the first that I found if a rail had not slipped from it as I approached. The three nests that I have seen in El General were at heights of from six to ten feet in dense, vine-laden thickets or light second-growth woods. Each contained three large, strongly ovate eggs, about two inches long by nearly an inch and a half in diameter, which were dull white, spotted and blotched with bright rusty brown and pale lilac. These markings were heaviest on the thick end but sparsely scattered over the remaining surface. All these nests were discovered in the early part of the rainy season, from mid-April to the first week of July.

On the island of Trinidad, according to Sir Charles Belcher and G. D. Smooker,[1] this wood-rail builds a deep bowl of small twigs, dry weed stems, fibers, and leaves, and lines it with green bamboo leaves. Nests are placed from three to twenty feet above the ground, or at times eight feet or more above the edge of a waterway. These authors found eggs from late May well into August, in sets larger than I have seen in El General. They considered five to be the normal

1. Charles Belcher and G. D. Smooker, "Birds of the colony of Trinidad and Tobago," part 2, *Ibis*, 13th series, 5 (1935): 279–297.

complement, but they found up to seven in a nest, and, at the other extreme, sets of only three or four eggs, which they surmised were second layings.

Belcher and Smooker believed that if a nest is touched by a human hand, the rail sometimes destroys the eggs and deserts it, and this may happen if the sitting bird is merely suddenly flushed.[2] My own experience is different. When I found my first nest, in a tangle of climbing Razor-Sedge in light woods near the coffee plantation where I saw the rails eat Pejibaye fruits, I measured the eggs. Nevertheless, the rails continued to incubate. On the following day, one watched me from the nest, while I looked at it from a distance of only three or four yards. Hoping to learn something about the *chirincocos'* domestic arrangements, I then set up a blind and screened it with leafy boughs, which caused the rails to stay away. When, later in the day, I found the eggs cold, I promptly removed the offending blind; but still the birds refused to return to their nest.

The second nest, ten feet up in a very dense tangle of vines that draped a spreading tree, was discovered by a laborer while cutting down light woods to plant bananas. The rail continued to incubate while he worked, noisily felling trees. It slipped from the eggs only when he cut two tall saplings so near that they fell against the vines in the midst of which it sat, hidden from view. When the boy took me to see his discovery, the rail, who had resumed incubation, remained at its post while we stood beneath the nest, but unobtrusively vanished when I turned away to cut a stick to which I attached a mirror that would reveal what the nest held. Next day incubation continued, at the very edge of the new clearing, where work had been suspended for the benefit of the rails and the studies that I hoped to make. But two days later the eggs had vanished, probably taken by some predator.

2. Ibid.

My third nest, situated eight feet up in a dense tangle of bushes and vines in a low second-growth thicket, not far from a rivulet, was without eggs when found on May 18, 1947. By half-past seven on the morning of May 22, three eggs had been laid. In the following days, I four times found a rail sitting on them, so well concealed by the leaves that clustered thickly around that I could see nothing of it except from a single point, where a gap in the foliage permitted a view of its head from the eye up and part of its bill—nothing more. It sat motionless and steadfastly returned my gaze. I never touched these eggs, viewing them only in a mirror raised on a stick; but by May 29 the nest was empty, with fragments of shells scattered over the ground below, apparently the work of some mammalian predator. Because of the premature loss of all my nests, I have never seen the *chirincoco*'s newly hatched chicks, nor have I ever met parents leading downy or half-grown young through the woodland or thickets.

My fragmentary observations at least demonstrate that the wood-rail is a shrewd bird, not fleeing from its eggs the moment a man comes into view, but sticking to its post until it is likely that it has been observed, then slipping away unobtrusively when the possible observer is not looking. I suspect that rails rank high in the scale of avian intelligence.

While prowling through dense bushy growth across the creek where the wood-rails live, in May some years ago, I discovered a platform composed of dead leaves, weed stalks, and coarse bits of vegetation, situated six feet up in a shrub at the edge of a marshy opening. It measured ten by twelve inches across the top and was about four inches thick. The top was hard and compacted, as though it had long been in use, and so flat, without the least rim, that an egg laid upon it would have been in danger of rolling off. Although canopied above by a tangle of vines, it was completely exposed on the side toward the marsh, from the farther edge of which it was visible.

Surmising that this was a rail's sleeping platform, after nightfall I waded the stream and stole up as silently as the tangled vegetation permitted. When in a favorable position, I threw the beam of my flashlight upon the platform. There, sitting beneath the canopy of vines, staring into the blinding rays with a big red eye and nervously twitching its short tail, was a *chirincoco*, whose sleep I had rudely interrupted. After taking one good look, I turned off the light and crept away as quietly as I could.

Next day, I returned to search for the dormitory of this bird's mate, or its nest and eggs; but my quest was fruitless. Since the surrounding thicket was so dense that I could hardly move without opening a path with my machete, and visibility was limited to a few yards, I might have passed close by what I sought without finding it. Or perhaps the rail's mate simply roosted in a bush, without a platform. In Panama, Alexander Wetmore discovered Gray-necked Wood-Rails resting at night two or three yards above water, or above the ground close by a stream or swamp, often in an exposed situation. He also found them moving about at night, usually in the hour or two after sunset, or while the moon shone.[3]

Since I discovered the sleeping platform, I often wonder, when the *chirin co co* song rings out in the night, whether the rails are performing on such platforms or wandering over the ground in the dark. This is one of the many questions about the life of the elusive *chirincoco* that will doubtless long await an answer.

3. Alexander Wetmore, "The birds of the Republic of Panamá," part 1, *Smithsonian Miscellaneous Collections*, vol. 150 (Washington, D.C., 1965).

18. The Flame-of-the-Forest Tree

WHEN I came to Los Cusingos, it certainly did not lack trees. Close by the site that I chose for my house was a large tract of rain forest that I was proud to call my own. Possibly some or all of this wooded land had been cleared and cultivated by the Indians who had left enigmatic carvings on the huge rock beside the creek. But if the aborigines had indeed cleared the land, it was so long ago that the forest now looked mature, with such a great variety of trees that, in nearly forty years, I have not identified all their kinds. Season after season, I have looked in vain for flowers on the lofty crowns of some of them. Among the hardwood trees grew many tall, slender palms, including Chontas with straight, columnar trunks propped high above the ground on spiny, spreading stilt roots. Great woody vines, sometimes as thick as my waist, hung from the massive boughs of the larger trees or lay coiled upon the ground, brought down by their weight.

The few trees with colorful flowers bloomed chiefly from March to May, as the short dry season gave way to the long rainy season. Then the towering Large-leaved Jacaranda displayed glorious masses of lavender flowers above the forest's roof, and the Mayos became a vision of delight in gold and glossy green. But through the long wet months from July to December, little color relieved the verdure that spread, in varying shades, from the sonorous mountain torrent in front of my home site almost to the craggy summits of Cerro Chirripó, which rose above intervening wooded ridges in the north.

Since color cheers the spirit, I set about to correct this deficiency. In a Guava tree beside the house I attached a board, on which I daily placed bananas. Little by little, birds formed the habit of coming for the ripe fruit, until I had an almost constant stream of brilliant visitors: eleven species of tanagers, five honeycreepers, two woodpeckers, Blue-diademed Motmots, and, in the months of the northern winter, Baltimore Orioles resplendent in orange and black. Including four less colorful resident finches, plainly attired Gray's Thrushes, Lesser Elaenias, Tennessee Warblers, and rarities such as Red-headed Barbets, Orchard Orioles, and migrating Indigo Buntings, my feeder eventually attracted thirty species of birds.

As I rode my horse about the valley, I sometimes saw colorful shrubs clustering around the thatched cabin of a settler. A request for a cutting or seeds was never denied. I brought back in my saddlebags, and planted around my new house on the terrace overlooking the river, hibiscus bushes with great red or pink flowers, Caña de India with broad leaves of red and green, Codiaeum shrubs with variegated foliage, Allamanda vines that bore large yellow trumpets, and, for a hedge, the straggling Stachytarpheta, whose clustered purple florets attracted a large variety of hummingbirds.

Although colorful shrubbery was what I chiefly needed, I had room for a few more trees. From a coffee planter in the center of the country, I received seeds of the Small-leaved Jacaranda and the African Flame-of-the-Forest tree. I made a nursery far from the house, on a plot of ground prepared for me by an old man, who in this manner paid me for its use in the preceding year. When showers were falling almost every afternoon and the seedling trees were a few inches high, I dug

them carefully, wrapped the ball of earth around the roots of each in a broad Shell-flower leaf, and carried them up to the house in my knapsack, a few at a time. Some were planted on the terrace where the house stood, others on the low, stony ground between it and the river.

The Small-leaved Jacaranda grew slowly but never flowered, doubtless because the climate was not right for this tree from northern Argentina. One of the chief adornments of Costa Rica's Central Valley during the dry season, this blue-flowered tree would be a welcome addition to the cultivated flora of El General if it flourished here. Although no more spectacular than the native Large-leaved Jacaranda, it could be planted closer to dwellings because it does not grow half as tall.

The Flame-of-the-Forest trees, or Tulip trees, thrived as though they were in their native Africa. They shot straight upward so rapidly that when three years old they were slender, branchless poles about twenty feet high. Then they began to put forth lateral boughs, heavy with pairs of long, compound leaves that reminded me of the foliage of the walnut. When the trees were only four or five years old, compact clusters of pointed, incurved flower buds appeared at the ends of the branches. Each brown, furry bud was turgid with a colorless, unpalatable liquid that spurted out when the bud was strongly squeezed. Although far from common, such water-filled buds are widespread among tropical plants and apparently protect the flowers, developing in a liquid medium, from the attacks of insects. When the buds were as long as a finger, each split along the outer side to release a great, bright red trumpet flower, as large as a tulip. Soon these trees of the bignonia family glowed with color.

Profuse flowering and fruiting did not retard the growth of the Flame-of-the-

Forest trees. When only nine or ten years old, they were from sixty to seventy feet high, with massive trunks and great, spreading domes of deep green foliage that made an effective background for the clusters of flamboyant blossoms. Through most of the rainy second half of the year, the trees continued to bloom generously, providing just the touch of color needed to enliven the wide, verdant landscape over which I looked from my front porch. In the dry season, the long, flat, woody pods split open, releasing masses of thin, winged seeds that the wind bore over neighboring fields and thickets. After a while, spontaneous seedlings sprang up here and there, and some survived to flower.

Color attracts color, especially in the tropics. To the bright red blossoms of the Flame-of-the-Forest trees were added the scarlet, orange, yellow, glittering green, deep blue, and turquoise of the tanagers, orioles, honeycreepers, humming-birds, and other feathered visitors that probed the trumpet flowers for insects and nectar or hunted through the foliage for caterpillars and spiders. What a brilliant display the birds and flowers made in the bright beams of the rising sun!

Sometimes, when I stood watching the birds in a Flame-of-the-Forest tree while the sun still hung low above the wooded ridge across the river, a flock of great Scarlet Macaws came from the east, as though riding down the level sun-beams. Two by two they flew, with steady, laborious wing beats, their long tails streaming like slender pennants behind their heavy bodies, their scarlet under-plumage glowing vividly where touched by the horizontal rays. As the macaws passed overhead, their raucous shouts made them as objectionable to the ear as they were pleasing to the eye. Often these flamboyant birds flew directly above the flamboyant crown of a Flame-of-the-Forest tree, in a gorgeous display such as one expects of tropical nature.

Sometimes a few of the macaws would settle to rest or eat high in trees at the edge of the neighboring forest, where, from the house, I could admire the bright yellow and blue of their wings, contrasting with the scarlet of their bodies. Most, however, continued over the crest of the ridge that rose steeply behind the house. After foraging all day on fruits in the forests to our west, the scarlet birds returned eastward in the late afternoon, often flying through rain, or beneath gloomy clouds that dimmed their splendor. Most of the macaws were in pairs that flew wing to wing, with an interval separating them from other pairs; but the larger flocks usually contained a few single birds who seemed to be trying to intrude into mated couples.

Like many trees that grow rapidly, my Flame-of-the-Forest trees did not live long. Only twelve years after I planted them, those in the rich but stony black loam beside the river began to die. After all their aerial parts were dead, some sent up numerous sprouts from their roots. Now I began to pay for the colorful displays that for seven or eight years they had given me. After they have provided us with shade, flowers, or fruits for many years, other trees end their bounteous lives by giving us firewood or timber. Not so the weedy Flame-of-the-Forest trees, whose wood, although tough, is too soft and sappy to make good fuel or boards. The removal of their leafless skeletons was strenuous, unproductive labor.

One of the dead trees, situated where its sudden fall would do no harm, was permitted to stand until it rotted away. After decay had softened the branchless trunk, a pair of Baird's Trogons came out of the neighboring forest and carved a nest cavity in it. The male, resplendent in metallic green and violet-blue upper plumage, vermilion abdomen, and white outer tail feathers, shared the labor of excavation with his duller mate, and each day he took a long turn on the two white eggs that she laid in it. These eggs were overrun by Fire Ants, which caused the interruption of incubation but failed to penetrate the shells. Although the trogons continued to warm them for fifty-one days, or three times the normal incubation period, they failed to hatch. The following year the trogons returned, laid three eggs, and hatched two nestlings, which were taken by some predator before they could fly. In four consecutive years, the trogons nested in this stub, each year carving their chamber lower, as decay reduced its height. All their attempts to rear a brood failed, but not before I had added to the scientific knowledge of the habits of these lovely birds.

The Flame-of-the-Forest trees on the terrace by the house lived longer than those on the richer soil near the river; but, seventeen years after I planted the seeds, all but one had died. This lone survivor was an exceptionally large specimen of *Spathodea campanulata*, about eighty feet tall, with an irregularly ridged and furrowed trunk two and a half feet in diameter at breast height. When covered with bloom in the wet season, its great, rounded dome was a landmark visible from afar. Each dry season, when it shed all its leaves and appeared to be dead, we felt sure that the patriarch had flowered for the last time. But in April or May, when rain was falling freely again, little green buds would push out from the sides of the thick, stiff terminal twigs, some distance inward from their lifeless tips. Growing rapidly, these sprouts soon covered the lofty crown with foliage as profuse as it had ever borne; and soon it was ablaze with flowers. Thus, for a number of years, the tree continued to put forth new leafy twigs without becoming taller, although it continued to increase in girth.

Standing in solitary splendor, the Flame-of-the-Forest tree still attracted a multitude of small, colorful birds. But no longer did huge-billed toucans with yellow breasts come from the neighboring forest to rest on its limbs; no longer did noisy flocks of macaws fly over its crown. These inhabitants of ancient forests,

along with many others, had been killed or driven away by the flood of hungry settlers that swept down the valley, felled the trees, and shot the larger wild creatures.

Ironically, this highest and longest-lived of my Flame-of-the-Forest trees
stood just where we did not want a tall tree. While it was still of moderate size,
we had built a laborer's cottage not far from it. Occasionally, the man climbed into
the tree and, with his long machete, lopped off branches that pushed out toward
his dwelling. There was little danger that it would fall on his house in calm weather. But, at long intervals, our sheltered valley, which for years may know only gentle breezes, is visited by a violent windstorm that may attain such intensity that it
blows over trees. As the oldest Flame-of-the-Forest tree grew more imposing, we
became increasingly concerned about what might happen if one of these miniature
hurricanes struck it. Since the tree could not be felled without doing much damage
in the garden, we planned a drastic pruning, in the dry weather when it was leafless. But, before this could be done, fiercely stinging wasps built nests high in the
Flame-of-the-Forest tree and in an avocado tree close beside it. Because these insects might have attacked anyone who began to chop in the treetop, causing his
fall, I would not run the risk of sending up a climber.

Accordingly, the big Flame-of-the-Forest tree continued to flourish into the
twentieth year of its life. In July of this year, while I was briefly absent from the
farm, a violent wind tore away half of the beautiful, elegantly foliaged Dipterodendron tree in front of the house, uprooted two Guava trees, destroyed some
Pejibaye palms, and damaged trees that shaded the coffee plantation. Since such
windstorms had been coming only at long intervals, I believed that they would not
afflict us again for many months.

In less than a fortnight, our confidence was rudely shattered. As we sat at early supper on Sunday evening, light clouds covered the sky, and the air was calm. Suddenly a tempest struck the house, driving light rain almost horizontally against it. The first blast completed the demolition of the Dipterodendron tree. I rushed to shut doors and windows, and, when next I looked northward, the big Flame-of-the-Forest tree was gone! Striking its wide, full-foliaged crown, a gust had uprooted it, throwing it upon the laborer's cottage.

It was distressing to think of what could have happened, but, at the moment, neighboring trees were bending so alarmingly before the gale that we did not dare to cross the garden and investigate. As soon as the rudest blast had passed, we ran to the scene of the disaster. The Flame-of-the-Forest tree had demolished the semi-detached kitchen at the rear of the cottage. Smoke was rising from the open fire. Our calls brought no response. Was the family pinned beneath the wreckage? Presently, however, the housewife appeared from a nearby shed, with her little daughter and a neighbor's boy. When the big tree bowed menacingly before the wind, they had rushed out just in time to avoid being crushed. The little girl was lightly scratched, either by falling boards or by the topmost twigs of the tree. The rest of the family had not been present when the tree fell.

Two walls of the kitchen had been shattered, and nearly all its roof tiles were broken, but the main part of the cottage was hardly damaged. While I brought water to extinguish the fire, my wife, Pamela, rummaged amid the wreckage, finding that, aside from a few glasses, scarcely any of the simple furnishings had been broken. After everyone else had left, I stood in the dusk, surveying the ruin and recalling how, nearly twenty years before, I had planted the tiny seed from which that great tree had grown. How readily do the things that we start, inno-cently or hopefully, pass beyond our control! The same depressing sense of our inadequacy to govern the spreading consequences of our acts had come over me once before, as I watched a fire that I had set to clear land leap its bounds and burn over several additional acres.

Days of strenuous labor with machete, axe, and poles were needed to cut up the fallen tree, carry off its branches, and roll away the segments of its thick trunk. Then the kitchen had to be replaced. For several years after the disaster, this amazingly vital Flame-of-the-Forest tree was far from dead. Although the stump was turned sideways and connected with the ground by only a few roots, it almost covered itself with vigorous green shoots. When removed, they were promptly re-placed by new growths. Even the short logs from the trunk sprouted, while callus tissue grew out from their ends, where wood and bark met.

Few trees reward one with such a brilliant floral display so soon after they are planted as does the Flame-of-the-Forest. But, on the whole, I prefer trees that grow more slowly, live longer, die more decisively, and are more useful after their sap has dried. I have planted no more Flame-of-the-Forest trees.

19. *Casual Visitors*

EACH year, as days grow short in the Northern Hemisphere, about twenty species of long-distance migrants, chiefly wood warblers, arrive at Los Cusingos. In addition to these birds, which I can confidently expect to appear between August and November, a dozen others that have come for the winter, or are passing through on their way to South America, may be found if I search diligently. Then, early in the following year, three species, the Swallow-tailed Kite, Piratic Flycatcher, and Yellow-green Vireo, come up from the south to nest, and the Lesser Elaenia arrives, probably from the same direction. As the sun swings northward, certain migrants that are rare or absent in autumn pass through in great numbers, including Swainson's Hawks, Cliff Swallows, and Olive-backed Thrushes.

In this chapter I shall tell, not of birds that arrive as regularly as sowing and harvest, but of the unexpected visitors, the real surprises, that I have seen on the farm, perhaps no more than once or twice. Let us begin with the greatest surprise of all. The drizzly morning of October 23, 1973, was followed by an afternoon of steady, hard rain. Looking out the window when daylight was already fading, I saw a Magnificent Frigatebird high overhead. Against the dim sky, it was wholly black; but its long, angular wings made it unmistakable. It came over the forest, from the south, and, flying steadily, disappeared above the house roof, headed toward the ten-thousand foot continental divide.

The oceanic wanderer vanished before I could focus my binoculars on it, and, despite its unique silhouette, I might have mistrusted my identification if I had not, earlier that same year, seen a frigatebird soaring high above Lake Atitlán in Guatemala, a mile high and fifty miles from the Pacific Ocean. Another frigatebird flew above dry woodlands in the Tempisque Valley in the Province of Guanacaste, Costa Rica, at a low altitude but well inland from the Gulf of Nicoya. In Honduras, Burt Monroe, Jr., saw a frigatebird four thousand feet above sea level and one hundred miles inland.[1] These birds often cross the Isthmus of Panama from ocean to ocean, following the forty-mile-long canal. This is understandable, because they are above water all the way, and if high enough they can see both the Pacific Ocean and the Caribbean Sea at the same time. But what are these marine birds seeking, or where are they going, when they wander far inland over high, mountainous country that supplies no food that they are known to eat?

In this high, well-drained valley, where I have never seen a wild duck, I have noticed only one other large water bird that comes up from the coast. Neotropic, or Olivaceous, Cormorants wander far up the wider streams that flow down from the Costa Rican highlands toward either ocean. Rarely, they reach an altitude of five thousand feet. Traveling by rail between San José and Puerto Limón on the Caribbean Sea, one sometimes sees them sunning themselves on rocks in the channel of the turbulent Río Reventazón. Here on the Río Peñas Blancas, I have found cormorants chiefly from July to February, always in the brownish olive plumage of immature individuals, never in their black nuptial attire. They stand in a statuesque attitude on exposed boulders or swim in the rushing current, doubtless in pursuit of fishes. When surprised, the long-necked birds flap along the surface with

1. Burt Monroe, Jr., "A distributional survey of the birds of Honduras," *American Ornithologists' Union. Ornith. Monogr.* no. 7 (1968): 1–458.

much splashing, until they gain enough speed to become airborne. Sometimes one circles up until far above the treetops, then flies off in a straight course, as if bound for some other river that it sees or remembers.

Hardly less surprising than the appearance of an oceanic bird flying over the forest twenty-five miles inland and twenty-five hundred feet above sea level is my failure ever to see here many birds that are abundant on the neighboring wooded slopes, a thousand feet higher and only a few miles away. Even when the clearings that they had to cross were fewer and less extensive than they are today, I never saw some of these species at Los Cusingos. The rare occurrence of a few of them suggests that no insurmountable barrier prevents their visiting us, and emphasizes the stubborn adherence of sedentary tropical birds to their preferred altitudinal life zones. Abundant at slightly higher altitudes, the little Blue-throated Toucanet has been recorded here only once, on November 28, 1963. Apparently it returned promptly to cooler heights, for I never saw it again. The only Immaculate Antbird that I have met here stayed longer, from at least September 6 to September 21, 1958. This almost wholly black follower of army ants is likewise not rare a little higher in the mountains.

Other birds from the higher hills come slightly more often. Rarely, an American Dipper descends the river from its higher reaches for a brief visit to the stretch of broken water beside our farm. It wades up to its flanks in the swiftly flowing current, immersing its head to pluck insect larvae from the rocks, or completely submerges itself to catch tiny fishes. Occasionally, in the interval from November to February, I hear in our woods the beautiful, calm notes that Black-faced Solitaires repeat more freely in the oak forests above us. Very seldom a Rufous-browed Peppershrike proclaims its presence in our treetops. Although in this region it is

◀ THREE-WATTLED BELLBIRD, MALE

rarely heard below three thousand feet, in other parts of its vast range the pepper-shrike lives near sea level.

At long intervals, Blue-hooded Euphonias used to come to eat the berries of a mistletoe that grew profusely upon an Aceituno tree in front of the house. After satisfying their hunger, the elegant blue-black, orange-bellied males would pour forth their rambling songs without set phrasing—a sweet sequence of weak, tinkling notes, now high, now low, that drifted unhurriedly down from the treetop for many minutes together. Since the Aceituno tree died years ago, I have seen no more Blue-hooded Euphonias here.

In July, 1949, while an arborescent melastome was laden with small black berries, Scarlet-thighed Dacnises came in numbers to feast on them, even bringing a well-feathered fledgling, who fluttered his wings vigorously while his mother gave him berries. How the glossy, blue-and-black plumage of the adult males shone in the sun's rays! This invasion was the nearest approach to an avian "irruption," well known in the North Temperate Zone, that I have noticed here. Since that notable visit, I have seen only an occasional Scarlet-thighed Dacnis at Los Cusingos. All of these five species of middle altitudes arrive so unpredictably that I cannot count upon seeing them every year.

A somewhat more frequent visitor from higher slopes is the Red-headed Barbet, a bird as solitary, silent, and unsociable as its relative, the more soberly attired Prong-billed Barbet, is gregarious, vocal, and sociable. Here we have Red-headed Barbets chiefly from October to March, when both males and females may be seen eating bananas at the feeder, although never together. In forest treetops they probe curled dead leaves for the insects and spiders that hide within them, sometimes holding a leaf beneath a foot while they pry it open. Last February, I watched a

AMERICAN DIPPER ▶

female barbet, and then a male, eat the flesh of a shriveled ripe orange that hung in the top of an orange tree at the woodland's edge, while a Speckled Tanager perched nearby, waiting for its turn. In some years, White-ruffed Manakins are not uncommon in our woodland, even in the breeding season, although I have never found them nesting here, where four other kinds of manakins regularly breed, nor giving the charming courtship displays that, at slightly higher altitudes, the males perform at mossy fallen logs in the depths of the forest.

At long intervals, large flocks of little Barred Parakeets have come down from the mountains. Usually they arrive just after sunrise, flying high. After eating for many minutes, they rest invisibly in the crown of a tree with dense foliage; then scores of them erupt all together, in the sudden fashion of parrots, to fly swiftly away. When the afternoon sun sinks low, they return northward toward the mountains. On certain days, these flocks, ranging in size from a few individuals to hundreds, continue to pass for half an hour, often, especially the larger flocks, so high that the birds are only small, vibrant motes against the sky. At other times, they fly so low that, with the sun behind me, I can distinguish the light green of their plumage and their short, rapidly twinkling wings. These low-flying flocks sometimes circle around to gain altitude, before they head northward toward the high cordillera. The parakeets fly with the bright, sharp chirping of innumerable small voices, which call attention to them even when they are hardly more than dark specks in the sky. On some afternoons a dozen flocks, large and small, pass over or in front of the house. Barred Parakeets come most often in February, to eat the seeds in the tiny rayed achenes of the Burío tree; but in 1962 multitudes arrived in July, when they feasted upon the small, black berries of an arborescent miconia, and perhaps other fruits. They were shy and difficult to watch while they ate.

Lately, these diminutive parrots, like other members of their family, have been coming less frequently, and in smaller numbers, than they did two decades ago.

Another visitor from the higher mountains, chiefly in the dry season, is the larger Sulphur-winged Parakeet. These parrots arrive in smaller, swifter flocks, flying lower, the yellow on their wings flashing, shrill voices causing me to look upward just in time to see them vanish over the treetops. After foraging for a while in the woodland, they return, as swiftly and noisily as they came, to the mountain forests where they roost. I have not learned what they eat in the forest at Los Cusingos, but at higher altitudes I saw them devouring the small fruits of a huge wild fig tree. Once, high in a mountain pasture, I watched five of them in a great oak tree. Instead of resting in obvious pairs, preening only their mates, as many parrots do, the five huddled together and preened or nibbled one another indiscriminately. At intervals, their peaceful companionship was interrupted by a noisy squabble, with much wing flapping; but whether they disputed for preferred perches or for partners, I could not tell. After each brief flare-up, they would settle down in a compact cluster once more. This behavior suggested that these little-known parakeets have unusual social habits that would well repay study. Perhaps the nest is attended by more than a single pair, or they may cluster together for warmth on frosty mountain nights.

No wanderer from higher altitudes is more erratic and unpredictable than the Three-wattled Bellbird. The male's stentorian calls, often sounding more wooden than bell-like, leave no doubt that he has arrived; but one may spend fruitless hours trying to glimpse the handsome, foot-long bird, for he perches at the top of one of the highest trees, where his bright brown body, pure white head and neck, and three dark, stringlike wattles hanging from the base of his broad black bill are all screened from earth-bound man by masses of foliage. In some years, bellbirds are present at Los Cusingos during certain months and in other years during other months; they may arrive unexpectedly at any season. Only once did I hear them throughout an entire year; and then they may have nested here, since I saw one individual in the streaked, greenish plumage of females and young birds. However, these cotingas that wander down to sea level appear to breed chiefly in highland forests above five thousand feet, where the males call most persistently in the first half of the year. Little is known of the nesting of this bird, which makes itself so conspicuous by its voice.

All these occasional visitors from higher slopes represent a small minority of the species that live up there, too few to invalidate the generalization that most tropical birds cling stubbornly to the altitudinal life zone where they nest. Of birds that reside on the mountains over which I look, I have never seen a Resplendent Quetzal here, nor a Collared Trogon, Band-tailed Pigeon, Acorn Woodpecker, Highland Wood-Wren, Slate-throated Redstart, White-winged Tanager, Common Bush-Tanager, Yellow-throated Brush-Finch, and many others that I might find a thousand feet or so—the height of the tallest skyscrapers—above my home.

Wandering hummingbirds give many surprises. Last May, while the young photographer Paul Feyling was making a nature film at Los Cusingos, he described a hummer that he had photographed at close range. Not recognizing it from his description, I went to see it. The large hummingbird, resplendent in glittering metallic green, deep blue, violet, and purple, was perching just where Paul had found it, in a large, spreading shrub of *Hamelia patens* beside the banana plantation. After visiting a number of the tubular red flowers, it consistently returned to the same perch, a slender dead twig of the shrub that supplied its nectar. Although it could be approached closely, I watched long before I saw it at just the proper angle to catch a fleeting glimpse of the small, intensely bright, orange-red patch that clinched its identity as a Fiery-throated Hummingbird—the first I had ever seen below six or seven thousand feet. Evidently it had come much farther than the dipper, the solitaire, the dacnis, the barbet, and other visitors that live only a little higher than Los Cusingos.

This amazingly tame hummingbird repeatedly permitted us to stretch up our hands above our heads and gently touch its tail. Once it remained on its preferred perch while I slowly closed a hand around it; but, just in time to avoid being caught, it slipped between my fingers and fled with squeaky notes of alarm—the only time I heard it utter a sound. Immediately after this narrow escape from a brief sojourn in my hand, it was slightly more cautious and alighted on more distant perches. Soon, however, it returned to rest where I could touch it again. Probably it had hatched in remote mountains where men never appeared. I surmised that it was a young bird seeking a territory, and I was certain that, although it had found abundant food, it would never remain so far below its life zone. After twelve days, it vanished.

Another rare visitor from higher altitudes is the Green-crowned Brilliant. For almost a month in late April and May of 1948, a female of this large hummingbird could be found almost daily in the same part of the forest, and, during part of this interval, a young male in immature plumage was present in the same area. Apparently, they were attracted by the white florets, displayed between two bright red bracts, of the *Cephaelis elata* shrubs then blooming abundantly. Between visits to the flowers, they caught insects in the air. After their departure, I did not see another of their kind until nineteen years later, when a Green-crowned Brilliant, so young that its cheeks, throat, and breast were still largely cinnamon, came to stay in the garden for just one day, in mid-March of 1967. Like the Fiery-throated

Hummingbird, all these Green-crowned Brilliants were much less wary than are our permanently resident hummingbirds. Although I could approach the Brilliants closely, I could not touch them. The Green-crowned Brilliants live at lower altitudes than the Fiery-throated Hummingbirds and probably did not come so far. The single Green Violet-ear (another resident of the highlands) that I have seen at Los Cusingos was in view for only one day in January, visiting the red flowers of *Hamelia patens*.

In a family of birds renowned for glittering attire, the Brown Violet-ear is an anomaly. The dull plumage of both sexes is relieved by a stripe of violet-blue on each cheek and a small patch of metallic green on the throat. Over the years, I have met a Brown Violet-ear in this valley only at long intervals, and rarely more than one in a day. Then, early in August of 1976, I discovered that these humming-birds were strongly attracted to a tall Cerillo tree, bent over into a clear space in the forest by the vines that burdened it, and heavily laden with small red flowers with incurved petals that gave them the shape of berries, so that the tree appeared to be fruiting rather than flowering. Until the tree passed from bloom two months later, I could depend upon seeing Brown Violet-ears every time I visited it. Often three or four were in view at one time, with probably more on the other side of the tree. Sometimes one chased another; but they did not make much effort to maintain exclusive territories in this tree crowded with nectar-drinking birds.

After the Violet-ears, the most numerous visitors to the Cerillo tree were White-necked Jacobins, who also are of sporadic, unpredictable occurrence and have never been found nesting at Los Cusingos. Strangely, the permanently resident hummingbirds came to the red flowers much less frequently than these two kinds of wanderers. The Violet-ears and other hummingbirds shared the Cerillo's nectar with Bananaquits, Shining Honeycreepers, Blue Honeycreepers, and Green Honeycreepers, without, as far as I saw, trying to drive away these small birds.

In early September, while the Cerillo was flowering most profusely, I found a Brown Violet-ear plucking nest material from the trunk of a tree in the pasture. She carried it into the neighboring forest, but did not return for more while I waited.

The Violet-ears continued to visit the Cerillo until, in early October, it shed its last flowers, after which I did not see another for ten months. This tree did not drop its heavy crop of fruit, many of which were diseased, until late June and early July of the following year. Like certain other trees that flower profusely and set many fruits in one year, this Cerillo failed to bloom in the following year; but neighboring Cerillos did so, beginning in late July of 1977. Soon after this, I found at one of these trees the first Brown Violet-ear that I had seen since the preceding October. Where these hummingbirds, which range from Guatemala and Belize to Bolivia and Brazil, had been in the long interval, I cannot tell.

The rain forests on the Pacific slope of southern Costa Rica and the adjacent Province of Chiriquí in Panama, now rapidly shrinking, are isolated from similar forests. The high Cordillera de Talamanca separates them from the Caribbean rain forests; to the northwest, the Pacific lowlands support lighter woodlands that endure prolonged dry seasons; while eastward lie the savannas and gallery forests of Panama's Pacific slope. In this location, the Valley of El General developed a peculiar avifauna, notable for what it lacked no less than for what it had. Among the species confined to southern Pacific Costa Rica and adjacent Panama are the Turquoise Cotinga, Fiery-billed Araçari, Baird's Trogon, Golden-naped Woodpecker, White-crested Coquette Hummingbird, and other splendid birds. On the other hand, the valley has no jay; and resident orioles, so abundant in other parts of Central America, are lacking here, where only the migratory Baltimore Oriole occurs regularly and the Orchard Oriole seldom arrives.

With the destruction of forests over much of this region, widespread species of open country are invading it. Among the first was the Smooth-billed Ani, which came up from Panama; until 1940, I did not find it in El General, where it is now abundant. By 1964, the parasitic Striped Cuckoo was sounding its distinctive whistle in the valley. Five years later, I first saw one of its principal hosts, the Pale-breasted Castlebuilder or Spinetail, which had long been resident in the savannas around Buenos Aires de Osa, lower in the Térraba Valley. Here it had been separated from El General by extensive forests that have been destroyed by axe and fire, preparing the way for its advance up the valley. I first saw another parasitic bird, the Bronzed Cowbird, in 1962, in a neighbor's pasture. Since then, I have noticed only one or two others; but the cowbirds will probably increase.

As the sun rose into a clear sky on December 7, 1974, familiar raucous cries caused me to look upward in time to see a lone Brown Jay fly high over the house and southward over the forest until it vanished—the first of its kind ever to be seen here. This aggressive jay of cleared and lightly wooded lands of Caribbean Middle America has been extending its range, eastward almost to the Canal Zone in Panama, and over the continental divide to the shore of the Gulf of Nicoya in Costa Rica. Probably, before long, it will establish itself here, along with Striped Cuckoos, Bronzed Cowbirds, and other invaders. Although the Brown Jay has interesting social habits, like other jays it is a nest robber that we do not need here. It is distressing to see our unique native birds yearly becoming rarer, as their sheltering forests dwindle, while widespread, commonplace species take possession of the land.

In addition to birds wandering up from the coast or down from the mountains, and those that are probably the vanguards of invading species, our casual visitors include long-distance migrants that appear to have deviated from their usual routes. Since I came to Los Cusingos, I have seen only one Ruby-throated Hummingbird, one Black-billed Cuckoo, one Yellow-billed Cuckoo, one Gray Catbird, one male Hooded Warbler, and one or two Bay-breasted Warblers—all, except the hummingbird, during the spring migration. I would not have seen the catbird if I had not been intently watching a vine of *Doliocarpus dentatus*, whose bright red pods were splitting into two hemispheric valves, to release two hard, black seeds, each enclosed in a soft, waxy-white, sweetish aril attractive to birds. The silent gray stranger kept itself well hidden in the dense tangle of vines, where it was swallowing the seeds whole.

How strongly arils, rich in oil, attract birds was impressed upon me two years ago, when a tall, slender *Dipterodendron* tree fruited copiously, its flattish pods opening by two valves to release black seeds partly surrounded by white arils. Among the thirty-one species of birds that ate the seeds—from parrots and araçari toucans to vireos and honeycreepers—were Sulphur-bellied Flycatchers, which nest at higher altitudes in Costa Rica, and northward to southwestern United States, but are rarely seen here. During the two weeks in late April and early May when the seeds were available, these flycatchers were among the most constant and conspicuous attendants at the tree, with sometimes five present at one time. They were particularly adept at snatching the seeds from opening pods while hovering on wing, more rarely while perching. As soon as the supply of seeds was exhausted, they vanished. In the following year, when this tree failed to flower and fruit, I saw no Sulphur-bellied Flycatcher. In the year after, when the tree flowered again but bore fruits that were mostly diseased and attracted few birds, I saw only a single representative of the species.

No casual visitor gave me a more pleasant surprise than the splendid male Prothonotary Warbler that, early in the morning of October 22, 1976, I found foraging over the mossy branches of a dead orange tree. From there he flew to a neighboring wild fig tree and plucked the pea-sized fruits, one after another. He did not swallow them whole, as Blue-crowned and Orange-collared manakins were doing, but mandibulated them to press out the softer parts, then dropped the skins. Tennessee Warblers, Bay-headed Tanagers, and Silver-throated Tanagers were eating the figs in the same way at the same time. The Prothonotary Warbler flew away; but soon he, or another equally yellow male, returned to eat more figs. By the following day, he or they had vanished, never to be seen again. By the exercise of faculties that we understand most imperfectly, birds that wander, or are driven by adverse weather, from their normal migration routes are able to reorient themselves and reach their proper destinations. Doubtless these warblers, which found themselves in an elevated interior valley, promptly flew down to the coast, where they winter.

The only migratory woodpecker to reach Costa Rica is the Yellow-bellied Sapsucker, which winters in the highlands above three thousand feet. The wintering sapsuckers are chiefly females. I never saw a sapsucker at Los Cusingos until the evening of February 12, 1970, when I noticed one clinging to the trunk of a dead Jacaranda tree. It had a bright red forehead and a whitish throat and was evidently a female. I watched her intently in the fading light, hoping that she would answer a long-standing question. How do woodpeckers, which usually sleep in holes that they have carved for themselves in their territories, pass their nights while migrating?

After clinging motionless for some time, the sapsucker climbed up to a depression, left by the fall of one of the huge, twice-compound leaves, in the side of an upright branch, sixty or seventy feet above the ground. Into this hollow, which appeared to have been slightly enlarged by the removal of bark and possibly also a little wood, the sapsucker inserted her abdomen and part of her breast, which seemed to fit snugly, while all the rest of her body was fully exposed and visible from afar. Her tail was pressed against the bark below the depression. In this upright posture, she remained motionless while daylight faded and the crescent moon grew bright. Finally, her head disappeared, evidently having been turned back and buried among the feathers of a shoulder.

I looked for the sapsucker on the following evening, but she did not come to the Jacaranda tree. After that, I did not see a sapsucker for more than two years. On the evening of March 25, 1972, I found the same or another female sapsucker clinging motionless in a tall Jacaranda tree, near where the first, now fallen, had stood. While daylight faded, she rested upright at a point where two thick, vertical branches diverged, beside (rather than within) the crotch—apparently the most protected nook she could find. Again, I failed to find her on the next evening. Doubtless, after a night's rest, she had resumed her northward journey.

20. *The Patient Puffbirds*

As I climbed a steep, forested slope at Los Cusingos, on a day in early June many years ago, a small bird flew up from close beside me, to vanish among the trees before I saw it well. Looking around, I found the burrow from which the sounds or vibrations of my footsteps had driven it. The straight tunnel descended obliquely for twenty inches, expanding at its inner and lower end into a roomy chamber, lined on the bottom and sides with large pieces of brown dead leaves. Here rested two spotless eggs that gleamed whitely in the beam of my flashlight. The mouth of the tunnel, slightly over two inches wide, was surrounded by a low pile of decaying twiglets, some of which were thorny, and dead leaves up to a foot long by four inches wide, which apparently had been placed there by the owners of the nest. On the long, leaf-strewn slope, thinly covered with saplings, shrubs, and small ferns, beneath tall trees that cast a deep shade, the burrow was so inconspicuous that I would have passed without noticing it if the bird had not flown out. I had never before seen such a nest.

Returning the following afternoon, I stood several yards in front of the burrow and stamped a foot. The bird in charge of the eggs flew out, rose to perch about twenty-five feet up, and repeated, over and over, a high, thin, long-drawn whistle. When I moved for a better view, it rose still higher and disappeared amid the foliage—but not before I had seen enough to identify it as a White-whiskered Softwing.

One of the thirty-two species of puffbirds that are related to the jacamars and toucans and confined to the tropical American mainland, from southern Mexico to northern Argentina, the White-whiskered Softwing is about seven inches long, with a large head and short, narrow tail. As in other members of the puffbird family, its stout body and loose, fluffy plumage give it a chubby or puffy aspect, like that of the Puffin. Although the male is considerably brighter than the female, in the dimly lighted forest the sexes are often difficult to distinguish. His general color is warm chestnut-brown or bright cinnamon, paler on the underparts than above. The female is decidedly more olive and grayish, although sometimes her breast is tinged with cinnamon. Both sexes are liberally spotted and streaked with tawny and buff on the head and upper plumage, and streaked with brown and dusky shades on the breast and sides. Both wear, at the base of the bill, long, slender, slightly curved, white or whitish feather tufts, which are sometimes inconspicuous, but in other lights or aspects stand out like old-fashioned drooping mustaches, and have reminded me of miniature walrus tusks. A less prominent whitish tuft adorns the forehead, above the base of the moderately long, strongly tapering bill, which is downcurved at the tip. The red eyes are remarkably large, evidently adapted for foraging in dim light. The legs and feet are gray, with two toes directed forward and two backward, as is usual in the woodpeckers and related families.

Puffbirds in general belong to that category of birds that are often called "stupid," simply because they have adopted a mode of foraging that involves a minimum of wasted movement and energy, and, in the wild woodlands where most of them dwell, they have not been sufficiently exposed to man's destructive habits to become innately wary in his presence. Singly or in pairs, never in flocks, softwings live chiefly at midlevels in the rain forest, from fifteen or twenty feet upward. They seem never to rise to the highest sunlit treetops. Sometimes one joins a mixed party of small birds. Their lethargic aspect as they perch motionless on a slender branch is deceptive, for they are watching with patient intensity. Suddenly they dart outward or downward to pluck their prey from leaf or bark, with a loud "clack" of their strong bill, and carry it back to the same or another perch, to be devoured at leisure.

The first softwing that I ever met was perching about ten feet above a trail through second-growth woods in the Caribbean lowlands of Honduras. From time to time it about-faced, all in perfect silence. Not only did it permit my companion and me to watch it for many minutes while, at intervals, it snatched small creatures from surrounding foliage, but once it darted straight toward us to capture an insect in the trailside grass, not ten feet from where we stood in plain view, commenting, in voices that it certainly heard, on this bird so different from any that either of us had seen. In shady clearings near forest, softwings not infrequently drop down to catch an insect amid low herbage. Their diet includes large orthopterons, moths, other winged insects, large caterpillars, spiders, and an occasional lizard, which may be as long as itself. I have never seen them eat berries or other fruits.

Like a number of other birds of deep forest, softwings stay within the forest most of the time and hunt on the outskirts chiefly in the dim light of dawn and evening, thereby lengthening their day and increasing their foraging time. They make longer excursions, in full daylight, so seldom that birds of neighboring clearings may not become familiar with them. One August morning, my writing was interrupted by a great commotion among the birds in our shady garden. Vermilion-crowned and Gray-capped flycatchers were making most of the noise, but the

WHITE-WHISKERED SOFTWING ▶

voices of many birds of other kinds swelled the excited chorus. I hurried out, ex-
pecting nothing less than a hawk or large snake, only to find a little White-whiskered Softwing, who had wandered out of the nearby forest. While the visitor rested
motionless, it was surrounded by a crowd of scolding or merely inquisitive on-
lookers, "mobbing" it. Whenever the puffbird flew to another perch, Gray-caps
shouted harshly, while hummingbirds darted in pursuit with low rattling sounds,
such as they make when they follow a hawk. Then the whole crowd gathered to
scold the doubtless bewildered softwing in its new situation. Finally, it flew across
a corner of the pasture into the coffee grove, still attended by its persecutors. This
display of hostility to a bird that superficially resembled a pygmy-owl surprised me
the more because owls of any kind have always been so rare here that most of these
birds had probably never seen one. Forest birds, who know the softwing better,
seem never to treat it in this discourteous fashion.

The high, thin whistle or "peep" that the softwing uttered after it left its burrow in the hillside is the note that I have most often heard from these birds, especially when their nests or young seem to be in danger. Occasionally they voice a
long-drawn, weak, plaintive *tzeee*, which seems to taper to a sharp point. Their
notes are most nearly imitated by whistling through the teeth rather than with the
lips. A more elaborate vocal performance was given by a male who, for hours together, perched motionless near his burrow with nestlings, while I sat in a blind
nearby. This was a rapid, undulatory twittering, almost a sizzling, in a weak, high-
pitched voice, *tweee, tweee twit a whit a whit, tweee, tweee*, which often continued
for many minutes without interruption. When first heard, I took it to be the insistent pleading of a hungry fledgling, perhaps a woodcreeper or ovenbird. Not until
I detected the slight vibrations of his bill was I certain that these notes came from
the parent softwing, perching in full view, sometimes holding food. Often I have

heard the softwing's thin notes floating down from leafy boughs, where the bird perched unseen. What a contrast between the softwing's weak voice and the ringing notes that its more sociable relatives, the dusky White-fronted Nunbirds, pour forth in a chorus, while they perch in a row on some high branch in lowland rain forest!

On my third visit to the softwings' nest on the hillside, I approached cautiously and, looking in with my flashlight, surprised a parent covering the eggs. It sat facing outward, staring into the blinding beam with deep red eyes. As soon as I extinguished the light and stood aside, it darted out and flew swiftly down the slope toward the rivulet, then rose high into the trees on the opposite slope. Several flies, as big as houseflies, alighted on the eggs when they were left uncovered.

Both parents repeated their thin notes almost continuously when I approached their burrow on the ninth day after I found it, but they stayed so high in the trees that I could not glimpse them—behavior that I later found to be typical of nesting softwings. Peering down the tunnel with my flashlight, I saw two newly hatched nestlings. Their pink skin was completely naked. Their eyes were tightly closed, and their short bills curved downward to sharp tips. They moved around rather actively, evidently trying to avoid the light. Two days later, they had vanished, probably having been taken by a snake, as the burrow was unaltered. I heard the parents complaining in the vicinity.

Five years passed before I saw my second White-whiskered Softwings' nest. This occurred during the 1948 revolution, when El General was ravaged by Nicaraguan mercenaries, sent by the government to punish the valley that supported the Opposition. One day in mid-April, when we heard that these ruffians were marching toward us—to plunder, burn, and kill, as was their custom—María, who cooked for me, hurriedly carried cooking utensils and tableware into the neighboring forest. While hiding them, she saw a small brown bird emerge from the ground. Going to investigate, I found a softwings' burrow, containing three blind nestlings with sprouting pinfeathers. This was the only nest with more than two eggs or young that I have seen, and likewise the earliest, the eggs apparently having been laid in the third week of March. Since the rumor that the raiders were approaching, like other similar ones, proved false, I set my blind in front of the burrow to watch it.

At dawn of the following day, I entered the blind. As daylight slowly seeped through the high forest canopy, a rather large snake took form in front of me, stretched motionless over a rotting log not two yards from the burrow. After an hour had dragged by, bringing no view of the puffbirds, whose plaintive notes came from the trees above me, I emerged from the blind to remove the snake. Before I could reach it, it fled. Now I could see one of the nestlings lying, cold and dead, in front of the burrow. Looking in with the flashlight, I found the floor covered with freshly dug earth, beneath which the other two nestlings were buried. I could not decide whether the snake or some other animal was responsible for this tragedy.

Another five years slipped by before I found my third softwings' nest. In thirty-five years, I have seen eleven of their burrows in the forest at Los Cusingos. Most were in slightly inclined ground; only the first was in a steep, but by no means precipitous, slope, up which I could easily walk. Three were in the sides of shallow depressions, made long before by the uprooting of a great forest tree, and now covered by moss and fallen leaves. From a round orifice in the forest floor, the burrows slanted downward at an angle of about thirty degrees with the horizontal, or somewhat less. Nine that I measured ranged only from eighteen to twenty-two inches in total length; five of these were between nineteen and a half and twenty and a half inches. In all these burrows, the dilated chamber at the inner end was well lined on bottom and sides with dead leaves, a refinement rather exceptional in nesting burrows, where the eggs are usually laid on the bare earth. However, at least one other puffbird, the White-fronted Nunbird, carpets its chamber with dead leaves. All but one of the softwings' burrows (which was deflected by a root) were so straight that I could easily see their contents when I peered in with a light.

Around the mouth of each tunnel was a low collar composed of coarse dead petioles, rachises of large compound leaves, and thin dead twigs. Mixed with the sticks, and overlying them, were usually a number of dead leaves, some fairly large. Since similar leaves covered the surrounding ground, I could not decide whether they had fallen upon the collar or been placed there by the softwings. A similar collar, through which the birds go in and out, surrounds the mouth of the White-fronted Nunbird's much longer tunnel in the forest floor. The Black Nunbird of South America is reported to collect a large heap of coarse dead twigs over the mouth of its burrow, leaving a passageway along the ground, through which the birds enter.

The uniformity in size and shape of all the White-whiskered Softwings' burrows suggests that the birds dig them rather than use holes that they find ready-made. Yet, with a single exception, I found no freshly dug earth in front of them. To carry all the excavated material away in their bills, as Prong-billed Barbets and certain titmice do when carving nest holes in trees, would be a huge undertaking for these small birds. Possibly, like the Blue-diademed Motmot and Buff-throated Automolus, softwings prepare their burrows so many months before they lay in them that the earth which they leave in front no longer appears freshly dug. The

single burrow before which I found recently moved earth, already well covered
with leaves, was occupied by a pair of softwings who had apparently first tried to
clean out and rehabilitate the burrow where they had successfully nested the preceding year, only to abandon it to dig a new one forty feet away. Another pair
nested at least twice in the same burrow, successfully in the first year, unsuccess-
fully in the second year. The reuse of old burrows decreases the probability of
finding one that has been recently excavated.

With the exceptions of the early nest with three young, already mentioned,
one that was prematurely abandoned, and one that had been dug out by some animal just before I found it, each softwing nest that I have found contained two spotless white eggs. The eggs were laid from late March to about the end of May, but
chiefly in April. Those that I found, with incubation well advanced, in early June
may have been laid to replace an earlier brood that had been lost. None of my successful burrows was used again in the same year, and I found no evidence for
second broods.

Because the softwings were so shy and suspicious, to study how they incubated was not easy. If the terrain and surrounding vegetation permitted, I could
set my brown wigwam blind six or seven yards from the burrow and watch
through binoculars, which required a viewing aperture at least an inch wide; or I
could place the blind closer and peer with naked eyes through a narrower slit.
Either way, these sharp-sighted birds seemed to detect my presence in it. Leaving
the blind in place for days did not wholly reconcile them to it, at least while I was
within. They often delayed for an hour, and sometimes for several hours, to enter
their burrow while I watched, with all but my eyes or binoculars hidden from their
view. Nevertheless, by matching their patience with my own, during long vigils at
two nests, I learned their peculiar pattern of incubation. Then, at several other

nests, into which I could peer with a flashlight and determine the sex of the sitting bird, often without causing its departure, I corroborated what I had earlier found.

The two sexes alternate in the care of the eggs, according to a very simple schedule, which requires long, patient sitting in the burrow. As in woodpeckers, anis, Ostriches, and a number of other birds, the male softwing incubates through the night. He leaves early in the morning, around half-past five, while the light is still dim beneath forest trees. The eggs remain unattended for about a half hour to an hour, or much longer if the female is suspicious. Usually, however, she enters the burrow around six o'clock, or soon after, and continues to incubate until around midday, or sometimes until after one o'clock—an interval of six to nearly eight hours. On the rare occasions when the male appears before she leaves, he does not enter the burrow until after her departure. The eggs again remain alone until, usually between one and two o'clock in the afternoon, he goes in to begin a session that will continue uninterruptedly until the following dawn. Never have I found a male with the eggs between sunrise and noon; never a female after two o'clock in the afternoon. Because the only nest that I found before the eggs were laid was destroyed, I did not learn how long incubation lasts.

After the nestlings hatch, naked and sightless, the parents' schedule changes completely. Now only the male broods them, while the female, during their first few days, brings all their food—a division of labor that is, as far as I know, unique among birds, for usually, if both parents do not begin rather promptly to feed the nestlings, then their mother broods them while their father brings their meals, as in hornbills and certain hawks and crows. For the first three days after hatching, the male softwing continues to leave the burrow in the dim light of dawn, but after an hour or two he returns, to pass all the rest of the day with the nestlings. On the day after the young hatched at one nest, I watched from early dawn to midday without seeing the male. Emerging then from my blind, I found him in the burrow, where he had either remained since the preceding evening, or, as seems unlikely, left and returned while the light was still so dim that I failed to see him.

After the nestlings are about four days old, they are brooded less continuously by day; but their father accompanies them at least part of the daytime until they are about eight days old and their pinfeathers are becoming long. Nocturnal brooding continues for at most a day or two longer; and at one nest the nestlings slept alone from their seventh day. During the second half of their time in the nest, the young softwings sleep alone. With the exception of species of which the adults use the burrow as a dormitory, burrow-nesting birds discontinue nocturnal brooding early, before their nestlings are feathered, as I have seen in birds as diverse as the Blue-diademed Motmot, Buff-throated Automolus, and Rough-winged Swallow. Huddled together in their sheltered nest, the young remain warm enough without the parental coverlet; and, by roosting apart from them, the adults reduce the risk that parent and young will be trapped and devoured together by a nocturnal predator creeping into the tunnel's mouth. If the nestlings are lost, the parents may live to rear another brood.

After the nestlings were no longer brooded by night, I sometimes went with a flashlight to look into their burrows in the dark forest. On some nights I could not see them, because they slept behind a screen of leaves that extended from the floor almost to the ceiling, just in front of their nursery chamber. On other nights, the screen was lower, leaving part of the young softwings exposed, and on still other nights it was lacking. Although I found this screen at all three burrows that I visited in the night or before a parent had arrived in the early morning, it was not consistently present.

Watching in the late afternoon, I did not see a parent come to arrange the screen that I found in this burrow after nightfall. Therefore, I concluded that it had been made by the nestlings themselves. Hoping to see them do it, I looked into the same burrow at five-minute intervals as darkness fell on the following evening. On one inspection, I discovered the nestlings making vibratory movements of body and wings. If their feet, which I could not see, were similarly active, these movements might have piled up the dead leaves that covered the chamber's floor and which had been broken into smaller pieces during the weeks when the softwings had been incubating and attending the nestlings. On this evening, no screen was formed, possibly because the flashlight had disturbed the nestlings at a critical time.

With the possible exception of White-fronted Nunbirds, whose long tunnels defied adequate inspection, no other of the many burrow nesters that I have studied has made such a screen. Indeed, the unlined burrows of most of these birds contained nothing suitable for making it.

How this screen, present only at night, helps the nestlings to survive is far from obvious. Even with a full moon, the inner end of the burrow, in the depth of the forest, must be dark. Accordingly, the screen would hardly be needed to conceal the nestlings from view. In any case, nocturnal predators commonly hunt by scent, or some sense other than vision. If the nestlings have a scent (which I never detected) the leaves that have been in such close contact with them must be impregnated with it, so that the screen would hardly shield them from a mammal that finds its prey with its nose. Possibly it helps to prevent their discovery by great, hairy "bird spiders," or by snakes that detect their victims with their tactile sense or, like the pit vipers, by heat radiated by birds and mammals. If the screen considerably increases the nestlings' survival, it should be more consistently raised at nightfall.

Of the many surprising features in the life of the softwings, not the least is the way they feed their nestlings. As we have seen, during the first few days after they hatch, their father stays most of the time in the burrow, brooding, while their mother brings all the food. She delivers it while standing in the doorway, with her head, or head and shoulders—rarely as much as half her body—inside, so that I could not see just what happened. With her mate inside, one might suppose that she passed the food to him, and he carried it down to the chamber and fed the nestlings. However, I am sure that, beginning at the age of three days, the blind, naked nestlings walk or shuffle up the inclined entrance tunnel, a distance of about fourteen to eighteen inches, and receive meals directly from their mother, for I saw food delivered so while their father was absent. And certain observations lead me to believe that they come to the doorway for their food from the day they hatch. When the nestlings were a day old, their mother took a minute or so to deliver a small object, which the young evidently had difficulty swallowing, although their father could have received it in a trice. On the same day, she brought a very large insect, tried for a minute or two to deliver it, then carried it away. Her mate would almost certainly have received it, had he been at the doorway. And, as I have clearly seen, White-fronted Nunbirds, still naked and sightless, toddle the length of their much longer burrows to take food at the entrance from the parents and their helpers.

Among hawks, crows, and other birds of which the male brings most or all of the food while his mate broods, the female shares it with the recently hatched nestlings. I could not learn whether the male softwing eats any of the food that his mate brings, but I believe he does not. Early one morning, while a male perched in front of his burrow on his way to brood day-old nestlings, the female, also on her way to the burrow, approached him and seemed to try to pass her food to him; but he showed no interest in it. Two days later, she tried even more obviously to give him food that she was bringing to the nest; but again he refused it. Apparently, during the few days when he stays almost continuously in the burrow with the nestlings, he finds all the food that he wants on his early morning outing, and through the rest of the day he fasts, while the young are fed by their mother.

Sometimes, when the female came to the burrow with food, I heard her utter faint, high notes, which probably served to bring the nestlings up the tunnel for their meals. Often, however, I failed to hear a note, while watching from my blind only eight feet from her. Either the notes were too low to be audible to me, or some other stimulus alerted the young to come for their meals. Possibly the sound of her wings as she alighted, or darkening the entrance by her body, brought the nestlings forward. One morning, when they seemed to be very hungry, they called when a bird of another kind flew past their burrow's mouth. But nothing that I could do, such as covering the entrance with a hand, or making a variety of low notes, elicited a response from the young softwings. Because of the danger of drawing predators to the nest, I did not persist in these experiments.

At two nests watched for many hours, I saw the nestlings receive only animal food, among which were small lizards; insects, including mantids and moths, with green, brown, or pink wings; caterpillars; and spiders. Only one item was brought at a time, and, except the lizards, most were so badly torn or mashed that I could hardly recognize them. Most seemed to be of kinds that would be plucked from bark or foliage instead of being caught in the air. Even when newly hatched, the nestlings were offered, and sometimes appeared to eat, surprisingly large objects. Once an *Anolis* lizard about four or five inches long was brought for nestlings only slightly over two days old. This contrasts with the behavior of kingfishers and many other birds, which adjust the size of the food items to the size of their young, bringing them larger articles as they grow older.

At one nest, I first saw the male bring food when the nestlings were six days old, and at another, when they were eight days old. Even afterward, he was a poor provider. In a total of seventy-three hours' watching at these two nests, covering all ages of the nestlings, I saw the males feed them only six times, three times at each nest. The two females fed a total of fifty-seven times, and twice food was delivered by a parent of undetermined sex. Thus, in seventy-three hours, the nestlings, always two, were fed sixty-five times, or at the rate of somewhat less than once per hour. Substantial meals compensated for infrequent feeding.

The rate of bringing these meals was surprisingly variable. On the evening when the nestlings in my fifth nest were three days old, their mother continued to feed them actively in the fading light. By six o'clock, when she was difficult to distinguish amid dripping foliage, she had brought food eight times in forty-seven minutes—the fastest rate that I recorded. On another evening, a female fed her nestlings after the evening songs of the Great Tinamou, swelling through the darkening forest, announced the end of the diurnal birds' day. The softwings' large eyes helped them to detect insects in the dim light. Concentrated feeding at nightfall was not habitual, and sometimes the nestlings received nothing in the last hour or two of daylight. In the forenoon, the highest rate of feeding that I recorded was nine times in the seven hours between 5:30 and 12:30, when the two nestlings were eight days old. At the other extreme, two fifteen-day-old nestlings were fed only once between daybreak and 11:00. The rate of feeding appeared to depend, at least in part, upon the size of the meals. When they were brought frequently, as on the evening when I watched exceptionally rapid feeding, the items tended to be small.

One reason why the males fed the nestlings so infrequently, even after they stopped brooding them, was that when they arrived with food they delayed long to deliver it. One rainy afternoon, a male sat around, on various perches in front of the burrow, for nearly three hours before he took to it the object he had held all this time. One morning I left him still clutching a green insect that he had brought more than two hours earlier. The females sometimes delayed for from half an hour to an hour to approach the burrow with food that they brought, but I never saw them procrastinate nearly as long as the males sometimes did. This hesitancy may have been caused by shyness in the presence of the blind, but they had already gone to the nest repeatedly while it stood there. What a contrast between these softwings and White-fronted Nunbirds, who fed their nestlings while we stood or sat unconcealed at no great distance from their burrows!

Looking into one burrow, I saw a blind, naked nestling trying to eat the shell from which it had just escaped, without success, as far as I saw. The empty shells soon disappear, but I could not learn what happens to them. Although I never saw a parent carry out a dropping, the nestlings continued to look clean in their expanding plumage. With my face at the tunnel's mouth, I detected no odor save that of moldering vegetation. After the young left one burrow, I scraped out the contents for examination. Among the fragmented leaves that covered the floor crept many fat white maggots, which may have helped to disintegrate the nestlings' wastes, for I found no droppings and scarcely any of the regurgitated shards and other chitinous parts of insects that accumulate abundantly in the burrows of jacamars and motmots. The litter smelled strongly of ammonia, but this odor had not reached the burrow's mouth.

When the nestlings were six days old, dark feather rudiments became prominent on their pink skins. Two or three days later, they bristled with long pinfeathers. At nine or ten days, their feathers began to expand at the tips of the horny sheaths, and their eyes were open. When two weeks old, the young puffbirds were well clothed with plumage, much like that of their mother. Even their white "walrus-tusk" mustaches, and the white tuft on the forehead, became prominent a few days later. Sometimes older nestlings fluffed out their plumage until it covered their eyes.

These nestlings never exposed themselves at their burrow's mouth; at most, I fleetingly glimpsed part of a head as one took food from a parent. Likewise, in strong contrast to nestling Rufous-tailed Jacamars, they were nearly always silent. Although I spent hours less than three yards from their burrow, I did not hear them until the day before they left. When an Orange-billed Sparrow flew past the burrow's mouth, and again when a Lowland, or White-breasted, Wood-Wren sang nearby, they began a high-pitched, rapid, rather plaintive trill, which continued for several minutes. On this and the following morning, their last in the burrow, they trilled briefly just after they were fed.

These two nestlings and two others flew from their burrows when twenty days old. Another left at twenty-one days, and two others when between twenty and twenty-two days of age. When I visited nests from which the young had just departed, the parents often started to complain as soon as I came into view, and they continued as long as I remained in sight. While they repeated without pause their high, thin notes, they twitched their tails nervously from side to side, and often held them tilted to the right or to the left. The protesting parents were sometimes hidden amid foliage, always well above my head. Only at a single burrow did I detect the newly emerged fledglings, already perching well above the ground. Like all other burrow nesters that I have studied, White-whiskered Softwings nev-

er "feigned injury" or gave any other distraction display. Nevertheless, their obvious concern for their offspring, and their whole comportment while I studied their
nests, convinced me that, despite their often stolid aspect, they are no less alert
and emotional than other, more demonstrative birds.

My fifth softwings' nest, which received most of my attention, was only two
yards from a Lowland Wood-Wrens' nest, a small, roofed structure with a side
entrance that had been built, a few inches above the ground, in a pile of fallen
branches and palm fronds, with which it blended well. I found the wrens' nest
first, and only after I had visited it several times did the sudden emergence of a
softwing, as I passed its burrow, lead to its discovery. The eggs of the wrens
hatched first, and their exquisite notes and frequent visits with food helped to enliven the long hours when I sat watching the burrow without seeing the softwings.
At daybreak on the morning when the puffbirds' eggs hatched, the young wrens
were safe in their nest. When I returned at noon, they had vanished, taken by a
snake, or perhaps the weasel that I had seen nearby a few days earlier. But the softwings' burrow escaped predation both on this occasion and through the following
three weeks.

The White-whiskered Softwings' burrows in the leaf-strewn ground of tropical forest appear to be excessively vulnerable, yet, of the eleven that I have seen,
six were at least partly successful, producing nine or ten fledglings. This is a high
rate of success for birds of tropical rain forest, where only one nest in five may
escape destruction, usually by predators. The safety of the softwings' burrows
depends upon their excellent concealment amid the ground litter; the parents' great
caution in approaching them; the infrequency of their visits while incubating eggs
and feeding young; the habitual silence and invisibility of the nestlings; the ab-

sence of a strong odor emanating from the tunnel; and perhaps also the screen of leaves that the nestlings raise in front of themselves after they are no longer brooded by night. White-whiskered Softwings belong to a very ancient lineage that was once more widely distributed over the Earth. One wonders how many thousands or millions of years were needed to adapt them so well to their life in the tropical forest. It is distressing to think how many other birds, equally well adapted and equally fascinating, are in danger of extinction before we know how they live.

21. *Flowers, Bees, Fruits, and Birds*

 THE melastome family, one of the largest in tropical America, is well represented at Los Cusingos, especially by woody species, which are among the most abundant low or tall shrubs and small trees in the old forest and taller second growth. Melastomes never, as far as I have seen, attain the stature of the giants of the rain forest; but the biggest species in our woods, the Cinnamon-leaved Miconia, occasionally grows to be one hundred feet tall and may have a trunk a foot thick at breast height. Although the wood of this and other species is hard and durable, it has the great defect of splitting readily, a quality that has earned for these trees the curious name of *canilla de mula* ("mule's leg"). One that an axeman is felling often begins to fall before it is cut through. As it bends over, the trunk splits lengthwise, and the severed half "kicks" upward, perhaps striking an unwary woodsman. Because they split as they dry, melastome trunks do not make good fence posts, and they are too thin to be sawn into boards. Among our melastomes, one, *Adelobotrys adscendens*, is a white-flowered vine that climbs high into trees, attaching itself by roots. Others are herbs, including the delicate little *Pterolepis trichotoma*, which, in December, adorns sterile patches in the pasture.

The distinctive venation of melastome leaves makes this family easy to recognize. These leaves are opposite, rarely in whorls, and always simple rather than compound. At the base of the blade, or somewhat above it, from one to three

strong lateral nerves spring from each side of the midrib and curve around to rejoin it at the tip of the leaf. Sometimes an additional, weaker longitudinal nerve
runs along each margin, without reaching the apex. The longitudinal nerves are
joined by many thinner transverse veins that are parallel and give the underside of
the leaf a ribbed aspect. Between these veins lie finer veinlets that often tend to be
parallel, too, but may form a fine network. Some species bear, at the base of the
leaf blade or on the petiole, curious hollow lobes that are regularly inhabited by
tiny ants.

The flowers of melastomes are usually white or pink, less often shades of red
or purple. Often they are small and densely crowded in large panicles, but some
species have such large, attractive blossoms that they are cultivated as ornamentals.
The huge genus *Tibouchina* contains many trees and shrubs that are planted for
their lovely flowers. Especially handsome are the species of *Blakea* that grow as
woody epiphytes in mountain forests and display large pink flowers of curious construction. The stamens of melastomes also distinguish the family, as their anthers
nearly always open by one or two tiny apical pores, instead of splitting lengthwise,
as most anthers do. Often the anthers have curious appendages whose function can
be clarified only by careful studies of how the flowers are pollinated. The fruits
of melastomes include fleshy berries and dry capsules, in either case with usually
many minute seeds.

A tree of the melastome family that grows abundantly on the sterile hillside
behind our house, but never in the old forest, is the Coronillo, which rarely attains
a height of forty-five feet and a diameter at breast height of six inches. When standing in the open, it is a handsome tree, with a shapely rounded crown and large,
smooth, elliptical leaves. The brown bark is rough and scaly. The white flowers,

CORONILLO, *BELLUCIA COSTARICENSIS* ▶

slightly over two inches wide, spring in small clusters from the trunk and thicker branches, as in many tropical trees with large fruits. Although not big or heavy as tropical fruits go, the berries of the Coronillo are by far the largest of any melastome I have seen. Up to an inch and a half in diameter, they are glossy, whitish, nearly globular, and are crowned by the five or six persisting calyx lobes, which are responsible for the name Coronillo, "little crown." The soft pulp, filled with a multitude of minute seeds, is pleasantly both sweetish and acidulous, reminding me of the fruit of the Pitahaya Cactus. These fruits have little attraction for birds, but children sometimes eat them, and horses and Agoutis gather them from the ground beneath the trees. Apparently, the seeds are disseminated chiefly by terrestrial animals.

The thick, fleshy petals of Coronillo flowers are asymmetric, usually with two curious, irregular projections on the right side, which is the inner side while the petals are rolled up in the flower bud. The ten or twelve thick, pale yellow anthers are closely pressed together in a ring, which is interrupted at one point, where the long style projects. Each anther has two minute apical pores, directed inward toward the style instead of opening in a more exposed position. These flowers, which are present from March to June, have a delicate scent, as of orange blossoms. Screened by foliage on the trunk and older branches, they are less conspicuously exposed than the flowers of many other woody melastomes, and they appear to have greater need of fragrance to attract insects.

Like other melastome flowers that I have examined, those of the Coronillo yield no nectar and are rarely, if ever, visited by hummingbirds or butterflies. They are frequented by pollen-gathering bees, chiefly the large, furry Black Bumblebee and a smaller black bee. While watching these bees fly from flower to flower, with conspicuous masses of pollen on their hind legs, I wondered how they extracted it from flowers that seem so reluctant to release it, guarding it in massive anthers that open by tiny pores situated where they are not easy to reach. I found it difficult to make the minute pollen grains emerge.

Because most of the Coronillo flowers were above my reach, I did not succeed in solving the mystery. However, it occurred to me that I might throw light on the problem by learning how bees extract pollen from other anthers with apical pores. I turned my attention to an arborescent Large-flowered Miconia that was blooming at the forest's edge. Its white flowers, about an inch across, were much bigger than those of many species of miconias and, accordingly, favorable for observation. Their five delicate petals appeared ragged or frayed on the right side, which was inside in the bud, a feature that reminded me of the irregular projections on the Coronillo flowers. The ten slender, yellow anthers, nearly a quarter of an inch long, stood up conspicuously in the center of the flower. Each opened by a single tiny pore, exposed at the tip instead of turned inward, like the pores on the Coronillo anthers. Nevertheless, I found it difficult to shake out the tiny, dry pollen grains, which under the microscope resembled grains of wheat. I could detect no fragrance from these flowers.

The chief visitors to this miconia were the same furry Black Bumblebees that frequented the Coronillo trees. They flew from flower to flower with great, pale-yellowish lumps on their hind legs. These bumblebees live in old rat burrows. Not long ago, a worker chopping down the weeds along the side of the road passing through our forest fled when angry black bees emerged from the ground, but not in time to avoid being stung painfully. However, while busily gathering pollen, these bees are not irascible, and I could watch them closely. Nevertheless, their rapid movements were difficult to follow, and I could never detect any pollen escaping from the pores. After much watching, I learned that they seize the slender anthers in their mandibles, one at a time, and pull outward with a vibratory or massaging movement. They appeared to extract the pollen much as one milks a cow. This treatment left prominent brown scars on the yellow anthers.

The long, slender style that held the capitate stigma above the anthers sometimes pushed up between a hind leg and body of a pollen-gathering bee. Probably, when this happened, pollen was rubbed onto the stigma from a leg. This did not appear to be an efficient method of pollination, because the bee could procure pollen without touching the stigma. Melastomes and other plants that attract insects by pollen rather than nectar necessarily provide a great excess of the fertilizing dust to pay for the pollinators' services. Most of the flowers of this miconia appeared to be pollinated and to develop juicy berries. Whether or not they were fertilized, they lasted but a single day, and by late afternoon all were discolored and shriveling.

After the miconia, I gave attention to *Lycianthes synanthera*, an epiphytic shrub of the potato family, which grows on the Madera Negra trees that I planted many years ago for living fence posts, on the shaggy trunks of African Oil Palms, on forest trees, and sometimes on rocks. On its drooping, crooked, woody branches, which become six or seven yards long, the *Lycianthes* bears clusters of lavender flowers that spring on slender stalks from the leaf axils. The five narrow petals spread outward, leaving exposed the five bright-yellow anthers, which, fused side by side into a tube, stand up prominently at the center. The pollen, shed through apical slits into the top of the tube, can escape only by way of the narrow opening through which the style projects. Although the structure of this flower is different from that of melastome flowers, it presents to its pollinators the same problem as they do: how to extract pollen through a narrow pore.

The *Lycianthes* blooms profusely early in the wet season, chiefly in May and June. The flowers start to open as the night ends and continue to expand until past midday. I marked some twigs and counted thirteen open flowers before sunrise, fifty-seven by half-past eight, ninety-seven by midday, and one hundred and three by two o'clock in the afternoon. Their method of opening was interesting. The edges of adjoining petals are sutured together by tapering, interlocking marginal cells. To pull apart, these petals must build up sufficient turgor on their inner or upper faces. They begin to bulge out and separate near their bases. Finally, when the turgor pressure becomes great enough, they suddenly fly apart at the apex, then bend steadily outward and downward with visible motion. The whole expansion takes only a few seconds. Flowers that open late on a sunny morning often do so imperfectly, two or three of their petals remaining stuck together, doubtless because in the drying air they did not become turgid enough. Whether they open early or late, all the flowers start to close soon after the middle of the afternoon, earlier when rain falls than when the sun shines. By nightfall, most are closed.

Since the petals of flowers that have already opened and closed are not sutured together, they tend to open earlier on their second morning than they did on their first morning. Most are now discolored. If the corollas do not fall during the day, they may close a second time in the afternoon. None that I marked opened the third day. In the morning, the *Lycianthes* flowers exhale a faint fragrance that reminds me of that of the liverwort *Conocephalum*, which forms flat, branching ribbons along shady streams in northern woodlands. Devoid of nectar, these flowers do not attract hummingbirds or butterflies.

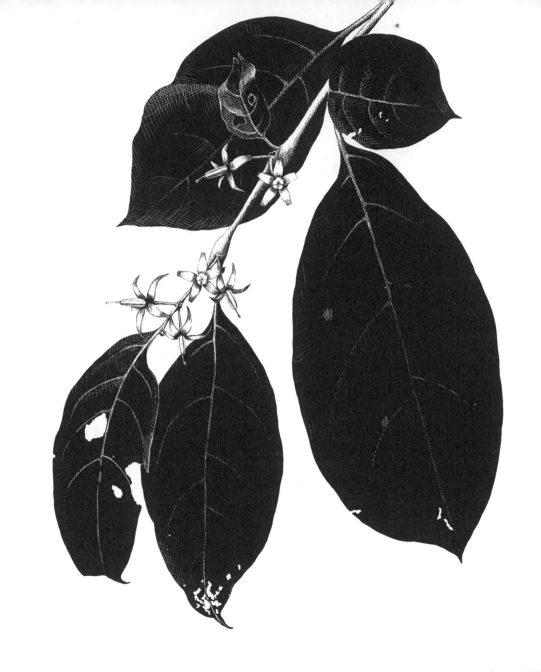

The same furry Black Bumblebees that visit the melastome flowers are the chief pollinators of the *Lycianthes*. They begin to arrive early in the morning, when the first flowers open and the light is barely bright enough to see exactly what they do. Steadily they increase in numbers, and well before sunrise many have large loads of pale pollen attached to their hind legs.

To gather this pollen, the bee curves her body over the top of the anther tube and the stigma that stands above it, with her abdomen on one side, the ventral surface of her thorax over the pore and stigma, and her head downward on the other side. Then, pressing her mandibles, which are often closed, against the yellow side of the anther tube, she vibrates it so strongly that the movement can be plainly felt in the woody twig on which the flower grows. She rotates around the yellow column, thereby giving this treatment to different parts, or she flies off a few inches, to return facing in another direction. She may slide her mandibles upward while she vibrates them against the anthers. Often, while so engaged, she emits a high-pitched buzz.

If the flower has just opened, little puffs of pollen escape from beneath her body, so effective is this treatment. If the flower has already been visited by one or more bees, the less copious stream of pollen all lodges upon the insect's ventral surface; at least, I could see none escape. While a bumblebee is visiting a flower, one or even two others of her kind may cling to her, eager to share the nutritious pollen. I never saw a fight result from such massing. The bees' treatment of the anther tubes leaves brown marks upon them, which doubtless help the insects to avoid flowers that have already been drained of their pollen.

While the bee is extracting pollen, some of the grains that had lodged on her ventral surface when she visited other *Lycianthes* shrubs would doubtless be rubbed

◀ *LYCIANTHES SYNANTHERA*

upon the stigma, thus effecting cross pollination. But each large shrub bears so many flowers that most of the time pollen is merely transferred from one flower to another of the same plant.

To move the pollen from her ventral surface to the pollen baskets on her hind legs, the bee has several procedures. Most often she does so while clinging to the flower, or nearby, by both front legs, one front leg, or the front and middle legs on the same side. Then, whatever legs are left free are moved so rapidly, all together, that it is difficult to distinguish details; but the end result is that the pollen that dusted her lower surface and forelegs swells the load on her hind legs.

By August or September, the pea-sized yellowish berries of the *Lycianthes* begin to ripen. They are slightly sweetish but rather more bitter. They are eaten by Green Honeycreepers and several kinds of tanagers, especially the lovely Bay-headed Tanager. The plant employs bees to pollinate its flowers and birds to disseminate its seeds, giving to each an appropriate reward.

Other plants with anthers that open by apical pores are the golden-shower trees and other members of the genus *Cassia*. The flowers of certain species have three or even four kinds of stamens, with anthers of different sizes and shapes on filaments of different lengths. Often some of these stamens are rudimentary or sterile. To learn the significance of this diversity requires prolonged, patient observation of the behavior of the insect pollinators, but the height of *Cassia* trees often makes such study difficult.

A *Cassia* favorable for observation is *bacillaris*, which may grow into a shapely, many-branched shrub eight yards high but often blooms when much lower. The flowers, an inch or more wide, have five bright-yellow petals, which, instead of falling, persist after pollination, turning straw color. In their midst stand four

hard, solid, almost stalkless anthers, each of which opens by two apical pores. Three much smaller stamens are doubtfully functional, and three more are minute rudiments. These flowers are devoid of nectar and have only a "polleny" odor.

Black Bumblebees visit these flowers also and appear to be their chief pollinators. Sometimes, just after they alight and vibrate the anthers, a dusty cloud arises from them. Soon the bees bear huge masses of yellow pollen on their hind legs. The long pistil curves over the bee's body and doubtless at times rubs over the pollen basket, scraping some of the grains into the tiny stigmatic pit at its end. A variety of smaller bees, including stingless *Trigona*, buzz around these flowers, gathering pollen, but appear unable to shake it from the anthers. Instead, they collect what is accessible at the pores and sometimes seem to gather it from the stigmas, thereby reversing the process of pollination. A bee of intermediate size does shake the anthers, as I could assure myself by feeling the vibrations in the supporting twig. But only the bumblebee is big enough to rub against the stigma and serve as an efficient pollinator. Probably the solidity of the four functional anthers is an adaptation to prevent bees too small to serve as pollinators from shaking the pollen from them; and this might be the explanation of the solidity of the Coronillo anthers. Hummingbirds ignore these *Cassia* flowers, and butterflies rarely visit them.

Later than *Cassia bacillaris*, the Candelillo, a medium-sized *Cassia* tree that I brought here from other parts of El General, covers its shapely, rounded crowns with a golden mantle. Through the pastures where it grows, it diffuses a delightful but elusive fragrance, which I detect chiefly in sunny middays, and in the evenings. These large flowers are also visited chiefly by the Black Bumblebee, but they are always too high for me to follow details. The Candelillo blooms in August and September, after which the bumblebees disappear. In mid-September I found one dying on the porch, evidently from age or exhaustion after a long season of harvesting pollen, as I could detect no injury. From late September until near the end of the following March, I saw not a single one of these big, furry bees.

Hummingbird-pollinated flowers, no less than bee-pollinated flowers, include species with anthers that open by terminal pores. They tend to be tubular, nectar bearing, and scentless, rather than open, nectarless, and fragrant, like the bee flowers. Among them are shrubby heaths that grow as epiphytes in tropical American mountain forests, such as species of *Satyria*. These white-tipped, red flowers open downward, so that the hummingbird must hover beneath them and insert its bill upward into the narrow tube while it sips the nectar. Probably the vibrations of its rapidly beating wings help to shake the pollen from the pores onto the hummer's forehead and bill, so that it may be carried to the next flower that the bird visits. Since hummingbirds are warier than bees, I have not been able to hold the stems and feel the vibrations.

The melastomes, with their distinctively veined leaves and anthers that open by apical pores, include many species, such as the Coronillo, Large-flowered Miconia, and the charming little *Pterolepis trichotoma*, that open a succession of flowers day after day over an interval of weeks or months, and some have blossoms large enough to attract that expert extractor of pollen, the Black Bumblebee. Many other melastomes, especially species of the huge genus *Miconia*, have flowers that are too small to interest the bumblebee, but which open in great masses. At least six species of *Miconia* at Los Cusingos bloom simultaneously. One day all, or nearly all, of the trees or shrubs of a certain species will be laden with unopened flower buds, with few or no expanded flowers. By the following morning, they will be covered with large, richly branched panicles of pure white flowers, exhaling a delicate fragrance. Dozens or scores of trees scattered over the farm—often every one that I can find—have burst into full bloom on the same day. A day or two later, tiny white petals drift down like thickly falling snowflakes, especially when I shake the small trees. The flowers are spent and discolored; only a trace of their fragrance remains. The multitudes of small, pollen-gathering bees that buzzed around them for a single day have gone.

These miconias compensate for the smallness and inconspicuousness of their flowers by opening nearly all at once, thereby making a display visible from afar and filling the air with fragrance. Prominent among them is the Wayside Miconia, which ranges from southern Mexico to Panama and western Cuba. It thrives on rather sterile soil and is perhaps the most abundant woody melastome along road-sides in El General. After two nearly rainless days in mid-September, 1976, every one of twenty-five small or large shrubs of the Wayside Miconia that I found at Los Cusingos was white and delicately fragrant with freshly opened flowers. Even suppressed plants in the shade of thickets had a few flowering panicles on straggling branches. By nightfall the stamens were becoming discolored, but the minute flowers did not close. Soon after sunrise next morning, myriads of tiny petals were raining downward. Only a few of the panicles, chiefly those at the tops of some of the larger shrubs, bore buds that would open later.

After September 18, 1976, I noticed no Wayside Miconia in flower until the following August 10, when a minority of the shrubs had very few open blossoms. Again, on August 19, a few flowers opened and were visited by bees, as though anticipating the grand efflorescence. This occurred the following day. I walked for two miles along the road down to the broad valley of the Río General, finding these shrubs and small trees in fullest bloom all along the way. Those that grew in the open, with plenty of space, had shapely, rounded crowns almost solidly covered with white. On distant hillsides they stood out prominently amid the verdure. On the farm of a friend who had instructed laborers cleaning a neglected coffee plantation to preserve these shrubs, scores were arrayed in purest white. Among the swarms of insects that visited all these shrubs were a few domestic honeybees, but I noticed no bumblebees. The only trees that I found with only a minority of their panicles in flower were a few that stood at the forest's edge, where they were shaded by taller trees. Here one slender Wayside Miconia had attained the exceptional height of about seventy feet.

Although the preceding week had been wet, with heavy afternoon showers sometimes prolonged into the night, the day on which the Wayside Miconias flowered was brilliantly sunny throughout the morning and early afternoon. In the late afternoon, a hard shower fell, with some wind. In the evening I was distressed to find that a large branch had broken from the shapely tree beside our entrance gate, the best specimen on the farm. The small, crowded flowers on many large panicles held so much rain water that their weight, aided perhaps by a little wind, snapped off the slender bough. Although the Wayside Miconia is in full flower only one day a year, it is well worth preserving for that day. I was pleased to see that a fine example had been preserved in San Isidro's central park.

Eight days after the grand efflorescence, belated buds opened, again simultaneously, on many plants. Here and there, a whole panicle was in flower; nearby, another inflorescence, that had bloomed earlier, might have only one or two open flowers. This was a very minor flowering; no Wayside Miconia that I saw was covered in white, as nearly all had been in the preceding week. On several days in October, a depauperate shrub bloomed feebly while all its neighbors were flowerless.

Other miconias, including the Cinnamon-leaved, the Glossy-leaved, the Furry, and the Scorpioid (so called from the shape of its inflorescence branches) are somewhat less tightly synchronized. A few inflorescences may have open flowers the day before the full blooming, which may occur on two consecutive days on different trees or shrubs. Nevertheless, by the third day, it is difficult to find a single tree in flower. Then, from a few days to six or seven weeks later, many plants of this species will come simultaneously into flower, again for only a day or two. Those that have flowered sparingly at the first efflorescence will be the chief contributors to this second general flowering; those heavily laden with developing berries may have only a few additional flowering panicles; and the same panicle that bears many fruits may display a few fresh flowers. The abundant Glossy-leaved Miconia flowered three times in two months. The smaller, shrubby Smooth-leaved Miconia, abundant in the forest, bloomed profusely from December 21 to December 23, 1976, more sparingly on February 10, 1977, again profusely on December 18 and 19, 1977, and once more from January 19 to January 21, 1978.

The main efflorescence of two species rarely occurs at the same time. Each responds differently to the prevailing weather, or requires a different stimulus to initiate flowering. If several common species bloomed simultaneously, competition for the services of pollinating insects could become intense. As it is, one wonders how so many trees of the same species, blooming synchronously, can attract enough small pollen-gathering bees and other insects to fertilize their myriad tiny flowers. Whether they are sometimes self-fertilized would be difficult to determine experimentally, because they are so small and crowded. In any event, always enough flowers are pollinated to produce an abundant crop of berries.

Five of our most abundant simultaneously flowering miconias bloom in the dry season or at the very beginning of the wet season, their efflorescence apparently triggered by occasional showers that interrupt the prevailing dryness. Their main flowering may vary by as much as two or three months in years with different weather. In all this they resemble coffee, which also flowers synchronously, usually nine or ten days after a shower, and repeatedly if occasional, copious, rather widely spaced showers punctuate the dry season.

About seven to ten weeks after flowering, from late March into June, these miconias ripen their berries. In spite of simultaneous blooming, these trees and shrubs ripen their fruits successively, over an interval of usually a month or more. Although insects may be abundant enough to pollinate the flowers in a day or two, birds could not consume the heavy crops of berries in such a short interval; many would be wasted if they matured all at once.

Melastome berries are most abundantly available to birds in their principal nesting season, from late March to June, and doubtless are among the factors that cause the birds to breed most freely at this time. Some birds, especially the abundant manakins, rely heavily upon berries to nourish their young; many others bring them to nestlings in smaller quantities. Even if the young are nourished principally with insects, the availability of easily gathered fruits to parents with mixed diets leaves them more time to hunt insects and spiders for their offspring.

Although melastome berries are most abundant in the principal nesting season, they are by no means confined to this season. As we have seen, different simultaneously blooming species flower on different dates, and they ripen their berries over an extended interval. Together with species that do not flower simultaneously, they provide berries for birds through most, if not all, of the year (although melastome berries and other small fruits are much less plentiful toward the end of the rainy season and through much of the dry season, when few birds that include much fruit in their diet are nesting, and when the bananas that we provide for them are most eagerly sought).

Melastome berries are exceedingly attractive to birds. Watching at a low, widely spreading tree of the Scorpioid Miconia in the pasture behind the house and at a tall, slender tree of the same species in the midst of the forest, I have seen thirty-eight species of birds eat the sweetish, deep purple or black berries, about a quarter of an inch in diameter. Among these thirty-eight were nine kinds of tanagers, including the wintering Summer Tanager; six flycatchers, ranging in size from the Lesser Elaenia to the big Boat-billed Flycatcher; five finches; four thrushes, including migrating Olive-backed, or Swainson's, Thrushes; four honeycreepers; four manakins; two vireos, including the migrating Red-eyed Vireo; one cotinga, the Rufous Piha; and three northern wood warblers, the Chestnut-sided, Tennessee, and Bay-breasted warblers. This last was one of the very few members of this species that I have seen on the Pacific side of Costa Rica.

Most of these birds plucked the berries while perching. The manakins seized them as they darted by. The Rufous Piha gathered them either on the wing or while perching. Even the flycatchers preferred to perch while they ate, but occasionally they plucked in flight a berry otherwise difficult to reach. These birds and most others swallowed whole berries. But the little Variable Seedeaters, among the most constant visitors to the miconia tree, and the Yellow-faced Grassquits, rare visitors, nibbled at berries still attached to the tree. Tennessee Warblers pierced attached berries with their sharp bills, to extract the juice or small bits of flesh. Chestnut-sided Warblers proceeded differently, plucking and chewing a berry before swallowing it.

While wandering through forest and thickets, I too have often eaten melastome berries, just as, long ago, I gathered blueberries and huckleberries in northern woods. I prefer berries of melastomes that open a few flowers at a time instead of all at once, as they tend to be bigger, sweeter, and easier to reach because many kinds grow on smaller shrubs.

Thus the long cycle is completed. In return for nutritious pollen, bees and other insects fertilize the melastome flowers, enabling them to set fruits. Birds eat the juicy berries and spread far and wide the small, indigestible seeds, from which more trees and shrubs grow to provide more pollen for industrious bees. This benign cycle, in which every participant is benefited and none is harmed, is one of evolution's finest accomplishments, proof that a blind, undirected process, which depends upon random variations and produces much that we abhor, and much that we regard with mixed feelings, can also create much that we unreservedly applaud.

22. Excursions to Guanacaste

I. THE UNSPOILED PROVINCE

ALTHOUGH Guanacaste, Costa Rica's northwestern province, is only a hundred miles in a straight line from the Valley of El General, the contrasts between these two regions are great. The two-mile-high barrier of the Cordillera de Talamanca shields El General from the northeast trade winds and favors the development of convectional showers. The Cordillera de Guanacaste consists of volcanos somewhat less than seven thousand feet high, widely separated by much lower ridges. Through these gaps in the range the trade winds, after dropping much of their moisture on the Caribbean slope, blow strongly and steadily through the long dry season from November to April, May, or June, adding to the stress of plants that have long been without rain. Where not growing on land with a high water table, the Guanacaste forests shed most of their foliage in the dry weather, in strong contrast to the much taller, heavier, evergreen forests of southern Costa Rica. Especially on abrupt limestone hills on the western side of the province, tall, columnar cacti stand prominently amid the stunted woods. At Los Cusingos, the only cacti are epiphytes whose broad, flat stems with scalloped or undulate margins hang high in trees and bear large white flowers on their edges.

The faunas of these two regions are as different as their floras. Guanacaste has the White-tailed Deer; El General, the smaller Forest Deer, or Brocket. Guanacaste has the large, elegantly attired Variegated Squirrel; El General, the plainer Cinnamon-bellied Squirrel. Aside from some wide-ranging, adaptable species, mostly of open country, the birds are also different. The avifauna of Guanacaste is composed largely of species that range up the arid Pacific coast of Middle America far into Mexico, and are found also on the Caribbean slope in dry interior valleys that lie in the rain shadow of high mountains. Few of these arid-country birds extend south of the Gulf of Nicoya, where rainfall increases. The bird life of El General is more similar to that of the Caribbean rain forests, with differences that can be attributed to its long isolation by the Cordillera de Talamanca.

The water birds present the most striking difference between the bird life of the two regions. In the well-drained Valley of El General, I rarely see one bigger than a kingfisher, never a spectacular aggregation of large aquatic birds. The low-lying basin of the Río Tempisque, which flows through the center of Guanacaste, is famous for its huge gatherings of ducks, storks, ibises, spoonbills, egrets, and other feathered inhabitants of ponds and marshes. To see some of these birds that I never meet here, I have, over the years, visited Guanacaste a dozen times, alone, with students, or as leader of groups of bird-sighting tourists. To my regret, I have never been able to stay long enough to make careful studies of some of its birds.

I first visited Guanacaste in mid-November of 1937, before I settled at Los Cusingos. At this date, before the Inter-American Highway made northwestern Costa Rica readily accessible by road from the center of the country, it could be reached either by launch up the Gulf of Nicoya from Puntarenas or by air from San José. I chose the second alternative, and left the capital at half-past six in the morning. With landings at Puntarenas and Las Juntas, the airplane reached the village of Las Cañas (now called Cañas), in southern Guanacaste, an hour later.

Guanacaste was still without the buses, trucks, and smaller cars that now run

nearly everywhere in the province and spoil much of the pleasure of horseback riding. The morning after my arrival at Las Cañas, I set forth on a hired horse for Tilarán, in the hills to the northeast. The road leading across the plain, between wide pastures shaded by scattered trees, was almost everywhere churned up by the hoofs of horses and cattle and the wheels of ox-carts. Now, at the beginning of the dry season, the stiff mud was nearly or quite dry, leaving the surface exceedingly rough with the pits and ridges into which it had been tortured while soft and plastic. These stretches of exceedingly muddy roadway were called *pegaderos* ("stickers"), an apt designation, as one readily stuck in the adhesive clay. To avoid sticking, travelers went around the sides of the worst *pegaderos*, thereby continuing to widen them. Some had become very broad.

After a few miles, the road converged with the Río Cañas, which flowed swiftly along a wide, rocky bed, beneath noble Espavel, Ceiba, Guanacaste, and Sandbox trees that shaded and delighted the traveler. The Espavel, which I found beside all the rivers that I visited in Guanacaste, is a truly impressive tree, attaining a height of a hundred feet, with a trunk six or seven feet thick and massive horizontal branches, heavy with large, dark green leaves. Its form and habit of growing along streams reminded me of the stately Sycamores that shade mountain torrents in northwestern Guatemala.

Leaving the river, the way began to climb into the hills, which became higher as I approached the main ridge of the *cordillera*. At a fork, I took the wrong branch and presently came to a *trapiche* (an ox-driven cane mill) where men were making *dulce*, or brown sugar. They gave me not only directions but a drink of cane juice hot from the boiling caldron, a welcome gift to a wayfarer who was becoming hungry and thirsty. I found the people of Guanacaste friendly and hospitable.

◀ HOWLING MONKEY, MALE

Returning to the fork, I took the other branch and wound up a steep hillside to a picturesque region of rounded hills and ridges of moderate height, covered chiefly with light green pasture grass, but with darker patches of forest on the summits and steeper slopes and along streams that flowed through narrow valleys. Ahead, the *cordillera* rose with a gentle profile. In the opposite direction, I enjoyed glimpses of the nearly level, wooded central valley of Guanacaste, stretching away to the low coastal mountains, blue in the distance.

At intervals along the road, as nearly everywhere in Guanacaste at this period, I met clans of Howling Monkeys. Their pelage was all black, except the long, golden brown hairs on their sides. By no means restricted to the heavier, more extensive forests, they seemed to thrive in small groves and tongues of woodland amid the pastures, and even on the outskirts of the villages, close beside houses. I heard their loud roaring everywhere. Evidently little molested by man, they showed little fear of him. I have long wondered why I never saw these widespread monkeys in El General, even while its forests were vast. Perhaps the early settlers ate them all. The more agile White-faced Monkeys, which take a wider variety of foods, were much rarer than the Howlers in Guanacaste, possibly because their habit of raiding fields of ripening maize caused them to be shot.

After a leisurely horseback ride of six hours, I reached Tilarán, a large village inhabited chiefly by settlers from Costa Rica's Central Valley, whose pale faces contrasted with the dark skins of the Indians and people of mixed race who predominated in the lowlands of Guanacaste. The village had many *pulperías*, or general country stores, and appeared prosperous, but the only inn was wretched.

The surrounding country produced cattle, upland rice, maize, beans, and *trigo de arley*. As a crop new to me, this narrow-leaved variety of Job's-Tears, of Oriental origin, more correctly called "adlay," interested me greatly. The grain, enclosed in a hard, white, glossy shell, resembled the Job's-Tears that grow wild along the rivers and are used as necklace beads, but it was only about half their size. Large bins of adlay were displayed for sale in the *pulperías*, where I bought some sweet cookies made of it. Had I not been told their ingredients, I would not have suspected that they were not made of imported wheat flour, as they tasted much the same. I was told that, unless mixed with wheat flour, adlay flour will not rise to make bread, probably because it is deficient in gluten. I have never elsewhere seen this cereal grown except as a rare curiosity.

At Tilarán I became familiar with the Guanacaste wind, which, during most of my sojourn, blew steadily and hard from the northeast, driving the remnants of dissolving clouds that it had swept across the continental divide, to descend in a fine drizzle on the leeward side. Juvenal Valerio, director of the Museo Nacional in San José, had given me a letter of introduction to his brother, a storekeeper of Tilarán. Don Juvenal's nephew, Carlos Luís Valerio, a boy of sixteen, agreed to serve as guide and companion on a visit to the Lago de Arenal. At eight o'clock in the morning, the two of us set forth on horseback beneath the prevailing drizzle. After riding a few miles, to the accompaniment of the raucous shouts of Scarlet Macaws and the deep roar of Howling Monkeys, we crossed the continental divide, where my aneroid barometer registered only twenty-three hundred feet above sea level, and began to descend into the Caribbean watershed. Here, on the windward side of the range, the forest was heavier, with a lusher, more tangled undergrowth. Much of this woods had already been destroyed to make pastures, fields of sugarcane or grains, and banana groves.

My first glimpse of the lake was not what I expected. From an elevation, I looked over, not an expanse of sparkling water, but a flat, yellowish-green meadow, about nine miles long, set amid low, rounded, darkly forested hills, which rose into the low ceiling of gray clouds that covered all the sky. I saw no open water. After lunch in a hut standing in a pasture above the lake, we rode down to its shore, where we found two dugout canoes. After bailing out the water, we embarked in one. Paddling along a narrow passage that had been cut through floating vegetation, we reached a broad avenue of naturally open water that stretched for a long distance parallel to the southern shore.

Our limited exploration revealed that the Lago de Arenal was more a swamp, with stretches of open water, than a lake. As we paddled and poled along, tall, slender reeds nodded over our heads. Amid large expanses of grasses, sedges, and cattails rooted in mud were areas where Water Hyacinths, a bladderwort with yellow flowers, and the ferns *Salvinia* and *Azolla* floated on the water. Other plants that I recognized were Royal Ferns, a lobelia with splendid red flowers, Marsh Pennywort, and the orange-flowered *Epidendrum ibaguense*, a most adaptable orchid that also grows on dry roadside banks and arboreal ants' nests. Equally surprising was the presence of an aquatic begonia.

A male Red-winged Blackbird that flew across the water, the first I had seen in Costa Rica, was here at the southernmost limit of the widespread species. Many Tropical Kingbirds perched on tall reeds, watching for insects to fly within their range. Pale-vented Pigeons rested on the bare branches of some drowned shrubs and small trees standing near the shore. A Marsh Hawk circled over the marsh. Now the marsh and surrounding areas have been drowned for a huge hydroelectric development.

After three nights in Tilarán, I walked down to Las Cañas, having sent my hired horse back to his owner with the mail carrier. I was impressed by the abundance of pigeons in the fields around this village. The very numerous Inca Doves were evidently recent arrivals from the north, as they were not included in the list of Costa Rican birds published by M. A. Carriker, Jr., in 1910.[1] Continuing to extend their range southward, they reached the country just west of San José, where I found a few in 1964. With them around Las Cañas were Common Ground-Doves, Ruddy Ground-Doves, White-winged Doves, and White-fronted Doves. Red-billed Pigeons rested in the trees.

Wintering Scissor-tailed Flycatchers were numerous. Scores of these lovely, graceful birds roosted nightly in tall orange trees in the heart of the village, in company with fewer Tropical Kingbirds. Shortly before sunset they flew into the village from all directions, high in the air. Soon they began to settle in the tops of the orange trees; but, alarmed by the passage of some person beneath them, or seized by a sudden unrest, they would dart swiftly out again and circle around, before returning to their sleeping places. Later, at the village of Nicoya, I found a smaller number of Scissor-tailed Flycatchers roosting amid the dense foliage of fig trees beside the plaza, along with more numerous Tropical Kingbirds. Years afterward, I watched Scissor-tailed Flycatchers flocking into the central park of San José, as darkness fell and the city lights shone out. Although so gregarious at night, in the morning they disperse. Voicing short, dry notes, they spread over the surrounding country one by one, flying high overhead like feathered comets with a sunset glowing beneath each wing. Delightful birds!

Another bird that came to Las Cañas to roost was the Yellow-naped Parrot. On the outskirts of the village, at least twelve pairs of these large amazonas slept in two low, spreading trees. With a flashlight, I saw them resting near the ends of branches, where they were exposed to the sky and readily visible from the ground. The two birds of most pairs perched closely side by side; two who may have been

1. M. A. Carriker, Jr., "An annotated list of the birds of Costa Rica including Cocos Island," *Ann. Carnegie Mus.*, 6 (1910): 314–915.

mated rested about a foot apart; and one parrot was quite alone. At dawn they flew over the village in pairs, wing to wing. Other members of the family abundant here were White-fronted Parrots, Orange-fronted Parakeets, and Orange-chinned Parakeets. Parrots, pigeons, and hawks are more prominent in dry, lightly wooded country than amid rain forests.

Proof that this region was still fairly wild were the King Vultures that I saw near the village, along with Black and Turkey vultures. Roadside Hawks, Crested Caracaras, and wintering Sparrow Hawks, or American Kestrels, were abundant, and Red-tailed Hawks were not rare. In light woods I found my first pair of Elegant Trogons, lovely birds that well deserve their name. Groove-billed Anis were common here, as everywhere I went in Guanacaste.

At the little hotel in Las Cañas I met Don Walter Saborío, who invited me to accompany him on horseback to the Hacienda Tenorio, where his brother, Don Luís, was overseer. Our way led northward from the village, over gently rolling terrain, between pastures and fields of beans, rice, and maize. After fording the Río Santa Rosa and the Río Corubicí, we rode for miles through forest, unbroken and uninhabited. Most of the trees were low and slender. The largest—Ceibas, Guanacastes, Ceibos, and Pochotes—were widely scattered, notable for the spread of their boughs rather than their height. Leguminous trees with twice-pinnate leaves and tiny leaflets were abundant. I estimated the average height of this woodland to be sixty or seventy feet, about half that of the rain forest in El General. The light undergrowth was not difficult to penetrate.

Few trees flowered at this season. A notable exception was the Madroño, which grows to be seventy-five or eighty feet high, with a full, spreading crown and an irregularly furrowed trunk that often sends forth large branches within a yard or two of the ground. The light brown bark peels off in large flakes that cling, partly detached, to the smooth, newly exposed bark and give the tree a shaggy aspect. Above the glossy leaves, the white flowers are borne in large cymes. In some flowers of each inflorescence, a single calyx lobe is expanded into a broad, stalked, petal-like, whitish appendage—a development widespread in the coffee family, to which the Madroño belongs. These enlarged sepals make the whole crown of a profusely flowering tree spectacularly white.

At last the rough road passed through a low line of loosely piled stones that ran through the woods and marked the boundary of Tenorio, a huge hacienda of some thirty-seven thousand hectares—probably originally a royal grant to some enterprising *conquistador*. We continued through unbroken forest for several miles more, before we came to a region where grassland interrupted the woodland. Then, for a long distance, we rode through larger or smaller open meadows, everywhere bordered by belts and tongues of low woods, while small clumps or scattered single trees diversified the irregular expanses of grass. The tall, pungent, purple-flowered mint *Hyptis suaveolens* grew profusely over all the meadows and was in full bloom. Resident Meadowlarks and wintering Killdeers flew up as we passed.

As we approached the big house of Tenorio, the meadows became more extensive and the patches of woods more restricted. These meadows were said to be of "natural" origin, which probably meant only that their formation by human agency had been forgotten. However they arose, they were perpetuated by annual burning in the dry season, despite which, according to the oldest employee of the hacienda, the woods had been slowly encroaching upon the grassland. Protected from fire, the pastures would probably revert to woodland.

After a ride of nearly five hours, we reached the big house. We had risen so gradually, over level or slightly undulating land, that I was surprised to find my aneroid registering twelve hundred and fifty feet, about eleven hundred feet above Las Cañas. I was made welcome and given a good meal, which included a food new to me—tortillas made of *castañas*, or breadnut, the seeded variety of the Breadfruit tree. They were delicious.

The second morning after my arrival, I rode with one of the hacienda's cowboys up through the pastures on the gently rising land behind the house. They covered low, flat-backed ridges, while the woods occupied the valleys between them. We rode into the northeast wind, which for the past week had continued to drive the clouds across the mountains. As the cloud wrack was driven down toward the plains, it broke into very fine droplets, too highly dispersed to obscure the sun or the blue sky, or to wet our clothes, yet not too tenuous to spread the beams of the rising sun into a brilliant rainbow. The great, vivid arch rose high into the blue heaven, with one end seeming to rest on the distant plain far below us, the other on the forested lower slopes of Volcán Miravalles to the northwest, while the rounded Cerro Cuipilapa was framed within it. It continued to accompany us, on our left, for the whole of our ride up through the pastures.

After riding for nearly two hours, we reached the upper limit of the pastures, at an altitude of about three thousand feet. From this point onward, the slope of Volcán Tenorio rose much more steeply. Tying our horses, we continued on foot through the forest that clothed the six-thousand-foot volcano to its summit. Beneath the light canopy spread by the slender trees, the ground was so open, with few ferns, dwarf palms, low herbs, or obstructing vines, that we climbed up nearly a thousand feet without once using our machetes to open a passage. I had never elsewhere seen tropical forest so easy to penetrate. The crowns of the trees bore a light growth of mosses and larger epiphytes. We saw few birds, but hardly had time to search for others. After this climb through the forest, we returned to our horses and rode down through the meadows, with almost the whole of Guanacaste spread before us, from the Gulf of Nicoya to the Nicaraguan border.

Within the memory of man, Volcán Tenorio has been quiescent, but it would be hazardous to call it extinct. After centuries of inactivity, Arenal, the next volcano to the southeast, suddenly awoke in 1968 in an exceedingly violent eruption, with incandescent gases and lava flows that destroyed forests, villages, people, and animals. Although the cone of Miravalles, the next volcano northwest of Tenorio, has long been inactive, the many fumaroles and solfataras at its base are proof that its fire is not extinguished. Miravalles is followed by the active volcano Rincón de la Vieja, which in turn is succeeded by the dormant Orosí, near the Nicaraguan border. As Miguel Salguero points out in his recent book, *Volcanes de Costa Rica*, the volcanos of the Cordillera de Guanacaste have been much less thoroughly explored than the far higher volcanos of the Cordillera Central. Remoteness from the older centers of population, forbidding cliffs and steep slopes of shifting rocks, scarcely penetrable vegetation near the summits, violent winds and sudden rainstorms make the ascent of some of these Guanacastecan volcanos a hazardous, exhausting undertaking.[2]

A family of four Rufous-naped Wrens lived about the big house at Tenorio, hopping over the porches and entering a nearby ruinous hut in search of insects. They had nests in two of the four compartments of a dovecote mounted on a pole in the dooryard, and a pocket-shaped nest with a side entrance in an orange tree. Nevertheless, they were building a fourth nest in the top of another orange tree, close beside the porch. In the evening, all four of these big wrens retired into one of the nests in the dovecote. When I shook them out for a recount, they entered the finished nest in the orange tree. When, after much shaking, I persuaded them to

2. Miguel Salguero, *Volcanes de Costa Rica* (San José: Editorial Costa Rica, 1977).

leave the orange tree, they returned to the dovecote. Along the roadside near Las Cañas, I watched three of these wrens enter at nightfall a bulky nest in a bull's-horn acacia tree, inhabited by fiercely stinging ants. In another nest, similarly situated, two retired to sleep.

Years later, on the Nicoya Peninsula, three Rufous-naped Wrens protested with harsh, grating and mewing notes while I examined their nest with three eggs, also situated in a spiny acacia tree. The same three were present when I returned an hour later. I regretted that I could not stay to watch this nest after the nestlings hatched, as I had little doubt that the third wren would help the parents to feed them. Such assistants have been found in the related Banded-backed Wren. In another family of Rufous-naped Wrens, I watched one member preen another, while a third rested nearby. In Guanacaste, this wren is called *salta piñuelas*, or "jump the Piñuela." The Piñuela is a bromeliad or wild pineapple with long, narrow leaves, armed with recurved marginal spines, that stand upright in close clusters. Planted in a compact row, the Piñuela forms a hedge, much used in Guanacaste, which only a wren or some other equally agile small animal can penetrate.

Another bird that slept near the house at Tenorio was the Crimson-fronted Parakeet, which flew in great, noisy flocks, and roosted among clusters of coconuts in the tops of tall palm trees, as, in a later year, Eugene Eisenmann found them doing at Almirante in western Panama. At sunset, scores of Montezuma Oropéndolas arrived in long, straggling flocks to roost in large mango trees in a neighboring pasture. Early next morning, they departed in the same fashion. I was surprised to find these oropéndolas, so common along the Caribbean slope of Central America, here on the Pacific side. Another Caribbean bird, the big, noisy Brown Jay, was also prominent at Tenorio. I saw it at Tilarán, but failed to find it any-

where farther west. These two birds of the wetter eastern side of Central America seemed to "spill over" to the opposite side where the continental divide was low, but their westward advance was stopped by increasing aridity. Here at Tenorio, the Brown Jay mingled with the equally big and raucous White-throated Magpie-Jay, widespread in Guanacaste and along the Pacific slope northward into Mexico. With its blue-and-white plumage and high crest of forwardly curved feathers, it is a spectacular bird.

After three nights at Tenorio, I rode back alone to Las Cañas, where, the following morning, I took the airplane for Nicoya, on the peninsula of the same name. As we flew over the great marshes about the mouths of the Tempisque and Bebedero rivers, the trees around them were white with thousands of water birds, too far below to be identified. I found Nicoya a small, unattractive village, situated in the broad, level valley of the Río Morote, between steep, wooded hills. The church, long and low, was started in 1677 and not finished until many years later. Although no architectural gem, the strength and sincerity of its construction contrasted refreshingly with the cheap tawdriness of the churches made largely of thin sheet metal, painted to imitate brick or stone, that had recently been springing up in Costa Rica. Since Nicoya lacked an inn, I lodged in a cubbyhole behind the office of a lawyer, to whom a government employee at Las Cañas had given me a letter of introduction. A prosperous Syrian trader gave me meals.

The vegetation around Nicoya was lusher than that about Las Cañas and flowered more profusely. The birds also indicated a somewhat more humid climate. Here the Rufous-tailed Hummingbird, which favors clearings in rain forest, mingled with the Cinnamon Hummingbird of semi-arid regions; and the handsome Blue-diademed Motmot met the lovely Turquoise-browed Motmot, which is the common species in drier regions farther north in Guanacaste. The black-and-white Barred Antshrike and his plain rufous-and-buffy mate were abundant in the thickets, where many Long-tailed Manakins and Slate-headed Tody-Flycatchers lurked. Rufous-naped Wrens, Banded Wrens, Lesser Ground-Cuckoos, and many other species were evidence that the avifauna of the drier side of Central America prevailed here.

At Nicoya, as at Las Cañas, Orange-fronted Parakeets flew in large, noisy flocks, which separated into pairs as they settled in trees, where mates perched side by side and preened each other. By late November, they had started to dig their nest chambers in the large, black, arboreal termites' nests so numerous in this region. I found three pairs so engaged, at medium-sized termitaries well up in roadside trees. They started to dig into these structures at a point on the side, below the middle, and directed their entrance tubes upward, as trogons do. Clinging below the termitary and biting into it with thick, powerful bills, the members of a pair worked alternately, for five minutes to a half hour at a stretch. While at work, they appeared to eat things they found in the termites' nest, doubtless the insects themselves, although I could not see this clearly. While one member of the pair toiled, the other perched quietly nearby, at intervals yawning, as though bored by inactive waiting.

I spent considerable time watching two of these pairs. After the pair at Las Cañas had worked for about an hour, another pair flew into their tree. In the lively fray that now began, all four parakeets joined, fighting with bills and much loud chattering. I feared that, with those strong beaks, they would injure each other severely; but, after five minutes of intermittent conflict, one pair flew away, without any of the combatants having suffered obvious injury. With the retreat of the invaders, the resident pair—as I believed them to be—perched side by side and affectionately preened one another's plumage. Soon after this, I left. When I returned late in the morning, work had stopped; but one parakeet perched near the termitary, guarding it.

While at Tenorio, Luís Saborío had shown me a newly published geography of Costa Rica that contained an account of the "Volcán" Barra Honda on the Nicoya Peninsula. The description convinced me that this volcano, if such it was, differed greatly from any volcano I had seen. Moreover, the mountains west of the Río Tempisque and the Gulf of Nicoya were not known to be volcanic. To settle my doubts, I resolved to visit Barra Honda on my way down to the Gulf of Nicoya. Leaving the village of Nicoya on foot at dawn, I took the road to Santa Ana. After crossing a ridge about a thousand feet high, covered with beautiful forest, I came to a pretty little woodland stream, whose pellucid water, charged with what I took to be carbonate of calcium or magnesium, had formed a series of shallow basins with smoothly rounded rims. As it flowed down its steeply inclined bed, the water trickled charmingly from one basin to the next. The deposit of hard, blue-gray stone that covered the sides and bottoms of these basins also sheathed the roots of trees that the water bathed. In places the rims of the basins had grown outward in foliaceous expansions or shelves with irregularly scalloped margins, blue-green in color, which reminded me much of the lichen *Cora*. Beneath these shelves small stalactites hung. Unfortunately, I carried no camera to photograph this enchanting rivulet.

When finally I reached the hamlet of Barra Honda and looked up at the mountain of the same name, I beheld a steep, nearly straight rampart about a mile long. Its lower slopes were wooded; above the forest, on the eastern half, were high forbidding cliffs; above the cliffs, a treeless expanse of grass. It looked more like a mesa or table mountain than a volcano. Don Pantaleón Díaz, who gave me hospitality in his humble cabin, found an Indian who knew the way to the summit but was reluctant to guide us there, perhaps suspecting that I was a government agent looking for illicit stills. However, after a careful inquiry into my motives for wishing to climb the mountain, he agreed to lead us up. Near the top, we passed over hard, white limestone with a conchoidal fracture and sharp, irregular edges and points, which promptly cut a toe of Don Pantaleón's small, barefoot brother, who had to stay behind, along with our barefoot guide, while Pantaleón and I continued to the summit. This harsh rock was concealed by tall, coarse grass, through which we advanced with great caution, feeling rather than seeing our way, for a fall could have been disastrous.

Leaving the open summit and its wide outlook, we descended into the forest that covered the tablelike mountain a few hundred feet lower. Without our guide, we might have searched long without finding the fissures in the rock. The one that he assured us was the largest was about ten by twenty feet at the mouth and extended vertically at least fifty feet into the ground. From this cavern issued a gas with an unpleasant odor, which was neither that of hydrogen sulphide nor that of sulphur dioxide. From the depths of the cavity came a continuous, fine, shrill whistle, as of gas escaping under pressure through a narrow orifice. We were shown another large hole and several slender fissures, but not the depression from which, as we were told, the gas escaped with sufficient volume and force to sway the boughs of the trees. Clearly these were sinkholes, such as one finds in many calcareous formations, rather than volcanic vents; but I cannot explain why so much gas issued from them.[3]

3. Recently Cerro Barra Honda was declared a national park, well described by Mario A. Boza in *Los Parques Nacionales de Costa Rica* (Madrid: Centro Iberoamericana de Cooperación, 1978). The numerous orifices in the top of the mountain lead by deep, more or less vertical shafts into caverns that are often spacious but not joined together. Some have picturesque limestone formations. Perhaps the noise and odor that issue from some of them are caused by hordes of roosting bats.

In the 1930s, by far the best way to travel in the more sparsely settled parts of Costa Rica was by horseback. Without a horse, it was more difficult, above all to cross the many rivers, which when swollen were less dangerous to riders than to pedestrians. After bathing in the river and eating an early supper in Don Pantaleón's house, I set off on foot for Las Letras, near the mouth of the Río Nacaome. The broad road, rough with mud that had been churned up and hardened, crossed the winding river four times. At each ford I removed puttees, shoes, and socks to keep them dry. After wading across the last ford, I lost my way, and with some difficulty found it again. Night had fallen, and as I groped along the unfamiliar road with a flashlight, I stepped up to my knee into a puddle of soft mud. For all my trouble, I kept only one foot dry!

On reaching the hamlet of Las Letras, I was told that the launch for Puntarenas would not leave until three o'clock in the morning, when the tide was favorable. I stretched out for a nap upon a huge squared log, one of the many deposited there for shipment across the Gulf. At about two in the morning, they started to load hogs into the launch that had moored beside the bank during the night. I was advised not to embark in this boat but, for a more comfortable voyage, to take another that arrived while loading was in progress.

After the first launch left, they filled the second with pigs, too, at least fifty of them, in the hold and tied over the deck. There was no remedy but to ride with the hogs. After we passed out of the estuary into the Gulf of Nicoya, high waves, raised by the unrelenting northeast wind, struck the small boat broadside, making it wallow wildly, while water entered through the scuppers and washed over the deck. Hogs broke from their moorings and slithered into the narrow space reserved for passengers at the stern. Before we reached Puntarenas, at ten o'clock in the morning, most of the passengers, including the owner of the pigs, were feeling rather sick from the movement and the stench. A most unpleasant ending to my pleasant and exceedingly interesting sixteen days in Guanacaste!

From Puntarenas, I took the electric train up to San José, then returned to Vara Blanca on the northern slope of the Cordillera Central, where I remained until the following August, studying the Resplendent Quetzal, Blue-throated Toucanet, Prong-billed Barbet, and other birds of the highland forests.

II. THE RAVAGED PROVINCE

Twenty-eight years passed before I again, in 1965, visited northwestern Costa Rica. During the following decade, I saw much of the region, from the ground and the air. Between my first and second visits, the Inter-American Highway was built through the length of Guanacaste, and from it lateral roads had been made, or were under construction, through much of the province. Everywhere I went, including the Peninsula of Nicoya, I was appalled by the destruction of the woodland. Where extensive forests had grown not long before were now wide, machine-cultivated fields of upland rice, maize, cotton, and other crops. Vast areas had also been cleared for raising beef cattle, of all forms of food production that which gives the least for human consumption in relation to the land and energy expended and is ecologically the most disastrous. While agriculture increased, severe, prolonged droughts blighted Guanacaste's crops and forced cattlemen to reduce the number of their starving cattle.

Here and there, usually far from the highways, stands of more or less undisturbed woodland remained. Beside one of these tracts, on the Hacienda Taboga near Las Cañas, I camped, for a few days in March, with a group of graduate students and professors who were taking a course in "Fundamentals of Tropical Biology." Our tents were set in a pasture shaded by noble Saman trees, whose massive, far-flung boughs formed wide, low domes of green, and by equally large Guanacaste trees with more open crowns. Beside the camp flowed a shallow stream of clear water, beyond which was a large tract of forest, growing above a high water table; the forest's persisting verdure and dense undergrowth contrasted strongly with the sere nakedness of the much lower and lighter woods with sparse undergrowth on neighboring ridges.

On this and other visits to Guanacaste in March and April, while the dry season was at its height, I was impressed by the bright, cheerful quality of the voices of its birds. Although the drier woodland supports fewer species than wetter forests, some of these species seem to be more abundant, but perhaps this is an illusion caused by the more open vegetation amid which they live and the freer use of their voices.

One of Guanacaste's principal songsters is the Banded Wren, amazingly abundant in thickets and light woods wherever I went. Throughout the day, but chiefly in the early morning, the beautiful, strong voice of this large wren rings out of thickets and vine tangles, now with loud, clear whistles, now with melodious slurred notes, now with bright trills—its repertory is large. When disturbed, the Banded Wren complains with a low rattle or ticking.

From the depths of the woods all around floats the cheery *to-le-do* of the Long-tailed Manakins; but the elegant, little, red-crowned, blue-backed, black birds are difficult to see. Their other notes include a *heer-ho*, clear and ringing; *weet*, short and sharp; and *waaa*, nasal and grating, contrasting strongly with the clear, cheerful notes. The manakins' dance, in which two male performers spring alternately straight upward, falling back upon the same low perch, is performed in dense thickets, where it is not easy to watch.

From open fields and light woods rings the high-pitched, bright *bob-bobwhite* of the Spotted-bellied Bobwhite. These quails with boldly patterned underparts travel in small coveys, which usually fly rapidly beyond view the moment they see a man. However, a flock of eleven that I met in an open copse near the Pacific Ocean permitted me to follow rather closely while they foraged, walking in wide circles through the sparse undergrowth. After a while, they all squatted down on the dry, fallen leaves to rest. In this flock, as with Marbled Wood-Quails that I have watched, I noticed no indication of a "peck order." All foraged in perfect amity.

Another cheerful sound is the *spring o' the year* of the Common Meadowlark, which lives in the open pastures and has a song very much like that of its northern relatives. Pleasant, too, are the high, clear notes of the abundant Brown-crested Flycatchers. Unlike many birds, they nest in the midst of the dry season. In early April, I found one of these flycatchers incubating four eggs in the deep, hollow center of a massive fence post. Another pair were feeding well-grown young that already followed them about.

Often heard, too, in the shrinking Guanacastecan woodlands is the accelerated rattle or roll of the Black-headed Trogon, which may be harder or softer, but seems never to be as mellow as the similarly accelerated song of Baird's Trogon, which replaces the Black-headed farther south, where the woods become more humid. At Hacienda Taboga in March, I found seven of the violet-tinted, yellow-bellied Black-headed Trogons noisily engaged in the business of forming pairs. They did not attack each other—which I have never seen any kind of trogon do—but they pursued one another through the tall forest, pausing to call while perching close together. The females' calls were lower and drier than the males'. Like the parakeets, these trogons often dig their nest chamber in the heart of a hard, black, arboreal termitary.

Another bird that nests in termitaries is the White-necked Puffbird. In March, I found a pair of these large, heavy-billed, boldly patterned, black-and-white birds digging into a big, black termites' nest, thirty feet up in a crotch of a leafless tree in light, open woods. They took turns at clinging to the side of the termitary, below the shallow depression they had made, and pecking audibly at the bottom of the hole, while small, black fragments fell to the ground. Their spells of work lasted from one to eight minutes. These birds were silent, except for the weak, dry notes that, on several occasions, the resting bird uttered as its partner flew from a perch beside it to resume work at the termitary. During the hour and a quarter that I watched, standing nearby without concealment, the puffbirds seemed to ignore me. Even the passage of a motorcar beneath one member of the pair did not make it move from its perch.

Five years later, I returned to Taboga to find that this fine sample of Guanacastecan forest on land with a high water table was being devastated by the axe. Another large tract of forest, near the station of the Organization for Tropical Studies at Palo Verde, was, at the time of my last visit, burning in many places, from fires that appeared to have been deliberately and repeatedly started. I wondered how the birds of Guanacaste could sing so cheerfully when the destruction of their habitats was threatening their extinction.

Although I found many water birds on a marshy area with large expanses of shallow, open water at Hacienda Taboga, and on a similar marsh in front of the station of the Organization for Tropical Studies at Palo Verde, I saw most when I went to Guanacaste, in March of 1973, as part of a survey of possible sites for national parks and nature reservations that the Tropical Science Center of San José conducted for the International Union for the Conservation of Nature and Natural

◀ WHITE-NECKED PUFFBIRD

Resources. Our party on this excursion consisted of Keith Leber, a Peace Corps volunteer attached to the Costa Rican National Parks Service; his wife, Teresa; and their friend Alfred Cuzan, a young man, now a doctor of philosophy in the social sciences, whose family had escaped from Cuba after Castro made it a Communist state.

In a rented Toyota with four-wheel drive, painted brilliant red, we speeded down the recently completed superhighway to Puntarenas—the most perilous part of our trip. At the port, the car was placed upon a ferry that took us across the Gulf of Nicoya to Playa Naranjo. Then we rode for many miles, over smoothly ballasted but unpaved and dusty roads, to Nicoya. The parched countryside was embellished by the golden crowns of flowering Guayacán trees and by the lovely Robles de Sabana, varying in shade from deep pink to almost white. Both of these small or medium-sized trees had shed their foliage, making their profuse display of large, trumpet-shaped flowers more effective. From Nicoya, which had grown from the sleepy village that I visited in 1937 to a bustling town, we continued to Puerto Humo on the Río Tempisque. Here, for four nights, we slept on the floor of a large but rather ruinous house on a big cattle ranch.

Next morning we set out in the car for the Laguna de Mata Redonda, north of Puerto Humo. Although we had been told that a car with four-wheel drive could reach the lagoon, we found the way so rough with projecting rocks that, to avoid damaging the vehicle, we parked it by the roadside. After walking several miles, we came in view of a large, shallow lake set amid low, steep, deforested hills. In the rainy season it had been much more extensive than we found it in March. Its receding water had left wide expanses of dry or drying mud, broken into small plates by innumerable deep, irregular fissures. Large areas of this rough surface were covered with the drying remains of Water Hyacinths.

This lake provided one of the finest displays of water birds that I have ever seen. Fifty Jabirus stood on a low, grassy island in the midst of the water, with at least as many more scattered around the shores and in the shallows. I had not seen this many of these great storks in five weeks of voyaging along the rivers of Peruvian Amazonia. About a hundred Northern Shoveler Ducks floated in the water, and in the distance we discerned huge flocks of Black-bellied Tree-Ducks and wintering Blue-winged Teals. I counted thirty-four Black-necked Stilts, forty Whimbrels foraging in a compact group, and a score of Roseate Spoonbills. Northern Jacanas, adult and immature, were too numerous and mobile to count. Wood Storks, Great Egrets, and Limpkins waded in the shallow water. A large flock of Semipalmated Sandpipers ran over exposed mud at the water's edge, busily picking up objects too small to identify. Amid the multitude of birds I detected a few White Ibises and an American Avocet, which was apparently the first to be recorded so far south.

All around this lagoon, as at every other marsh and pond that we visited in Guanacaste, many cattle and horses grazed, leaving the mud flats honeycombed with their hoofprints. Our visit was too brief to determine their impact upon the water birds, whether by fouling the water they had an adverse effect or perhaps increased the number of small aquatic organisms that the birds ate. Probably they trampled nests of some of these birds.

For the following day, we planned a voyage down the Río Tempisque in Keith's green fiberglass boat with an outboard motor. For safety, the boat was locked up in Puerto Humo's tiny jail, which at the moment was without a prisoner. Unfortunately, the policeman had gone to Santa Cruz with the key in his pocket, and the boat was unavailable. We spent the morning watching land rather than water birds.

By the following morning, the policeman had returned with the key. Keith, Alfred, and I started down the river early, with a falling tide to help us onward. Opposite Isla de Pájaros ("Bird Island"), we found about three hundred Wood Storks and a few Roseate Spoonbills in tall trees along the river bank, resting idly at eight o'clock in the morning. Landing, we pushed in through low mangroves and other small trees on this little "Bird Island," where Keith had been studying the nest life of the storks and spoonbills. Apparently because of insufficient rain, near-ly all the nests had been abandoned early in the year. The only young birds we found were two well-grown Wood Storks in the same small tree, but possibly from neighboring nests. What ugly creatures they were, with sparse down on their black-skinned heads and necks! Keith had built a tower to overlook the nests on the island, but somebody stole all the lumber of which it was made.

From Bird Island we continued downstream on the swiftly ebbing tide. The estuary became very wide, and in its midst was a large, recently formed island overgrown with low shrubs and trees. Among the birds foraging on exposed mud around this island were a multitude of Black-bellied Plovers, less numerous Semi-palmated Plovers, many Semipalmated Sandpipers that seemed fearless of us and our boat, many Limpkins and Roseate Spoonbills, White Ibises, and a few Tri-colored and Little Blue herons.

From this point we turned back, moving slowly upstream against the strong tidal current. Soon Keith announced that, unless we waited for the tide to turn, we would not have enough gasoline to take us to Puerto Humo. We approached a shore that appeared higher and firmer than most; but, when Keith stepped out of the boat, he promptly sank above his knees in the ooze. We moored the craft to a clump of Mangle Piñuela that jutted farther into the water than any of the others

◀ JABIRUS

that lined the shore. The trunks of these small trees of the tea family are enveloped by aerial roots and expand so strongly toward the base that they become almost conical. While we ate our lunch and discussed philosophical questions, the ebbing tide left our boat resting firmly on the muddy river bottom.

In mid-afternoon the tide came in again, silently and smoothly rather than with the audibly advancing low wall of water or bore that I have seen higher upstream, where the river is narrower. After waiting five hours, we were afloat in enough water to use the propeller, and resumed our upward voyage. Even far from shore, the propeller churned up mud beneath the shallow water. The Tempisque, even far inland, is an exceedingly muddy river, its brown water heavily laden with silt, probably in large part from wet ground loosened by the hoofs of the thousands of cattle pastured in its basin. The inflowing tide carried us slowly back to the port, with little use of the motor. As the sun sank low, many Mourning Doves flew across the river. After we landed, a great flock of Bronzed Cowbirds alighted in bushes along the shore, while some dropped down to hunt over exposed mud.

Next morning we embarked early to ascend the river with the strongly flowing tide. With the motor's help, it bore us swiftly upstream to where the narrowing channel was bordered by pastures, separated from the water by only a narrow fringe of trees instead of by scarcely penetrable stands of mangroves. Red-winged Blackbirds and huge iguanas were frequent in these trees, and at intervals we passed clans of Howling Monkeys resting in them. Although these monkeys, formerly a familiar sight beside the rough, unpaved roadways, are now seldom seen along the highways where motorcars speed, they are still not rare in the remoter areas where trees remain. Scarlet Macaws, the *lapas* of the Guanacastecans, once so numerous and obvious to eyes and ears, are now seldom seen. They are disappearing along with the trees that furnish their food and nest cavities.

At the highest point we reached on the Tempisque, we walked through a tract of dry woodland, where Streaked-headed Woodcreepers hunted over the trees, while we waited for the tide to turn and help us downward to Puerto Humo. At midday we took the road to Santa Cruz, where Teresa and Alfred boarded an airplane to return to their work in San José. Keith and I spent the night at Motel Diría, an excellent hostelry that contrasted greatly with the best accommodations I could find in Guanacaste three decades earlier. But, in those days, the hospitality of the people compensated for the lack of inns.

The following morning, we visited the lagoons of the Río Cañas, a few miles north of Santa Cruz. Here the small stream broadens into a series of wide, irregular, shallow lagoons, surrounded by the broad belt of drying mud typical of Guanacaste lakes at this season. Doubtless, at the height of the rainy season the lagoons are joined by flowing water, perhaps forming a single lake miles long. Here we saw no Jabirus or Wood Storks; but most of the other birds we had seen at the Laguna de Mata Redonda were present in numbers, along with Anhingas, Neotropic Cormorants, Least Grebes, Pied-billed Grebes, Snowy Egrets, Yellow-crowned Night-Herons, Common Gallinules, Snail Kites, and Ospreys. Black-bellied Tree-Ducks rested on the water in compact, elongated rafts that together contained many thousands of birds. Many Barn Swallows and a few Mangrove Swallows circled over the water and surrounding pastures, where the ubiquitous cattle grazed.

Guanacaste was as windy in March as I had earlier found it in November, and even hotter. One night rain fell, but next morning not a trace of it was visible. Walking beneath that burning sun, constantly buffeted by a desiccating wind, one accustomed to a cooler, calmer, more humid climate developed an insatiable thirst. The abundant watermelons helped to quench it. On our way back to San José,

Keith and I, with the help of a boy we encountered by the roadside, consumed all of a large one, except the seeds and the rind.

As in other arid regions, the sunsets of Guanacaste are superb, above all in the dry season. A truly impressive sunset requires a wide stage for its display; and the broad central plains, rimmed in the west by low, abrupt hills that fade to rich purple against the orange glow, provide an excellent setting. On my last day in Guanacaste, we sat on a hilltop at Palo Verde while the sun set and watched Scissor-tailed Flycatchers go to roost in the low trees that grew in the drier parts of the broad marsh. From the surrounding country over which they had scattered by day, the flycatchers streamed across the hilltop toward the marsh, traveling independently rather than in flocks, in an open stream that continued to pass for over a quarter of an hour. At first, most of them flew at no great height above the treetops, where the horizontal beams of the sinking sun set their lovely orange sides aglow. As the sun fell lower and the shadows rose higher, the flycatchers flew higher and higher, continuing to pass overhead in the sunshine that still illuminated their sides, while we sat in deepening twilight. With them flew many Barn Swallows that also roosted in the trees around the marsh. Not until the birds who flew highest were in the Earth's shadow did the procession cease. A memorable display!

23. Photosynthesis and Predation

In a country and a world that contain much to overwhelm a thoughtful mind with gloom and despair, I look over a valley nearly everywhere green. In my mind's eye, I see this color stretching far beyond the range of my vision. It covers vast expanses of all the continents and major islands, varying chiefly in shade, according to whether it is the green of broadleaved or coniferous forests, grassland, or fields cultivated with different crops. It is absent chiefly from the frozen polar caps, the highest peaks, arid deserts, and man's growing sprawl of cities, industrial plants, and highways.

This green is the color of chlorophyll, the most beneficent, constructive substance on Earth. During every daylight hour, it is silently, steadily engaged in photosynthesis, the process that supports all the life of this planet, except the minute fraction of obscure organisms that depend upon chemosynthesis. Every movement that we make, every thought that we think, every pulsation of every heart uses the energy that this wonderful substance captures from sunlight and stores in life-supporting compounds. Moreover, we owe to its ability to decompose carbon dioxide the atmospheric oxygen without which most organisms could not live. Even in the oceans, where it mostly passes unnoticed because it is distributed among minute planktonic organisms or is masked by the browns and reds of algae, chlorophyll is present in vast amounts, synthesizing food in quantities comparable

to that produced on land. How can evil predominate, how can pessimism prevail, how can a thoughtful mind sink into ultimate despair, on a planet colored green with a substance so beneficent as chlorophyll, engaged with quiet efficiency in the constructive work of photosynthesis?

Here in the humid tropics, especially in the rainy season, nature's constructive activities overshadow and mask its destructive aspects. Yet I know that amid the verdure of forests and thickets, by day and by night, predators are actively stalking their prey, rending the quivering flesh of animals that desperately cling to their lives, or swallowing them whole. Hordes of parasites suck the vital fluids of their hosts or invade their living tissues, causing sickness and death. We need not read newspapers or listen to radio announcements to learn of events and situations that distress us; the fair face of nature conceals much to cast gloom over a sensitive spirit.

As photosynthesis is the basic good of the living world, upon which all its constructive processes, its beauty, and its joy depend; so, predation is the basic evil, the cause of most of the ills that afflict it. The contrast between these two activities so widespread in nature is extreme. By photosynthesis, plants elaborate the primary materials and sources of energy that support them; by predation, animals wrest from other living things the nutrients that they need to grow and survive. Photosynthesis is economical, making good use of everything that enters into it; predation is wasteful, often using only a fraction of the bodies of its victims. In the broadest sense, predation includes parasitism in all its diverse modes: the crude predator crams itself with the tissues of other organisms; the parasite often invades the tissues of other organisms, the more efficiently to extract nutrients from them; or else it accomplishes the same end by attaching itself to the surface of its host.

◀ THE CABIN BESIDE THE FOREST WHERE THIS BOOK WAS WRITTEN; ITABO TREES

The predator typically kills its victim; the well-adapted parasite keeps its host alive, to serve as a continuing source of nourishment.

On the wider view, even wholly vegetarian animals are predatory if they consume living plants. The only animals that are in no sense predators are the relatively few that eat only fruits, like certain birds, or nectar and pollen, like bees. Since these creatures take only what plants offer them in return for their services as disseminators of seeds or pollinators of flowers, they cannot be classed as exploiters. Perhaps scavengers that eat only organisms for whose deaths they are not responsible should also be excluded from the category of predators.

Although, broadly interpreted, the predators include all creatures that consume the tissues or vital fluids of living organisms or those that they slay, we often restrict the designation "predatory" to animals that kill and devour others in the same broad zoological category as themselves: vertebrates that eat other vertebrates, arthropods that eat other arthropods, and so forth. The more like ourselves the victim of predation is, the more its violent death distresses the sympathetic onlooker, the fiercer and more unfeeling the killer appears to us. The red blood that flows from the mangled body of mammal or bird shocks us more than the paler fluids that ooze from an invertebrate or a plant. The more beautiful the creature, the more hideously revolting its dismembered remains appear to us; for there, where we expect symmetry and grace, a formless mess offends our vision. No inorganic bodies, no structures made by man, however crushed and distorted they may become, are quite so distressing to behold as the torn remains of what a short while ago was a beautiful living body.

The ultimate predators—those that prey upon other animals, which may also be predatory, but are themselves rarely or never victims of predation—are commonly said to be at the tops of food chains. However, a more accurate description would give this position to green plants, which create the primary foods on which nearly all life depends. From this source, there is a continuous waste of materials and dissipation of energy, or increase of entropy, as food passes down the chains to the ultimate predators. As dregs settle to the bottom of a liquid, so the poisons that man increasingly pours into the environment accumulate in the predators at the bottoms of food chains, sometimes depressing their reproduction and threatening their extinction. Man, especially carnivorous man, is at the bottom of a food chain and pays the penalty by the retention of toxins in his tissues.

Widespread in the animal kingdom, predation is rare among green plants. Most obviously predatory are the bladderworts, pitcher plants, sundews, Venus's-flytraps, and a few other insectivorous or carnivorous plants, which catch and digest small creatures on glandular leaves or in diverse traps, thereby procuring a nitrogenous supplement to the carbohydrates that they synthesize in the sunlight. We might even designate as predatory the figs and similar growths that germinate high on trees, whose trunks they envelop in a network of roots, which, after strangling the host, coalesce to form a false trunk that upholds the usurping tree. In the same category we might include the more aggressive tropical lianas, which embrace the host tree with a constricting spiral and spread a smothering blanket of alien foliage over the highest crowns. Only because it is very much slower does the strife between strangling figs, or the more aggressive lianas, and the supporting trees appear less violent than that between predatory animals and their animate prey.

With these few exceptions, green plants are in no sense predatory. Their competition for a place in the soil and sunlight, an inevitable consequence of the immense numbers of seeds and other propagules that they produce, takes milder forms; it is quietly persistent rather than violent and destructive. Able to elaborate their own food, green plants neither devour nor attack one another. They never expel rivals from territories many times their own size, but tolerate individuals of the same or different species in closest proximity. Not the fiercest or most aggressive plants, but those whose more productive photosynthesis supports more rapid growth, win a place in the sunshine, flower, and set seed, while they permit humbler vegetation, able to carry on photosynthesis in subdued light, to flourish in their shade. The nonviolent competition among green plants might be compared to that which prevails among men in an orderly, civilized society for markets, professional advancement, or social status; whereas the strife between predator and prey more closely resembles the internecine warfare among savage and cannibalistic tribes.

Because the struggle for existence in the vegetable kingdom, although certainly no less prevalent than in the animal kingdom, takes milder forms, natural selection is less stringent and more permissive, and evolution follows a somewhat different course. The forms of vegetable organs are not so strictly tied to their functions as are those of animals. For each animal and each particular type of locomotion, limbs of a certain definite construction are most efficient, and deviations from this form are likely to be eliminated. A similar relation exists between teeth or bills and kinds of food, between digestive tracts and diets, between hearts and circulation, and so forth. But a wide diversity of forms is consistent with the efficient performance of the same essential function in plants. Consider the great variety of the shapes of leaves all efficiently engaged in photosynthesis in the same woodland or meadow; or the immense diversity of the forms and colors of flowers that can be adequately pollinated by the same insects or birds; or the immense variety of devices that plants employ to disperse their seeds. Apparently, in the vegetable kingdom selection acts more stringently on characters less conspicuous than those that botanists use to classify plants, such as photosynthetic efficiency and toleration of deficiencies or excesses in the constituents of the soil. Thus, in a realm of nonviolent competition, evolution promotes efficiency in constructive activities, whereas in a realm infected by predation it too often promotes efficiency in destruction.

Predation, the exploitation by one organism of another to supply its vital needs, is a major source of the ills that afflict the living world. In its subtle form of parasitism it causes prolonged suffering rather than sudden death. In its more spectacular modes, as when a lion pounces upon an antelope or a hawk strikes down a bird, it is responsible for more insidious evils. More than the occasional violence of the elements or the competition between individuals of the same species for territory, food, or mates, predation has brought fear and hatred into the world. Doubtless it is because man's ancestors were for ages not only fiercely predatory animals but also frequent victims of predation by the larger carnivores that his passions are today so violent and difficult to control, his rage so intense, his hatred so implacable, his fear so enervating. Man, the omnivorous predator, became man, the merciless raider and warrior. The clubs and stones he employed to kill his prey slowly evolved into spears and arrows, and, finally, into artillery and atomic bombs.

Reluctant to concede that predation is an evil, biologists point to its functions in the living world. In the absence of predators, animals would increase until they exhausted their means of subsistence and died slowly by starvation instead of more swiftly by predation. Some, especially the larger herbivores, would destroy their habitat, as elephants today are wrecking woodland in parts of Africa where, under protection, they have become too numerous. Moreover, predation has been a potent positive factor in the evolution of animals. By placing a premium on senses keen to discover prey on one hand, or to detect approaching predators on the other hand, it has helped to perfect the sensory organs of both the predators and their prey. Similarly, cunning to surprise a meal, or to avoid becoming one, has doubt-less sharpened the wits of animals in both categories. Strength and endurance have likewise been promoted by the agelong conflict between predator and prey. But for these advantages animals have paid an excessively high price, not only in the form of physical suffering but, even more, in the fear and other distressing passions that the strife between predators and their prey has engendered.

To recognize the role of predation in preserving the balance of the living community and in promoting certain aspects of evolution is not to deny that it is an evil. It is merely to concede that it is a necessary evil, such as, certain philosophers have held, even an omnipotent, omniscient Deity could not avoid when he created a complex world. But predation is necessary only in relation to certain other features of nature as we actually find it, especially the tendency of organisms to multiply indefinitely, regardless of their progeny's prospects of survival. Predation would not be necessary if evolution had taken a different turn, and developed more universal feedback systems to adjust the reproductive effort of a population to its available resources and actual need of recruitment, such as V. C. Wynne-Edwards has contemplated in his book *Animal Dispersion in Relation to Social Behaviour*.[1]

As I have long maintained, and as biologists are increasingly recognizing, animals long established in a fairly stable environment, such as tropical rain forest, tend to have a restrained rate of reproduction, adjusted to their average annual mortality. With a different course, evolution might have made such adjustment more widespread and refined. Moreover, predation may itself be responsible for the excessive production of individuals that it must remove to preserve ecological balance. We have abundant evidence that "predation pressure" powerfully acceler-

1. V. C. Wynne-Edwards, *Animal dispersion in relation to social behaviour* (Edinburgh and London: Oliver and Boyd, 1962).

ates the embryological development of birds, thereby shortening their incubation periods, and it probably has the same effect upon other aspects of the reproductive rate of animals. The species that persistently fails to reproduce fast enough to replace its losses becomes extinct. Predators have made it imperative for many species to reproduce at a rate higher than they might have maintained in their absence. The fact that they continue to reproduce at the same rate when suddenly protected from predation proves nothing. Genetically determined reproductive rates can change only slowly in response to altered circumstances.

The role of predation in refining the sensory organs, sharpening the intelligence, and increasing the strength and endurance of animals is easily exaggerated. Man owes his exceptional endowments, physical and mental, to the arboreal stage of his long evolutionary history, when our ancestors were largely frugivorous, far more than to the subsequent terrestrial stage, when they became formidable predators. While tree dwellers, our remote progenitors developed forwardly directed eyes to judge the distance of their leaps from bough to bough, color vision to distinguish fruits from foliage, hands adapted to cling to branches and pluck fruits, and at least a rudimentary social life, such as many monkeys and apes have. Our versatile hands needed intelligence to guide them in life-preserving activities, some of which required social cooperation, which stimulated the growth of language. Every improvement in manual dexterity raised the survival value of intelligence; every increase in intelligence gave greater value to skillful hands; every refinement of language favored intelligent cooperation: intelligence, speech, and dextrous hands, the three outstanding characteristics of man, evolved together by reciprocal enhancement. Predatory animals that never passed through an arboreal stage, or which climbed by means of claws, like the cats, instead of by hands that grasp, never developed endowments comparable to ours. Anthropologists tend to overemphasize the role of the terrestrial hunting stage in the making of man and, ungratefully, to forget what we owe to the trees that for a long age supported our ancestors.

For all these reasons, and despite the contrary view of many evolutionists and ecologists, I steadfastly maintain that predation is an evil, the greatest that afflicts the living world, necessary in present circumstances, but not absolutely necessary, for it might have been avoided. Furthermore, I hold that not to recognize evil where it exists, not to call it baldly by its true name, is itself an evil, and not the least of them. We do not demonstrate our loyalty to nature by refusing to proclaim the evil it contains, nor do we raise our estimate of evolution by denying that it has produced much that is horrible and revolting. On the contrary, by such refusal and denial, we stifle one of the most precious things that evolution has yielded, our ability to pass moral judgments on its methods and products, to stand aghast as we contemplate much that it has done, to feel compassion for the victims of its harshness, to resist with all our might some of its unfortunate trends. More than all else that evolution has accomplished, more even than all its beautiful creations and marvelous adaptations, this capacity for moral indignation gives me hope for its future course. Holding a thoroughly monistic or naturalistic philosophy, regarding man as wholly a product of evolution, in the same sense that the plants and animals around him are its products, I regard our condemnation of much that evolution has done as a judgment that evolution or nature itself, at its higher levels, passes upon the crudities of its earlier stages. To refuse to pass this judgment is to resist the forward march of life. To condone everything we find in nature is to repudiate one of nature's finest achievements.

Much of my life has been a quiet revolt against the harsher aspects of nature, especially predation. This attitude is certainly not new nor confined to me. On the contrary, it is very ancient and has profoundly influenced whole civilizations, notably that of India, with its doctrine of *ahimsa* or harmlessness toward all beings, and to a lesser degree that of ancient China, where compassionate Buddhism took root and gentle Taoism arose. It is encouraging to watch the same attitude slowly spreading in the West, especially among the younger generation. This revolt by some of evolution's more advanced products against nature's harshness, together with our appreciation of beauty, our ceaseless quest of enlightenment, our striving to create a more harmonious and happier world, and all the admirable and lovely things that nature contains, sustains my firm conviction that the cosmic process, of which organic evolution is a phase, is not random or meaningless but a persistent striving to actualize all the high values—all the beauty, love, joy, and whatever else can make existence precious—that were latent in primal Being. The world process is an unremitting movement to transform bare existence into significant, richly endowed existence.

But how could the universal striving to realize positive values give rise to so many disvalues; how could the beneficence of photosynthesis lead to the nightmare of predation that afflicts our planet? To understand this, we must go back to the beginning. Atoms are social beings that persistently seek to unite with other atoms. Their social impulses are of two kinds. The first is an undiscriminating gregariousness, an inclination to join with other atoms of whatever kinds, in masses that often become huge but may lack finer structure. As gravitation, this gregariousness condenses thinly diffused matter into great spherical bodies, the stars and planets. Gravitation is a force so weak that, without the most delicate instruments, we can detect it only when exerted conjointly by immense numbers of atoms, like those composing the Earth. The second kind of sociality that atoms exhibit is both stronger and more discriminating, causing them to unite only with certain other atoms in definite patterns, thereby giving rise to the immense variety of molecules and crystals.

A vastly extended universe containing an inconceivably great number of social atoms, able to influence each other across intervening space by several kinds of radiations, is set to develop in wonderful ways. Without guidance by anything external to themselves, they will, wherever possible, unite in patterns of ever-increasing coherence, amplitude, and complexity; and this increase in organization will be accompanied by increased value. In cooling magmas and drying seas, atoms form crystals that delight us by their symmetry and radiant beauty. If atoms find a favorable environment, they will, with time, give rise to life in all its immense variety. The living state appears to be the ultimate expression of the atoms' social nature, the end toward which they spontaneously move. In it we find the maximum of complexity with the maximum of coherence. One of the higher animals contains a greater number and variety of parts, all more closely integrated and dependent upon each other, than one will find in any inorganic structure of whatever magnitude. And, as far as we can tell, in this state, and perhaps only in this state, are the highest values realized.

The human body is composed of elements widely distributed in the universe. Atoms everywhere appear capable of entering the living state, which appears to be the highest expression of their creative power, if they encounter a suitable environment. But such environments are few, far separated, and, it appears, always very small when measured in astronomical units. Accordingly, in any cosmic era, only a minute fraction of the matter in the universe can participate in the adventure of living. Much is so thinly diffused in gaseous clouds in intergalactic space that it cannot form complex molecules. Much more is gathered in incandescent stars, far too hot for large molecules to arise. Indeed, toward the centers of the denser stars, even complete atoms cannot exist; the tremendous pressure strips them of their electrons.

On the surface of certain favored planets that are neither too near their sun nor too far from it, neither too hot nor too cold, massive enough to retain an atmosphere yet not so huge that they hold a very dense one, and probably only where water collects in the liquid state—only in such special circumstances, it appears, can life arise in any form that we would recognize. Recent explorations of the solar system by means of space probes, plus the older astronomical data, make it increasingly certain that our planet is the only one of the nine that now supports life, except possibly in the form of very simple organisms. This gives to Earth a special importance. It is an expression point, apparently the only one in a vast expanse of space, of what the creative forces of the universe can accomplish in favorable circumstances. Those who measure the importance of our planet by its size use the wrong yardstick. The explorations of the universe that have dethroned Earth from the central position that our ancestors ascribed to it, and shown it to be hardly more than a speck in the immensity of space, have likewise demonstrated its uniqueness. Our tiny planet is a center from which questing minds reach out toward the farthest limits of the universe and the most remote epochs of past and future time. It is a gem, green and blue and wrapped in soft white clouds, that sparkles in the radiance of its sun. Will we ever learn to cherish it as it deserves?

When, at some small point in the immensity of space, for some brief interval in the infinitude of time, a small fraction of the immense number of atoms in the universe find conditions that permit them to give full expression to their social nature and creative powers, they do so with astounding intensity, as though to compensate for the long ages when they were denied this privilege, for the countless trillions of other atoms that may never have such an opportunity. In their frenzy to create, the social atoms unite in so many patterns, so close together, that they compete for the space, matter, and energy that they need to complete themselves. Thus, by its very intensity, the striving for order and value gives rise to strife, disorder, and disvalue. In broadest terms, evil is a secondary effect of the universal striving toward the good.

Before the creative movement destined to cover the Earth with life could proceed far, it needed a continuing source of energy. The most widespread and dependable source of energy on our planet's surface is solar radiation; but to capture and store it in forms that can nourish living cells is so difficult that man, for all his chemical wizardry, has not yet learned how to do it. Nevertheless, the restless permutations of the social atoms finally brought some of them together in the molecule of chlorophyll. This most momentous event in the history of our planet probably occurred, two or three thousand million years ago, in some unicellular organism floating in a tepid sea. Now the possessors of this precious substance could, by photosynthesis, absorb the energy in sunlight and store it in compounds composed of carbon dioxide and water. With the addition of other elements, the carbohydrates could be transformed into a great variety of molecules, including proteins; they could be transported from one part of an organism to another, used to build its tissues, and serve as a source of energy for all its activities. Photosynthesis prepared the way for the vast development of the vegetable kingdom, which from the seas, where it originated, advanced over the land, and finally covered all except the driest and coldest parts with luxuriant verdure.

The *eobionts*, as the earliest forerunners of the living world are called, were probably nourished by compounds of inorganic origin, formed, at least in part, by discharges of lightning in the primitive atmosphere, and washed by rain into the primal seas. Our contemporary atmosphere, almost devoid of ammonia and methane and poor in carbon dioxide, probably no longer produces such nutrients; and, in any case, before they could accumulate in the oceans in detectable quantities, they would be consumed by swarming microorganisms. Doubtless, at an early stage in the evolution of life, the eobionts consumed these nutrients faster than they were formed, and life would have stagnated if it had not developed photosynthesis or some equivalent process. While certain organisms thereby became able to nourish themselves, others, lacking this capacity, may have passed directly from dependence upon nutrients diffused through the water to dependence upon the self-supporting green cells. Another road to such dependence is the loss of chlorophyll to become saprophytes or parasites, as has happened repeatedly.

Thus, in the primitive seas, while the living world was still at a low level of organization, began the great dichotomy that we recognize today in the separation of the vegetable kingdom, most of whose members are able to nourish themselves, from the animal kingdom, dependent upon plants for food. In many ways, this is a tragic dichotomy, the source of a large part of life's toils and woes. Conceivably, all the advantages of animals, including their ability to move and create, to perceive and think, to communicate and love, could be enjoyed by creatures able to spread photosynthetic tissues to the sunshine and make their own food. How much toil and sweat, how much strife and bloodshed, how much ugliness and terror, might have been avoided if evolution had taken this kindly path!

If I am right in interpreting the cosmic process, of which organic evolution is a phase, as a striving to enrich Being with ever higher values, then animals carry this process to a higher stage than plants can attain. The psychic life of plants, if such they have, is hidden from us, but it obviously has many limitations. Lacking eyes, they cannot perceive their own beauty; lacking all but the most rudimentary nervous systems, they can hardly become integrated individuals; lacking brains, they cannot think; lacking muscles, they cannot move freely and explore the world that they bless with their loveliness and productivity. As they evolved to higher levels, animals acquired all these and many other capacities that plants lack. A world without animate creatures to appreciate its grandeur and beauty, to know and try to understand it, to be grateful for the privilege of living in it, would be a poorer world, devoid of something necessary to fulfill it.

All might have been well if animals, failing to become autotrophic or self-supporting, had continued to depend upon the primary producers, the plants, for their nourishment. If a benevolent Intelligence had guided evolution, he might have done on a vast scale what horticultural man has done on a modest scale. Just as man, by intelligent selection, has developed plants capable of supporting huge populations; so the Intelligence might have caused plants to yield fruits in sufficient quantity and nutritive value to support the whole animal kingdom, which then, of course, would have a character very different from what we now find. Moreover, he would have ensured that populations of animals did not exceed the plants' ability to sustain them. Although evolution has proceeded in a definite direction, which is toward ever higher levels of organization and awareness, it has obviously lacked guidance, such as an almighty, benevolent Intelligence might have given it. Depending upon random mutations for its advance, it has had to grope its way forward, as through a labyrinth, by means of trial and error, and much that it has done is tragic.

Multiplying excessively, animals found plants inadequate for their nourishment and began to devour one another. Thereafter, every mutation that made them more effective as predators gave them an advantage in the struggle to survive. They developed penetrating fangs, grasping talons, tearing beaks, and poison glands to immobilize their prey, along with the strength, speed, or cunning needed for the effective use of these weapons, and emotions appropriate for the hunter and the killer. For self-protection, the victims of predation developed an equally impressive array of devices and reactions, including tough integuments, horns, poisonous spines, repellent scents or tastes, swiftness to flee, or cryptic attitudes and colors, along with emotions appropriate for the fugitive and the victim. A planet made habitable and fruitful by green plants silently absorbing sunlight became the stage for carnage on an incredibly vast scale, for violence, hatred, and fear.

When I reflect upon this tragic turn that evolution has taken, I gaze over my verdant valley with mixed feelings. The sight of countless green leaves steadily engaged in an activity wholly beneficent and constructive dispels black pessimism but not all dark misgivings. Everywhere, photosynthesis, nature's brighter aspect, is decreasing as man covers larger areas with his highways and constructions, destroys thriving forests to make cultivated fields and pastures for his beef cattle, contributes to the spread of deserts by overexploiting arid lands, and poisons seas with his wastes. Simultaneously, predation, nature's darker aspect, grows apace, as increasing areas are devoted to raising cattle for slaughter and the oceans are more thoroughly scoured for the flesh of their living inhabitants. Moreover, to satisfy his carnivorous cravings, man has adopted methods that far exceed most natural predation in the prolonged misery they cause, as when he callously confines his prospective victims from birth in constricting pens, applying to sensitive living animals factory methods of production.

The exuberant tropical vegetation that I survey reminds me that nature's boundless creativity is not tempered by restraint. Its excessive multiplication of species and individuals is responsible for the gravest ills that afflict the living world, including the prevalence of predation. Unrestrained creativity is the precursor of destruction. Life would be so much more pleasant if there were fewer living things! What has been most conspicuously lacking, in the natural world as in human society, is moderation, which Plato and other Classical philosophers held to be the highest good, the key to every virtue. Moderation, which requires thoughtfulness, measure, and self-control, could be man's most important contribution to the life of his planet. Without moderation, life will never rise, upon the firm foundation of photosynthesis, to heights that this foundation might support, nor will man realize all the splendid values within his reach. Unless we exercise restraint and moderation, in reproduction, in consumption, in our exploitation of other organisms and the demands we make upon nature's bounty, the fairest planet in the solar system will not long remain a fit abode for life.

For man, who has devised so many means to titillate his appetites and excite his acquisitiveness, who in modern society is exposed to so much seductive advertising and salacious entertainment by the mass media, moderation does not come so easily as it does to many other animals. Even in the presence of abundant food, most animals do not often impair their fitness by overeating—a tendency to do so would be severely checked by natural selection. And in many species, whose ability to reproduce is strictly limited to a definite season, they do not breed immoderately.

Lacking these innate restraints, man has, nevertheless, acquired through a long evolution certain sources of strength that other animals may lack. He can foresee the disastrous consequences of excesses of all kinds and, if his will is strong enough, avoid them. The very physiological versatility that makes us, potentially, one of the most omnivorous of animals enables us to live long and healthily on foods that we can morally approve and that can be produced with the least detriment to the Earth's productivity. With a vast diversity of occupations and recreations available to us, we can choose those most compatible with a healthy, satisfying life and least wasteful of natural resources. We can limit our reproduction by chastity and restraint or by other means. Man has too long undervalued the freedoms inherent in his physiological versatility and mental flexibility, which are his inalienable birthright, while clamoring for greater political liberty, of which he is readily deprived, and which he often uses unwisely when he has it. The truest freedom is freedom from excesses of all kinds. We can will to be moderate and free. If enough of us could make this determination, a steadily improving, happier humanity should continue for a long age to flourish on a planet that remains fruitful and beautiful.

Index

Designer: Randall Goodall
Compositor: G & S Typesetters, Inc.
Printer: Vail-Ballou Press, Inc.
Binder: Vail-Ballou Press, Inc.
Text: VIP Janson
Display: Typositor Palatino
Cloth: Joanna Arrestox B53000
& Process Materials Elephant Hide
Paper: 60lbs. P&S offset A69